Studies in applied regional science

This series in applied regional, urban and environmental analysis aims
to provide regional scientists with a set of adequate tools for empirical
regional analysis and for practical regional planning problems. The
major emphasis in this series will be upon the applicability of theories
and methods in the field of regional science; these will be presented in
a form which can be readily used by practitioners. Both new
applications of existing knowledge and newly developed ideas will be
published in the series.

STUDIES IN APPLIED REGIONAL SCIENCE 17

TELEPEN

60 0326096 0

DATE DUE FOR RETURN

ECONOMIC—
ENVIRONMENTAL—
ENERGY
INTERACTIONS
Modeling and
Policy Analysis

T.R. LAKSHMANAN
P. NIJKAMP
Editors

Martinus Nijhoff Publishing
Boston / The Hague / London

326096

Distributors for North America:
Martinus Nijhoff Publishing
Kluwer Boston, Inc.
160 Old Derby Street
Hingham, Massachusetts 02043

Distributors outside North America:
Kluwer Academic Publishers Group
Distribution Centre
P.O. Box 322
3300 AH Dordrecht, The Netherlands

Library of Congress Cataloging in Publication Data

Main entry under title:

Economic-environmental-energy interactions.
  (Studies in applied regional science; v. 17)
  Bibliography: p.
  1. Environmental policy—Mathematical models—
Congresses.   2. Energy policy—Mathematical models—
Congresses.   3. Economic policy—Mathematical models—
Congresses.   I. Lakshmanan, T. R., 1932–
II. Nijkamp, Peter.   III. Series.
HC79.E5E27   301.31′01′51   79-19016
ISBN 0-89838-023-5

Printed in the United States of America.

CONTENTS

INTRODUCTION   1

1. INTEGRATED MODELS FOR ECONOMIC-ENERGY-
   ENVIRONMENTAL IMPACT ANALYSIS   7
   T.R. Lakshmanan and Sam Ratick

   1. Introduction   7
   2. The Evolution of Economic-Energy-Environmental
      Modelling   10
   3. SEAS: An Integrated Economic-Environmental-Energy
      Model   14
      3.1 General   14
      3.2 National Economic Subsystem   17
      3.3 National Environmental Subsystem   20
      3.4 Regional Environmental Subsystem   21
      3.5 Energy Subsystem   22
      3.6 Raw Material Subsystem   22
      3.7 Concluding Remarks   22
   4. An Application of SEAS   23
      4.1 Introduction   23

                                                          v

4.2   Economic Effects   26
4.3   Environmental Effects   31
4.4   Concluding Comments   35
5.   Notes   36
6.   References   37

2.   OPERATIONAL METHODS FOR STRATEGIC
     ENVIRONMENTAL AND ENERGY POLICIES   40
     P.J.J. Lesuis, F. Muller, and P. Nijkamp

1.   Introduction   40
2.   An Integrated Input-Output Model with Energy and
     Pollution   41
3.   Price Effects and Technology Shifts   44
4.   Composite Scenarios for Long-term Environmental and
     Energy Policies   49
5.   Applications   57
6.   Conclusions   61
7.   Appendix: Preliminary Estimates of the Parameters of
     the Translog Price Possibility Frontier   65
8.   Notes   71
9.   References   71

3.   COSTS AND BENEFITS OF WATER POLLUTION
     CONTROL   74
     William D. Watson, Jr.

1.   Introduction   74
2.   Methods   77
3.   Results   83
     3.1   Emissions and Regional Damages   83
     3.2   Control Costs, Damage Costs, and Benefits   89
4.   The Gains from Additional Information   110
5.   Implications and Conclusions   113
6.   Notes   113
7.   References   114

4.   LONG-RUN ENERGY POLICIES IN AN ECONOMIC
     SETTING   117
     L.H. Klaassen and J.H.P. Paelinck

1.   Introduction   117
2.   Preliminary Thoughts   118

2.1   Energy as a Production Factor   118
2.2   Energy Price and Level of Knowledge   121
2.3   An Analytical Model   122
2.4   Provisional Conclusion: Testing of Raw Material
        Models Required   126
3.   Further Investigations   127
3.1   Economics of Alternative Energy Sources   128
3.2   A Simple Model   130
3.3   A One-period Horizon Programming Model   131
3.4   A Two-period Transition Model   133
4.   Prices Revisited   135
4.1   Prices of Raw Materials   135
4.2   Compensating for Price Increases   137
4.3   Measures Against Inflation   140
4.4   A Model   142
5.   Conclusions   144
6.   Notes   146
7.   References   147

5.   AN INTEGRATED INTERREGIONAL MODEL FOR
     POLLUTION CONTROL   149
     Wim Hafkamp and Peter Nijkamp

1.   Introduction   149
2.   Multidimensional Welfare Profiles   150
3.   An Integrated Interregional Model of Production
     and Pollution   153
4.   Interactive Compromise Policy Models   157
5.   An Empirical Illustration of an Interactive
     Compromise Model   162
6.   Concluding Remarks   169
7.   Notes   170
8.   References   170

6.   THE ENVIRONMENTAL IMPACT ISSUES IN ENERGY
     DEVELOPMENT IN THE UNITED STATES   172
     Peter House

1.   Introduction   172
2.   The 1977 ERDA National Plan   173
3.   To the Present   179
4.   EDP System   179
5.   EDP Contents and Procedures   180

6. Technology Descriptions   181
7. Identification of Environmental Concerns   182
8. Determination of Significance of Environmental
    Concerns   182
9. Technology Assessment   183
10. Summary and Conclusions   184
11. Notes   185

7. DUTCH ENERGY POLICIES FOR THE FUTURE   186
    A.A.T. van Rhijn

    1. Introduction   186
    2. Energy Supply and Energy Policy in the Netherlands   188
    3. Availability and Security of Supply   189
    4. Feasibility of Application   191
    5. Economics of Energy Sources   192
    6. Environmental Impact and Risks of the Source   194
    7. The Energy Mix Policy: Spreading Negative Effects   196
    8. Guideline for Future Energy Policy   197
        8.1 Natural Gas   197
        8.2 Coal   197
        8.3 Nuclear   198

ECONOMIC-ENVIRONMENTAL-ENERGY INTERACTIONS

INTRODUCTION

This publication is concerned with two major current debates in public policy in all affluent societies. One is the widespread concern with the quality of the natural environment — the quality of air, water, land, and wilderness areas — which has expressed itself in the passage and implementation in recent years of a variety of environmental laws and regulations. A second debate concerns the adequacy of energy resources to meet the requirements of a growing economy.

The requirement that industries must abate environmental pollution leads to increased costs of production and, in turn, to higher prices, falling output in those industries, and reduced employment and income in the region where such industries are located. There may be, at the same time, growth in industries that supply pollution abatement equipment and services in those or other regions. Over time, the health and economic benefits of higher environmental quality express themselves in changing patterns of consumption. Thus, as environmental standards pertaining to industries, automobiles, and municipalities are implemented, the combination of goods and services produced in the nation changes. These changes are reflected in the regional economies, depending upon their industrial mix, incomes, and consumption patterns.

1

The concern with energy problems stems from the unrelenting growth of energy use, the multitude of specific public policies seeking to affect the various components of the large energy industry, and the necessity for placing some degree of constraint upon energy use and supply. The major effect of the public awareness of shortfalls in energy supply is a (significant) increase in the price of all sorts of energy and consequently in the price of all products to the degree they have energy embodied in them. Increases in costs of transportation, resulting from higher energy prices, will affect industries where the share of transport inputs is high. A rise in space heating costs will lead to higher utility bills and cost of living. All these effects will be incident to different degrees on various industrial sectors and regions. The long-run effects of such changes, stemming from higher costs of energy per se and the costs of transportation, may be regional shifts of industry and population.

Further, the production, distribution, conversion, and use of all forms of energy are inherently and heavily associated with environmental impacts — air, water, land, and thermal emissions. Since a significant part of the short-falls in environmental quality in contemporary societies derive from energy use, issues of "trade-off" between additional energy supplies and environmental quality frequently arise. To what degree will people reduce their use of electricity in the interest of cleaner air? How small a car will people accept to reduce the incidence of smog in the big cities? What incremental costs will be tolerated for energy supply to prevent further spread of strip mining or to prevent reduction of a given fish type in the Rhine, the Thames, or Lake Michigan?

These are the kinds of questions that illustrate the "energy-environment trade-off." The market does not, unfortunately, perform its equilibriating and allocating task in this area since different environmental attributes are not traded or available for appropriation (except perhaps when individuals shop around spatially in an urban area for choice environments). The alternative of collective choice is slowly developing, handicapped in part by our limited knowledge of physical processes that transform energy production and use into environmental changes and the effects of the latter on flora, fauna, property, and humans.

In spite of such limitations of knowledge and market failure, major decisions affecting environmental-economic-energy decisions get made. An analytical framework to help improve the quality of such decisions and make explicit their value judgements is emerging. This is the flexible framework of conditional (what if . . .) analysis. It would estimate consequences of a given set of policies in terms of the level and composition of output of goods and services, the pollution emissions, and environmental quality. These consequences can be next valued in common terms in some way (with all the difficulties in such a process) to provide some measure of the resultant welfare levels. This process, when repeated for alternative assumptions of policies or future states of technology, resources, and so forth, can be used to compare alternative policies and to choose the "most desired."

In the last several years a number of economic-environmental-energy models have been built around this framework at the national and regional levels. These models, given the complexities in the field, are necessarily elaborate, combining the best features of the methodologies of many disciplines. These models, reflecting in some cases cooperative endeavours of social scientists, engineers, and physical scientists, use a combination of methods — econometric, optimization, physical process models, and others. The resulting models, despite their limitations, evidence an increasing ability to deal with complex aspects of energy-environmental decisions.

In so far as integrated models are used for analytical purposes (description, projection, and so on), they require a close cooperation between scientists from several disciplines in order to achieve a fruitful coordination in the field of data collection, data analysis, model building, and future scenario analysis. When these models are used for policy analysis, the spatial scales of the various phenomena are to be taken into account, both at an interregional and at an international level. A closer cooperation between various institutional levels is a prerequisite for a further balanced development of our Western societies.

Therefore, a twofold research agenda may be proposed. In the analytical sphere, more attention has to be paid to an integration of environmental assessment analysis, technology assessment analysis, and social assessment analysis. Economic-environmental-energy models should also be oriented to weaknesses in the data base, so that qualitative approaches, fuzzy methods, and stochastic procedures deserve a great deal of attention. In the policy sphere, the research agenda would contain inter alia an extensive operational analysis of institutional procedures, an evaluation of individual and group preferences, an operational analysis of intangible impacts, and a consideration of long-term social and spatial distributive impacts. Both resarch agendas constitute a great challenge to future economic-environmental-energy model building.

While these developments in economic-energy-environmental modelling improve our analytical capacity to address policy issues, paradoxically, at the same time they pose serious difficulties for the user of these models. For the decision makers, who are the consumers of these models, the increasing complexity of modelling poses barriers to comprehension and assimilation of the significance of this expanding research.

If the marketplace of environmental-energy research and policy making is to be effective, the modeller (producer) must be in touch with the policy maker (consumer), and the policy maker should understand the attributes of the models. While the modellers have a lot to offer, they need directions on the nature, priority, and constraints of policy problems. The policy makers, on the other hand, must understand not only the strengths of these models, but also their assumptions, weaknesses, and the nature of operations of these models. The need for such bridges between producers and consumers of models is becoming widely recognized.

The International Conference on Economic-Environmental-Energy Interaction: Modelling and Policy Analysis is one more recognition of this need.[1] It brought together modellers and policy planners on both sides of the Atlantic to explore jointly the key analytical issues in the field of integrated economic-environmental-energy research. The specific focus of the symposium was twofold:

1. the analytical issues involved in the integrated treatment of economic growth, energy demand, and environmental protection at the national and regional levels and
2. the potentials and problems of policy analysis in such integrated modelling efforts.

The papers presented in this volume reflect this dual orientation to modelling and policy analysis. They illustrate the emerging trends in integrated modelling of economic-environmental-energy interactions. Such trends include cooperative endeavours, on the one hand, between economists, geographers, engineers, and physical scientists and, on the other, active bridge building between modellers and decision makers.

The topics related to such an integrated assessment of economic energy and environmental issues that are treated in this volume fall roughly into three areas. The first area dealing with different modelling systems for comprehensive and systematic analyses of energy and environmental problems is represented by the first three papers. The second field, covering analytical frameworks for formulating and addressing long-run structural changes likely to result from energy price increases in various nations and for addressing regional environmental issues, is illustrated by the next two papers. The last two papers in the volume reflect the perspectives of top-level energy policy administrators in the United States and the Netherlands as they attempt to structure and organize the formulation of energy-environmental policies in their respective institutions.

Lakshmanan and Ratick open the volume with the presentation of a large system of interlinked models of the economy, energy, and environment termed the Strategic Environmental Assessment System (SEAS) model. The SEAS model, an extension of the input-output model to include environmental and energy sectors, has been used for the assessment of a wide range of public environmental and energy policies in the U.S. Environmental Protection Agency and the U.S. Department of Energy. This paper presents one such application of SEAS to estimate the likely economic and environmental consequences of two alternative future national and regional energy supply scenarios in the United States.

The last decade has witnessed the growing realization that economic, environmental, and energy decision making takes place in the context of a wide variety of conflicting political priorities (e.g., maximizing employment, preserving environmental quality, assuring energy supplies, and so on). Lesuis, Muller, and Nijkamp respond to this challenge by developing a decision model that is interconnected with an economic-environmental model capable of incorporating price effects and shifts in technology. The conflicts between different objectives are analyzed in the Netherlands by means of learning strategies for conflicting objectives based on the concept of displaced ideals.

In the assessment of complex pollution abatement policies, failure to develop estimates of the broad range of benefits and costs in a systematic and dynamic framework can lead to poor policy choices. A case in point is provided by Watson in his review of the recommendation of the National Commission on Water Quality (NCWQ) to delay the implementation of the legal deadlines for municipalities, agriculture, and industry to meet 1983 water quality requirements in the United States. Watson demonstrates that NCWQ, by ignoring the effects of some key pollutants (chemical oxygen demand and dissolved solids) and effects of population and economic growth over time, has undermined the empirical basis of its policy recommendation. By using the SEAS model to estimate the additional benefits and costs in a dynamic framework and quantifying the uncertainties associated with such estimates, Watson arrives at conclusions quite different from those of the National Commission on Water Quality.

Klaassen and Paelinck outline analytical models to help formulate energy and raw materials policy or, in more general terms, a policy associated with energy and materials production and consumption. Such models should take into account the long-term effects (e.g., substitution behavior, technological change, spatial patterns, and others) of increased energy price. Klaassen and Paelinck present a broad analysis of the effect of increasing energy prices on the general price level, and they highlight the hard political choices that must be made in controlling inflation in oil, or raw materials in consuming (affluent) and producing (poor) countries.

The spatial aspects of a multiregional production system are addressed in the next paper by Hafkamp and Nijkamp. They characterize the states of economic environmental systems by means of quality profiles. These quality profiles are integrated into comprehensive multiregional, multisectoral programming models. They proceed then to these models in a multiobjective decision framework and further elaborate the interactive choice strategies. Hafkamp and Nijkamp demonstrate the operational character of the approach by means of a two-region model for the Netherlands.

A central issue for energy policy matters is the environmental-energy trade-off. In the U.S. Department of Energy, where a number of emerging energy technologies are being regularly assessed, House outlines the institution of a systematic procedure for incorporating environmental components with technology assessment. Such procedures include the conduct of a set of integrated analyses and data collection activities that cut across the broad range of impacts — socioeconomic, indirect community, regional needs and institutions, environmental quality degradation, and so forth. What is innovative is the fact that assessment of environmental effects is built formally into the technology assessment of all emerging technologies to be considered by the U.S. Department of Energy.

Van Rhijn concludes the volume with his paper on the future energy policies for the Netherlands. He identifies the four major criteria that would govern the choice of energy policies in the Netherlands. He identifies in this regard such criteria as availability and security of supply, the feasibility of energy source application, the economics of various sources, and the environmental impacts of energy development. His application of these criteria to elucidate future Dutch energy policies has a much broader applicability, beyond the Netherlands to the situation in many affluent countries.

NOTE

1. This conference was held at the Netherlands Institute for Advanced Studies in the Humanities and Social Sciences (NIAS) at Wassenaar.

1 INTEGRATED MODELS FOR ECONOMIC-ENERGY-ENVIRONMENTAL IMPACT ANALYSIS

T. R. Lakshmanan and Sam Ratick, *Boston University*

1. INTRODUCTION

The last decade has witnessed a growing concern with the adequacy of energy resources and with the quality of the physical environment. This concern stems from such factors as the unrelenting growth of energy use, the end of an era of abundant and cheap energy, adverse environmental effects of economic growth, and the increasing participation of government in decisions pertaining to energy supply and environmental protection.

A beneficial externality of this concern has been the enormous stimulus provided to modelling and analysis of environmental and energy policies. A significant portion of this research by social scientists and other professionals focuses on the interactions between energy, economy, and the environment (Figure 1.1).

The environment performs valuable economic service — as a habitat, as a source of supply of materials (fuels, fish, water, and so on), as a receptor and assimilator of pollutants generated by economic activities, and as a source of amenities (recreation, for example). These services are crucial to the conduct of economic activities. The latter — production, consumption, and energy conversion — generate residuals that affect environmental quality adversely

7

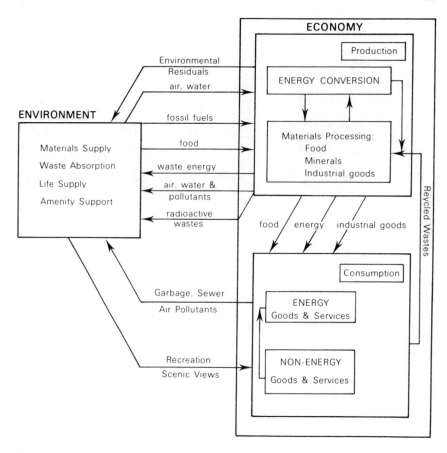

Figure 1.1.   Economic-Environmental-Energy Interactions

if they exceed its waste absorption capacity. The maintenance and improvement of environmental quality (e.g., pollution abatement and material recycling), in turn, requires energy.

In the context of this intimate association between the economy, environment, and energy, recent developments in energy and natural resource supply have raised a number of analytical issues that may be grouped into three classes:

1.   The effects on the economy of (and the policies to facilitate) the transition from cheap, or abundant, energy and a reliance on oil and gas to other more expensive sources of energy.

2. The trade-off between additional or lower cost energy for environonmental quality.
3. The incidence of the costs incurred in the trade-off decisions on different socioeconomic groups in society.

While considerable analytical effort has been devoted to, and some action taken on, the first and the second class issues, little attention has been devoted to the income distributional issues associated with energy supply and protection of the environment.

However, the range of problems that have been addressed even in the models pertaining to the first two classes of issues — at the interfaces between economy and energy and between energy and environment — is quite broad. Contemporary modelling efforts in economic-environmental-energy matters is concerned not only with economic matters but with issues of public sector policy, environmental quality processes, and technological development, which (while having economic effects) extend beyond the scope of socioeconomic theory.

This broader scope of energy-environmental modelling beyond the traditional confines of economic theory, is traceable to the basic structure of economic-energy-environmental interactions. A large number of these interactions are encompassed in physical processes. Examples of such processes are the emissions of pollutants and their spatial diffusion in the environmental media (which will be reflected as economic damages) and the flow of energy and alternative technological processes of energy supply.

This overwhelming diversity and the intermingling of socioeconomic and physical relationships in energy-environmental modelling poses for the analysts the question of the appropriate approach or "angle of attack." Since the analysts engaged in modelling the economy-energy-environmental interfaces are drawn from social sciences, engineering, and physical sciences, a variety of approaches flourish. The different approaches reflect the different perspectives and frameworks of the various analytical traditions.

Thus, the analytical framework of the economist depends on viewing the market and technology as dynamic forces that tend to be self-correcting and can be corrected, if malfunctioning, by proper management. The analysts of the environmental processes emphasize the physical processes of emission, transport, and abatement of pollutants. The energy technologists focus attention on the description of energy flows, conversion efficiencies of different energy forms, and on engineering studies of different technologies.

The strategy of recent economic modelling of energy and environment has been to focus on description of economic behavior and to bring in some physical factors by representing their economic ramifications by aggregate parameters. This paper argues that the resulting description is incomplete due to the lack of vital physical science inputs that may invalidate these aggregate descriptions. It presents the view that an appropriate strategy for modelling economic-energy-environmental interactions for purposes of policy analysis is to integrate the economic and physical process models.

The paper begins with a brief survey of past modelling efforts so as to highlight the necessity for the integrated approach presented here. The models reviewed illustrate the traditions of both the economic and engineering perspectives and include representatives of two popular classes of energy-environmental models: the global models that focus on economic growth, environment, and natural resources (including energy) and the major economy-energy models.

In the light of this discussion, the paper presents a model that integrates economic and physical process models so as to address a number of strategic policy issues in the interfaces between the economy, energy, and environment. This model — termed the Strategic Environmental Assessment System (SEAS) model — has evolved from a test version implemented in 1973 in the U.S. Environmental Protection Agency (EPA) to a large system of interlinked models of the economy, energy, and environment (Lakshmanan and Krishnamurthi [1973], House [1977], Lakshmanan and Ratick [1977]). It provides a framework for assessment of a broad range of policies pertaining to energy supply, energy technologies, and environmental standards.

The paper closes with an application of the SEAS model to provide a strategic assessment of the economic and environmental implications of alternative national policies of energy consumption and supply.

2.   THE EVOLUTION OF ECONOMIC-ENERGY-
ENVIRONMENTAL MODELLING

The current brisk pace of modelling of energy and environmental phenomena reflects the bewildering variety of public policy choices to be made regarding the incentives to promote energy conservation, or to augment energy supply, or to meet environmental standards. While these models provide, to varying degrees, information on the efficiency of the alternative policies to meet the specific objectives sought, a broader assessment of the effects of these policies on *other* valued objectives in society is often necessary.

For example, the choice of policies to stimulate new technologies may well be an efficient means of increasing energy supply and reducing dependence on foreign sources of energy supply. However, it may pose severe environmental damage in the form of air, water, or land pollution. The maintenance of environmental quality in the face of these increased pollution emissions will require additional investment for pollution abatement; further, the requisite large capital investment for energy production and pollution abatement may require a very high level of savings or dampened consumption or a reduction of capital going to other productive sectors in the economy, with adverse consequences on output and price levels. An assessment of energy supply policies requires, consequently, a consideration of these broader contexts of effects on environmental quality and economic growth. Indeed, many energy, natural resources, and environmental policies need to be viewed in a broad context and over the long term so that constraints and fundamental choices are revealed.

Such a strategic perspective in economy-energy-environment interactions modelling has been stimulated in the last decade by two distinct strands of modelling:

1. the "survival" type, global models, which have contributed to an improved analytical representation of economy-environmental relationships, and
2. the "strategic" economy-energy models, focusing on the interrelationships between the economy and energy demand and supply. Originating from various perspectives, these models have identified the role of both economic and physical processes models in aiding broad policy analyses.

The survival type global models focus on the interactions between population, economic growth, natural resources, and environment, so as to identify the long-run outlook for continuation of a high-income, high-amenity society. While the early representatives — Forrester's World 2 and Meadows' and Meadows' World 3, often termed the MIT models — of this type have been greeted by responses ranging from vociferous enthusiasm to derisive dismissal, their basic utility has been to highlight attention on the resource-environment-economy interactions and galvanize professional attention to the relevant issues (Forrester [1971], Meadows and Meadows [1972]).

Our objective is not to address the assumptions, structure, or policy implications of those models. They are discussed extensively in the literature (Carter [1974], Cole et al. [1973], Nordhaus [1975a, 1975b], World Bank [1972]). Instead, we draw attention to their modelling strategy as a stage in the evaluation of the field of interest to this paper.

The MIT models attempt to link the future population growth, natural resource depletion, food supply, capital investment, and pollution in the world at a very high level of aggregation. The modelling perspective derives from engineering, with physical engineering relationships dominant.[1] There is hardly any explicit specification of socioeconomic relationships—the implicit ones often turn out to be glaring misspecifications of widely accepted demographic and economic relationships.[2] The biggest drawback of these models is that there are no central behavioral notions, nor economic parameters such as prices, nor any conscious choices made by society—in fact, no automatic or deliberate corrective mechanisms come into play to avoid impending world collapse.

Subsequent efforts either to elaborate on or to provide countermodels to Forrester and Meadows have made world modelling a growth industry in the last half a decade. Some of the models have attempted to improve the MIT framework by disaggregating the variables in the Meadows model and the world into regions and, in addition, improving the specification of economic (e.g., prices, production functions, international trade) and demographic (age-specific fertility and mobility trends) phenomena (Mesarovic and Pestel [1974], Okita and Kaya [1973]).

Other global models have explicitly started from a different perspective — that of economic theory—in modelling the future growth of industrial production, food supply, and selected "quality of life" variables (e.g., housing, education, and so on) in the world and its regions (Herrera, Scolnik et al. [1974], Leontief et al. [1976]).[3] The Leontief model extends, in addition, its input-output framework to encompass descriptions of natural resource consumption, urbanization, pollution generation, and costs of and economic effects of abatement of pollution.

The main contributions of these world models—as they have evolved and continue to be worked upon—is that they have thrown light on the key interactions between economic growth, natural resource use, and pollution and assisted in the development of some analytical methods for representing these interactions—particularly the links between the economy and environment. Such analytical models include the integration of economic and physical process models.

A second strand of modelling activities relevant to our area of interest is the new generation of models that have been developed to describe, in a sophisticated fashion, energy-economy interactions.

Since energy is used in the production of all goods and services, constraints in the supply of energy or significantly higher prices of energy will affect production processes, energy demand, sectoral composition, and level of GNP. The different models addressing this broad range of analytic issues in economic-energy relations have chosen alternative approaches—some econometric, others physical process models (Hogan and Parikh [1977], Greenberger [1977]).

The strengths and weaknesses of the econometric models can be illustrated in the case of the Hudson-Jorgenson model (Hudson and Jorgenson [1974]). This model is a macroeconomic and interindustry model of the United States economy, where flows of economic activity, including energy flows, are described in terms of economic accounts in current and constant prices. The feedback between energy and economy is through substitution across labor, capital, material, and energy as represented econometrically. Energy technology is represented in terms of behavioral and technical responses of production patterns to alternative prices (rather than through physical flows or engineering descriptions of technology). However, this representation is not possible for either new technologies or commodities not currently demanded.

The class of models that emphasize physical processes and optimization approach (e.g., the PILOT model or the Brookhaven DESOM model), on the other hand, describes energy flows and energy conversion processes in physical terms (Danzig and Parikh [1975], Marcuse et al. [1974]). This permits the representation of all kinds of technologies — current and future — in a form in which alternative technologies and physical supply constraints can be evaluated. For such assessments, those models are clearly superior to the econometric models. However, the energy output of sectors is delivered to other industries rather than to final consumers, so that the larger economic impact of energy technologies had to be assessed in the context of a larger economic model.[4]

What emerges from this review of previous modelling efforts is that the traditional distinctions between energy models that emphasize physical processes and the supply side and econometric models that focus on the demand side are no longer useful. Models capable of assessing a broad range of policies in the economic-energy interface must incorporate both the econometric and physical process approaches. The design of separate models for assessment of energy technologies, or of economic impacts of energy policies, or for the medium or long term reduce their usefulness for the policymakers. Models of energy technologies must be linked to models of the larger economy.

The need for integration between economic and physical processes in economic-environmental modelling was identified earlier. Evaluation of physical damages, such as the health effects of emissions (from energy conversions or general economic activities) of sulfur oxides or radioactive residuals, requires inputs from physical (e.g., diffusion of pollutants, durations of effects, and so forth) and biological (e.g., effects on flora and fauna) effects.

Thus, intelligent decisions pertaining to the interface of the economy, energy, and environment require models that are no longer the private preserve of a single discipline. Engineers, economists, operations researchers, technologists, and physical scientists need to join together, work cooperatively, and begin to appreciate the significance of one another's efforts.

These different disciplines bring to this task a diverse and rich assortment of methods such as input-output models, econometric models, optimization models, diffusion and flow modelling, engineering process descriptions, institutional and financial relationships, and a variety of judgments exercised with different balancing frameworks. If the workers from the different disciplines work together, their different analytical traditions expand and merge as they learn from and borrow from one another. An integrated economic-environmental-energy model provides a basic framework for such cooperative research from different fields that is directed to policy evaluation.

3.   SEAS: AN INTEGRATED
ECONOMIC-ENVIRONMENTAL-ENERGY MODEL

3.1   General

The objective of this paper is to present such an integrated model of the economy-energy-environmental interactions, termed the Strategic Environmental Assessment System (SEAS) model. From a test version implemented in 1973 in the U.S. EPA, SEAS has developed over the last five years into a large system of interlinked models of the economy, energy, and environment.

A large number of individuals drawn from different disciplines — economics, geography, engineering, operations research, systems analysis, policy science, and energy technology — have cooperated in the development of SEAS.[5] These individuals have formed an interdisciplinary team drawn from universities, private research organizations, and the United States Government. This interdisciplinary and multiinstitutional development environment of SEAS has required close links between model and policy analysis. Unlike the typical modelling effect, the modellers in the group have been regularly alerted to the nature of the decision problems, their constraints, and what are and what are not critical issues as perceived by the top-level government policymakers. At the same time, policymakers were provided a better understanding of the model, its assumptions, strengths, and limitations. Thus, the need for bridges between the producers and consumers of SEAS was recognized early and their creation has been a shared responsibility. This explains continued use of SEAS for analysis of a wide range of public policies in the U.S. EPA and the U.S. Department of Energy. Examples of such policies are: the annual economic effects of the implementation of the Clean Air Act and the Clean Water Act, the environmental consequences of the proposed Carter National Energy Plan, and the economic and environmental consequences of Resource Recovery policies.

The evaluation of SEAS over this period also reflects the keen sensitivity of modelling choices to emerging and current public policy issues. Thus, the test version of SEAS implemented in 1973 was an economic-environmental model that provided a systematic assessment of the emissions of more than twenty pollutants (including radioactive wastes) into air, water, and land and demands for fuel and nonfuel resources as a natural consequence of production and consumption processes (Figure 1.2). It was an early effort at linking population and economic growth, natural resource use, and environmental pollution at the national level starting from an economic perspective (a 185-sector dynamic I-O model of the United States). The prototype version of SEAS elaborated the model by a disaggregation of both the economic submodel and the environmental submodel. The input-output model sectors were disaggregated further both by process and sector as were the environmental sectors (Figure 1.3). In the last three years, the energy sub-

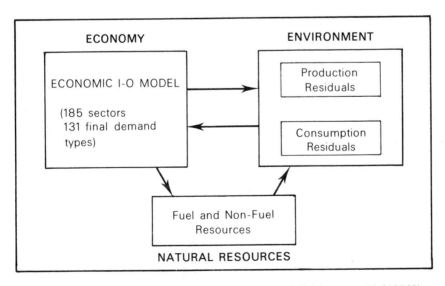

Figure 1.2. SEAS Test Model (Lakshmanan and Krishnamurthi [1973])

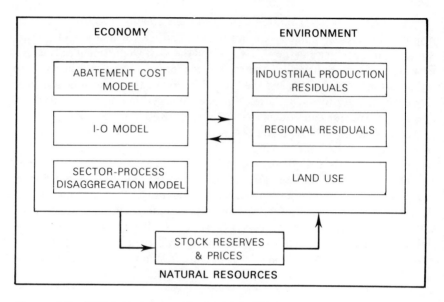

Figure 1.3. SEAS Prototype Model (U.S. EPA [1975])

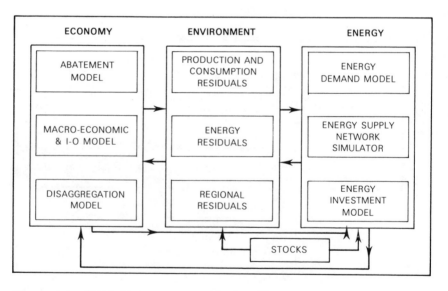

Figure 1.4. SEAS Model System (House [1977], Lakshmanan and Ratick [1977])

system comprising a demand and supply system and an investment model has been added, so that SEAS can describe economic-energy-environmental interactions. Figure 1.4 presents the current state of SEAS in a schematic fashion. A more complete version of SEAS appears in Figure 1.5, where the four component subsystems — the national economic subsystem, the national environmental subsystem, the energy system, the regional environmental subsystem, and a raw material subsystem — are identified. We will briefly describe each of these in turn.

3.2 National Economic Subsystem

This subsystem has three components: a national I-O model, a sector-process disaggregation model, and a pollution abatement cost model. The center of the national economic subsystem is a 190-sector, dynamic, inter-industry forecasting model of the U.S. economy, known as INFORUM (*In*ter-industry *For*ecasting Model of the *U*niversity of *M*aryland). INFORUM views the American economy as a set of 190 producing and consuming sectors linked to one another by the flow of goods and services and to (131 types of) final consumers — households, government, capital equipment, construction, and inventories and net exports.[6] It is maintained as a forecasting system that can be driven by alternate national macroeconomic forecasts to generate projections of the detailed structure of economic activity annually to year 1990. The SEAS project has extended this system to the year 2000, and in one application to the year 2025. INFORUM data base is continually maintained and updated; the production structure is revised and projected based on industry studies and econometric methods. The final demand components are estimated by an elaborate econometric forecasting system. Exogenous trends (e.g., population, labor force, federal government expenditures, labor productivity, interest rates), coupled with the specified structural relationships, are used to generate annual economic forecasts.

Since INFORUM is an economic model that was not designed with environmental issues in mind, INSIDE, or the Sector Disaggregation model, has been developed to adapt INFORUM to the forecast of environmental residuals. A number of side equations are developed in INSIDE to enable the system to take into account product and technological mix problems.

Product mix problems arise from different products of an I-O sector having significantly different residuals generation and demand trends. An example of a product mix problem is the emissions from nitric acid production. INFORUM Sector 55 (the industrial chemical sector) is responsible for 36 percent of the nitrogen oxide emissions from stationary fuel combustion

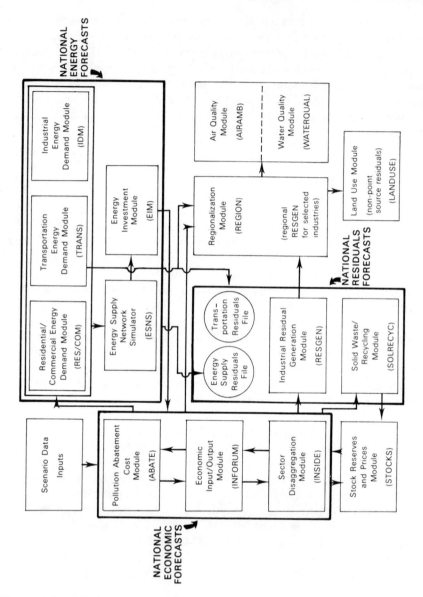

Figure 1.5.   SEAS Model System

sources. It would be possible to relate the future output of nitrogen oxides from the chemical industry to the economic activity of Sector 55. However, there are several hundred major chemicals within Sector 55, and the manu-facture of nitric acid generates the vast majority of nitrogen oxide emissions produced by this industry.

About 80 percent of the nitric acid manufactured is sold to fertilizers (Sector 59) and miscellaneous chemicals (Sector 61), whereas Sector 55 sells over 50 percent of its total volume of products to plastics, noncellulose fibers, cleaning and toilet preparations, miscellaneous chemicals, and paints. The growth rate of nitric acid does not parallel the aggregate growth of all major chemicals in Sector 55. Thus, relating the nitrogen oxide emissions to nitric acid demand rather than to the aggregate of Sector 55 gives a more accurate projection of nitrogen oxide emissions.

Furthermore, the side equation permits a clearer understanding of economic relationships to environmental concerns. Suppose that environ-mental considerations require a decrease in the use of nitrogen fertilizers. One result would be a decrease in the stationary nitrogen oxide emissions. This result would not have been predicted unless a side equation had been constructed for nitric acid.

An illustration of a technological mix problem is that of steel production by the competing processes of the electric-arc furnace, open hearth furnace, and basic oxygen furnace. Side equations allow the pollution coefficients to be linked with the particular type of steel production rather than with steel production as a whole (Sector 83). Thus, more detail is built into the model to allow residual forecasts as a function of relative growth among processes.

The side equations serve to disaggregate INFORUM sector outputs to the subsector level, where the outputs are expressed in physical units rather than in monetary units. Side equations are dependent upon the output of INFORUM; however, the output of a side equation is rarely significant enough to affect the INFORUM results. The output of certain side equa-tions, however, is sufficient to alter the INFORUM results. For these cases, techniques have been developed that place the side equations directly within INFORUM, thus providing for automatic feedback and correction.

The SEAS Abatement Cost module has two primary functions. The first is to serve as a means for aggregating and generating costs associated with meeting environmental standards for water pollution (including thermal pollution), air pollution (excluding control of automobile emissions), and radiation wastes. In this role, it utilizes user-supplied input data and scenario parameters for each sector, together with information generated elsewhere in SEAS, to develop abatement expenditures by sector on a year-by-year basis, as well as aggregate costs for each standard specified.

The second function is to incorporate the feedbacks of purchases for abatement within the SEAS forecasts (particularly within INFORUM). These data include the direct impacts on the supplying industries as well as on abatement-related employment; moreover, indirect feedbacks are also included. The more important of these are the effects of abatement costs on sectoral prices and outputs and on consumption and investment.

The model does not calculate abatement costs associated with automobile emission controls, solid waste disposal, and the control of pollutants in other modules of SEAS. For these categories, the cost module is used in its second role as a feedback mechanism. Using the abatement costs from these other modules, the cost module can capture the feedbacks of these costs on economic and other SEAS forecasts in a manner similar to those for other categories.

The key factor in determining feedbacks is the specification of vectors that allocate a dollar of capital and operating costs by abating sectors. Different vectors can apply to different standards. The total costs for a given year are broken down into demands from supplying industries using vectors. Operating expenditures for industrial sectors are bought on intermediate account and do not affect GNP directly. Effectively, they modify the A-matrix because of the additional purchases of chemicals, energy, and so forth. Abatement expenditures by industries on capital account and all municipal costs are added to final demand. The intermediate and final demand purchases lead to changing outputs by industries that affect investment and other variables. In the process, abatement costs are also impacted.

At the same time, price changes are occurring due to the cost-push caused by abatement expenditures as well as demand-pull effects in sectors that are abatement suppliers. The cost-push effects are captured by including the additional annual costs due to abatement in the price equations. Annual costs are the sum of operating costs and capital costs converted to an annual basis by means of a user-specified rate. These price changes lead to changing relative prices which then affect consumption by sector and, hence, output and other variables; they also lead to some input substitution. The net effects of all these changes essentially represent the feedbacks of abatement costs.

3.3 National Environmental Subsystem

This submodel generates forecasts of pollutant tonnages obtained from the National Economic Forecasts and the pollution abatement regulations. It computes national estimates of water and air residuals associated with activity in each of more than 400 pollutant-producing economic sectors and subsectors. A reasonable accounting can thus be made of the residuals produced in a specified year at both the national and regional levels, with this output being sensitive to changes in the mix and level of economic activity.

Additionally, RESGEN provides a means of assessing the environmental benefits of national pollution control standards by measuring the efficiency of waste treatment in both present and future years. A third objective of the module is to determine the amount and type of secondary residuals created as a result of pollution control in a medium.

RESGEN consists of a set of matrices and vectors for each year of the model's economic forecast. The starting point of the module is the definition of a coefficient relating generation of a specific pollutant to the output of an industrial sector/subsector in a given year. These gross, or uncontrolled, residual coefficients are expressed as tons of pollutant per million dollars of production if the industry in question is an INFORUM sector, or as tons of pollutant per million units produced (tons, bushels, or million BTUs) if the industry is an INSIDE subsector. The coefficient multiplied by the sector/subsector output provides the total gross residual for that year. An estimate of in-place treatment is then made. Both the extent (percentage of wastes receiving treatment) and efficiency (percentage of wastes removed by treatment) of treatment are estimated. The product of these two values equals the amount of gross residuals captured, with the remainder representing the net effluent discharged to streams, land, or the atmosphere. Two other pieces of data are also developed: the rate at which captured waste materials are recycled and the rate at which nonrecycled captured residuals are converted into secondary residuals (e.g., sludges). Both factors are expressed as a percentage of captured residuals.

SOLRECYC provides solid waste tonnages, with separate accounting for materials recycled. Other submodels estimate the residuals from energy supply and transportation usage.

3.4 Regional Environmental Subsystem

All the above modules make forecasts for the entire nation. A special module, *Region*, takes output from the national pollution-forecasting modules and breaks it down to produce regional forecasts — by state (Air Quality Control Region: AQCR), major control region, minor river basin, and several other schemes.

The region forecasts are arrived at from the top down; that is, the distribution of national pollution tonnages to the various regions is done by using the OBERS projections of economic activity by various regional groupings (OBERS [1974]). OBERS projections, developed by the U.S. Department of Commerce, are based on the use of a shift-share technique and suffer from a variety of drawbacks (Lakshmanan et al. [1979]). Currently an effort is underway to develop a multiregional *M*odel of the *R*egional *E*conomy and *E*nergy *D*emand (MREED) to provide a better basis for regional forecasting of economic activity in a framework that relates spatially the economies of different regions in the United States (Lakshmanan [1977]).

3.5 Energy Subsystem

In view of the recent concern with energy conservation and the impact of environmental policies related to energy, a special set of five modules has been developed to provide forecasts of energy-related data.

Three of these modules forecast the demand for energy resulting from the levels of economic activity forecast by SEAS/INFORUM. RES/COM forecasts residential/commercial energy demand, IDM forecasts industrial energy demand, and TRANS forecasts energy demand for transportation. These forecasts are in BTUs.

Based on the outputs of RESCOM, IDM, and TRANS, energy resource requirements are calculated by ESNS, the energy system network simulator, which is based on a Brookhaven Laboratories model. (The Brookhaven model provides an energy reference system and supply network from energy resources to energy end uses. The model allocates energy supplies to energy demands to minimize cost). A fifth module, EIM, then predicts the level of investment required to supply the required resources.

Energy prices forecast by EIM are fed back to RESCOM, IDM, and TRANS, and the entire energy package is run repeatedly until successive price forecasts converge, indicating that the results take changes in energy prices sufficiently into account. The final results are then fed back to SEAS/INFORUM, and the input-output matrix is modified to allow for the indicated energy demands.

3.6 Raw Material Subsystem

A separate module, STOCKS, takes into account the effects of raw material depletion. Both domestic production and importation of raw materials are figured into the stocks output, as are the effects of recycling.

3.7 Concluding Remarks

This is quite an elaborate model that brings together relationships and data pertaining to the economy, environment, and resources in a flexible framework that permits *conditional* (what if . . .) estimates. Because of the general interdependence among all parts of the SEAS system, the level of each type of economic activity or environmental residual loadings or energy and natural resource use (if not fixed by explicit assumption) will respond in some degree to changes introduced in any other part of the system. Further, many coefficients — production, residual generation, energy use, other natural resource consumption, abatement efficiency, and so forth — in the model are subject to change, in response to exogenously specified change in relative prices, supply constraints, preferences, technology, or endogenous changes due to feedbacks of another part of the system or on the basis of statistical studies of trends. This characteristic allows the flexible use of the model, permitting the estimation of requirements of meeting specified levels of a wide variety of target variables. For instance, it is possible to estimate the generation of various pollutants in air, water, and on land, the level of energy use, and the critical natural resource consumption that are consistent with a given projection of economic and population growth and changes in labor force participation rates.

4. AN APPLICATION OF SEAS

4.1 Introduction

We present next an application of SEAS to assess the economic and environmental consequences of two alternative future national energy supply scenarios (Table 1.1). The first of these is the U.S. Bureau of Mines (BOM) view of the energy future. The BOM scenario is a high-energy use and business-as-usual variety, assuming a general continuation of current trends in the patterns of energy use. It is typical of the assumptions of a number of leaders in the energy industry and government. The second scenario is the Ford Technical Fix (FTF), which assumes that vigorous efforts will be made to switch over to practical, economical, and energy-saving technology that is currently available or soon will be.

The macroeconomic assumptions — population, labor force, disposable income/capita — are the same for both the BOM and FTF scenarios. So are the pollution abatement assumptions of both scenarios. The differences arise in the specification of energy demand and energy supply in the nation and in one region — Ohio River Basin (ORBES, consisting of Ohio, Illinois, Indiana, and Kentucky).

The total energy demand in 1985 and 2000 is assumed respectively at 78 and 110 Quadrillion BTUs (Quads) for BOM and at 75 and 93 quads for FTF. Since FTF stresses electricity use less, in terms of resource consump-

Table 1.1. Scenarios for the ORBES Study

	Scenario	
Dimension	Bureau of Mines (BOM)	Ford Technological Fix (FTF)
A. ECONOMIC		
Population	Census Series D: 235.7m (1985): 264.4m (2000)	Same
Labor force	BLS 106m (1985): 123m (2000)	Same
Dispos. income/capita	(1958 prices) $4306 (1985): $6581 (2000)	Same
Productivity	Moderate to high	
B. ENVIRONMENTAL		
National	Delay in standards: Clean Air Act provisions through 1/1/77; State Implementation Plans (SIP) to be met by 1985, as will the BAT requirements of Fed. Water Pollution Control Act of 1972; BPT delayed by 2 years	Same
Regional	Pollutant removal efficiency related to individual State Implementation Plans	Same
	Gross emission coefficients related to mix of fuel supply assumed (see D below)	
C. ENERGY DEMAND	Historical growth patterns	Conservation in the use of energy
	Historical electricity use patterns trended	Transportation energy savings through mpg changes
	Aggregate demand: 78.2 quads (1985); 110 quads (2000)	75.4 quad (1985); 102.2 (2000)
	Aggregate resource use: 112.6 quad (1985); 180 quad (2000)	93.0 quad (1985); 141 quad (2000)

D. ENERGY SUPPLY

National	Greater use of electricity		Greater use of coal and gas	
Regional projection of new (post-1955) elec. generating plants	*Case 1*	*Case 2*	*Case 1*	*Case 2*
	80% coal	50% coal-fired	100% coal-fired	50% coal
	20% nuclear	50% nuclear		50% nuclear

tion, the energy savings over BOM in the year 2000 is even higher — 22 percent in the year 2000. Much of this savings stems from the transportation sector (improvements in vehicle miles per gallon), greater direct use of fossil fuels, and other conservation measures.

The procedures for simulating the two scenarios in the SEAS system is an iterative process between the model and the policy analyst. First, the model is targeted on the GNP/capita forecast of the BOM scenarios, by adjusting the annual per capita disposable income (PCDI) (the same population labor force forecasts are used in both scenarios). The PCDI levels in turn determine consumption and government purchases and industry output levels. If the perturbations introduced by other exogenous inputs in the model lead to aggregate expenditures that are higher or lower than the targeted GNP, a disposable income is iteratively lowered or increased to obtain convergence on the targeted GNP. (The mix and level of investments in producer durable equipment required to satisfy the BOM national energy demands were included in the economic forecasts prior to GNP targeting.) For the FTF scenario, the same PCDI as in the BOM scenario was used and the GNP allowed to float. (The expenditures for energy conservation were included in the FTF scenario.)

Further, existing regulations and state-level implementation plans were used to devise abatement efficiencies and modify the net emission coefficients for regional industries. The energy demand and supply assumptions of the two scenarios were input to the Energy System Network Simulator (ESNS) component of the energy modules, so as to determine the level of energy supply activity — by specific fuel category — needed to meet the forecasted energy demands.

4.2 Economic Effects

The overall performance of the national economy corresponding to the two scenarios appears in Table 1.2. While the FTF scenario represents a savings of more than 20 percent in energy resource use over BOM, the BOM scenario has only a slightly higher GNP/capita — less than 1 percent higher in 1985 and 2000. Real GNP/capita more than doubles in both scenarios. Since the disposable income per capita was kept constant for both scenarios, all changes in GNP and outputs are the result of changes in the industrial mix resulting from energy supply (BOM) and energy conservation (FTF) activities.

Gross private domestic investment (GPDI) as a percentage of GNP is higher in the BOM scenario (16.2 percent versus 15.6 percent) for the year 2000, due mostly to the larger capital investments necessary to supply the

Table 1.2. Comparison of Economic Growth Paths in the BOM and FTF Scenarios[1] (In 1971 dollars, except as indicated)

Item	Base Year 1975	Bureau of Mines Scenario (BOM) 1985	2000	Annual Growth Rates% 1975-1985	1985-2000	Ford Tech. Fix Scenario (FTF) 1985	2000	Annual Growth Rates% 1975-1985	1985-2000
A. Macro Indicators									
1. GNP/capita ($)	5360	7787	11,282	3.8	2.5	7749	11,200	3.78	2.50
2. Disposable income/capita ($1958)	2579	4306	6,581	3.75	2.87	4306	6,581	3.75	2.87
3. Gross private domestic investment as a % of GNP	13.0	17.9	16.2	3.3	-.01	17.5	15.6	3.0	-.01
4. Total output ($ Billions)	1877.8	3070.3	5034.3	5.0	3.35	3038.7	4,938.8	4.7	3.29
5. Civilian unemployment rate (%)		5.3	4.5			5.7	5.2		
B. Composition of Capital Investment ($ billions)									
Energy	45.2	64.93	82.84	3.7	1.6	42.91	54.09	0.0	1.2
Construction	4.1	4.98	6.60	2.0	1.9	9.48	15.75	8.7	3.4
All sectors	137.1	198.84	305.6	3.8	2.9	186.1	284.6	3.1	2.9

[1]Source: Computed from SEAS Simulation, September 1977

higher energy demand. The composition of capital investment is highly suggestive of the difference between scenarios. In the BOM scenario, output and capital investments are heavier in electric utilities and other direct related energy sectors. Capital investments in energy grow 3.7 percent a year in 1975–85 and 1.2 percent per year in 1985–2000 in the BOM scenario. In both 1985 and 2000, half the investments in the utilities in BOM are for nuclear plants. By contrast, FTF investment is focused on conservation — household appliances (energy-saving devices), stones and clay products (insulation), and service industry machinery. The rapid growth in "new construction" (Sector 18) capital purchases reflects the growth in national gas sector.

A more rapid change in GNP, investment, and output is in the decade before 1985, and a slowing down thereafter is evident. Investment rises faster than GNP throughout the forecast period, more so in the BOM scenario.

The unemployment rate is higher in the FTF scenario, partly a reflection of the use of the same productivity assumptions in the two scenarios. The implicit assumption is that energy-saving capital can be developed by year 2000 so as to maintain output and productivity at levels that would have otherwise been reached. If this assumption is not valid for the earlier period (1985), our unemployment estimates for FTF would be high.

What changes in the composition of output and employment emerge in response to our energy conservation scenario? Again energy industries dominate the picture (Table 1.3). The highest relative changes between the two scenarios are in electric utilities (29 percent) and mining (23 percent) and natural gas (21 percent), used more in FTF. The increased expenditures for energy conservation in FTF are reflected in greater output in relevant industries such as household appliances, services industry machinery, and stone and clay products.

The employment changes replicate the national output patterns with one difference (Table 1.4). In the FTF scenario, jobs increase in the energy conservation-oriented sectors (employment sectors are aggregates of the output sectors, there are ninety employment sectors) and drop in the energy production sectors, with a net loss of over 9,000,000 jobs in the year 2000. However, this job loss would have been greater but for the greater capital intensity and greater output per worker in industries such as electric utilities.

Next we consider the effects of these national growth patterns on the economy of the Ohio River Basin (ORBES) region (Table 1.5). As in the nation, the major output differences between the two scenarios are in those industries that generate energy or contribute to energy conservation. Some of these industries — electric utilities, household appliances, and petroleum refining — are dominant (ORBES) regional industries. In addition, energy-intensive sectors such as steel and structural metal products have larger out-

Table 1.3. Changes in the Composition of National Output between BOM and FTF, Year 2000

| | Year 2000 | | |
| | (Billions of $, 1971) | | BOM-FTF/FTF |
Sector	BOM	FTF	(% Difference)
Electrical utilities	149.10	108.55	37.4
Coal mining	19.0	14.73	29.2
Structural metal products	41.19	36.58	12.6
Transformers & switchgear	9.206	7.85	17.3
Natural gas	20.41	22.23	-8.2
Other stone & clay products	11.60	12.55	-7.6
Household appliances	22.77	24.46	-7.5
Service industry machinery	31.33	32.21	-2.7
All industries	5034.27	4938.79	1.9

Source: Computed from SEAS ORBES simulation, September [1977]

Table 1.4. Changes in the Composition of National Employment between BOM and FTF, Year 2000

| | Year 2000 | | |
| | (000 persons) | | BOM-FTF/FTF |
Selected Sectors	BOM	FTF	(% Difference)
Electric utilities	752.4	533.6	41.0
Mining	388.2	350.7	10.7
Railroads	473.7	450.0	5.1
Natural gas, water, & sewer	347.1	356.6	-2.7
Household appliances	240.8	257.2	-6.4
Service industrial machinery	203.9	210.9	-3.3
Stone & clay products	850.5	866.5	-1.8
All industries	121,472.5	120,559.0	0.76

Source: Meyer et al. [1977], pp. 27, 28.

puts in the BOM case. However, some other large regional industries such as motor vehicles, crops, and food products evidence little or no differences in

Table 1.5. Effects of National Growth Patterns on ORBES Region, Year 2000

Selected Sectors	ORBES Region, Year 2000 ($ 1971 Mill.)			Illinois, Year 2000 ($ 1971 Mill.)		
	BOM	FTF	BOM-FTF/FTF (% Difference)	BOM	FTF	BOM-FTF/FTF (% Difference)
Steel	9,383	8,911	4.9	1,597	1,516	5.5
Petroleum refining	10,451	9,949	5.0	4,309	4,102	5.0
Structural metal products	7,610	6,762	12.5	2,821	2,507	12.5
Coal mining				1,873	1,450	29.2
Electrical utilities	43,206	31,452	37.4	15,980	11,630	37.4
Household appliances	12,521	13,446	-6.9	2,620	2,814	-6.9
Service industry machinery				2,476	2,544	-2.7
Other stone and clay products				582	630	-7.6

Source: Meyer et al. [1977], pp. 30 and 31

the two scenarios. It may be noted that the percentage differences in output in the ORBES region and Illinois are not very different for most sectors (Table 1.5). This low variation is partly due to the inflexibility of the top-down regionalization procedures currently embedded in SEAS. These procedures involving the allocations of national output by sector are expected to be replaced by a multiregional model that captures regional growth and interregional effects.

In the national economy, primary energy inputs form a small proportion of GNP (less than 4 percent). Consequently, the effects of scenarios that differ in the use of energy, even to the degree BOM and FTF do, are most significant only in the relevant energy supply, energy conservation, and energy-intensive manufacturing (e.g., primary metals) sectors. The impacts on the rest of the economy are not pronounced, and hence, the small effect on the GNP.

However, this may be only part of the story. The level of capital investment envisaged (to generate energy, to conserve energy, and to protect the environment) is very high (16–18 percent of GNP), much higher than that of the previous history of savings in the United States, although comparable to that of Japan or European countries. Such a high level of savings will increase the competition for "productive capital" in the economy, leading to inflationary pressures as well as a fall in the output and labor productivity (over what it might be otherwise). Those indirect effects of energy developments on the economy have to be reckoned with, in addition to the direct ones, and they have been explored elsewhere.[7]

We have only explored the compositional changes in the GNP and in particular in the regional industrial mix. We proceed now to the environmental consequences of energy development.

4.3 Environmental Effects

While per capita real disposable income and GNP more than double betwen 1975 and 2000, the gross emissions for some pollutants do not keep pace due primarily to process mix changes. While the gross pollutant emissions increase significantly, the net emissions in most cases decline (except for oxides of nitrogen and sulphur, both of which are higher in 2000 than in 1975). The standards for mobile sources embedded in SEAS do not reflect the latest delays of the Clean Air Act Amendments. The net figures may be an understatement of the likely total pollution emission into the environment for the nation (Table 1.6).

The ORBES region is part of the industrial heartland of the United States. Its industrial mix has a greater weighting of energy-intensive indus-

Table 1.6.   National Residual Emissions

	2000	
Pollutant Category	Gross	Net
Particulates	263,342,096	12,751,296
Sulfur oxides	84,434,720	29,728,032
Nitrogen oxides	28,553,392	27,592,608
Hydrocarbons[a]	23,762,848	11,484,086
Carbon monoxide[a]	195,033,312	54,711,200
Biochemical oxygen demand[b]	30,492,400	1,759,618
Chemical oxygen demand	29,610,864	2,505,460
Total suspended solids	379,952,192	4,691,203
Total dissolved solids	34,424,352	14,234,192
Oils and greases	2,438,487	241,759

Source: Meyer et al. [1977]

[a]Hydrocarbons (HC) and carbon monoxide (CO) emissions are primarily derived from mobile sources of pollution. The decline in HC and CO emissions over the forecast period is due to a decline in the mobile source emissions over the period.

[b]In the case of biochemical oxygen demand, the municipal waste that has been *treated* becomes an effluent. Thus BOD declines over time as more secondary and tertiary treatment is assumed.

tries (e.g., steel) and energy conversion. This is reflected in its higher than average levels of air and water residuals in 1975. While the four-state ORBES region accounts for only a seventh (14.2 percent) of the population in 1975, its share of net pollutant discharges is much higher—from a fifth to almost half—for many pollutants (Table 1.7). By year 2000, except for total dissolved solids (TDS), nitrogen oxides (NOX), and sulphur oxides (SOX), the situation improves significantly in the ORBES region.

NOX and SOX and TDS are associated most closely with industrial activity, especially energy extraction and conversion technologies. Since the ORBES region will be experiencing a large increase in these energy activities, we would expect the emission values for these pollutants to be effected. The mix and level of energy consumption and the industrial mix in the region account for the high levels of SOX, NOX, and TDS that are maintained throughout the forecast period. The levels of coal-fired utilities and industrial combustion (primarily coal) account for SOX and NOX emissions not declining. The location of industrial chemicals—sodium carbonate, phos-

Table 1.7. Residual Emissions in the O Region (for the BOM scenario)

	Gross	% of Nat'l Total	Net	% of Nat'l Total
1975				
Particulates	19,519,059	18.2	4,265,892	29.8
SOx	6,820,388	15.9	5,752,306	23.7
TSS	26,664,133	22.7	6,485,752	46.2
TDS	2,608,821	14.6	2,247,479	18.8
2000				
Particulates	41,036,566	15.6	1,810,094	14.2
SOx	17,533,643	20.8	6,320,602	21.3
HC	3,539,787	14.9	1,674,729	14.6
CO	74,010,708	37.9	9,671,750	17.7
TSS	67,823,071	18.1	132,927	2.8
TDS	6,451,360	18.7	4,119,862	28.9

Source: Meyer et al. [1977]

phoric acid, chlorine, and such—and mining and coal processing in the region account for the high level of TDS emissions. Net emissions NOX, SOX, and TDS are shown to increase over the forecast horizon, as does the national emission figures for these pollutants. However, in the ORBES region the "gross emissions" for SOX, NOX, and TDS show a greater increase than the national figures; only for TDS does this hold true for the net emission figures. Since the growth in the ORBES region will require new capacity to be built, the assumptions about meeting the SIP standards, with their stricter emission requirements for new sources, is important in keeping net emissions (those released to the environment) in the region from growing faster than the net emissions nationally.

The environmental effects of the two alternative scenarios are presented in Table 1.8. Since both scenarios assume the same national and regional populations and economic growth forecasts, the differences in residual emissions are traceable to the energy demand and supply assumptions. It is quite clear that energy conservation is better for air and water generally. In many cases, the level of gross emissions of air and water residuals is lower in the FTF scenario. There is less difference between the two scenarios in the level of net pollutants from stationary sources. One reason is the greater efficiency of pollution abatement assumed to be associated with the capital to be installed in the BOM scenario. For primarily mobile source pollutants—

Table 1.8. Environmental Effects of the Two Scenarios in the ORBES Region, Year 2000

Pollutant Category	BOM Gross	FTF Gross	% Difference[a]	BOM Net	FTF Net	% Difference[a]
Particulates	41,036,566	37,326,901	– 9.0	1,810,094	1,755,108	– 3.0
Sulfur oxides	17,533,643	14,409,203	–17.8	6,320,602	6,334,145	+ 0.1
Nitrogen oxides	4,589,850	4,088,158	–10.9	4,324,810	3,866,242	–10.6
Hydrocarbons	3,539,787	3,050,650	–13.8	1,674,729	1,314,270	–21.5
Carbon monoxide	74,010,708	68,852,424	– 7.0	9,671,750	7,688,257	–20.5
BOD	2,262,202	2,234,212	– 1.2	112,033	107,968	– 3.6
COD	1,862,233	1,719,292	– 7.7	165,717	106,113	– 3.4
TSS	67,823,071	60,379,442	–11.0	132,927	129,337	– 2.7
TDS	6,451,360	5,750,643	–10.9	4,119,862	3,998,757	– 3.0

Source: Meyer et al. [1977], p. 78.

[a]FTF-BOM/BOM

hydrocarbons and carbon monoxide—the significantly lower level of pollution in the FTF scenario is due to the type of savings assumed in the transportation energy sector (e.g., more use of mass transit).

Overall, the high energy use BOM scenario, as compared with the FTF scenario, registers a slight (0.7 percent) increase in GNP in year 2000, but leads to a higher level of pollutant loadings on the environment. There are significant increases (11 to 22 percent) of emissions in the environment in the case of nitrogen oxides, hydrocarbons, and carbon monoxide in the BOM as compared with FTF in 1985 and 2000.

Though BOM generates twice as much electricity as FTF, 50 percent is assumed to be supplied by nuclear reactors. The latter generate special residuals not reported in Table 1.8. It would be prudent to conclude that the high energy use BOM scenario, as compared with the FTF conservation scenario, leads to a higher level of overall environmental pollutants in the ORBES region, with its particular industrial mix. Also, the higher level of activity in coal mining in the BOM scenario would cause a greater amount of mine waste to be produced. The land burden and concomitant environmental problems associated with mine wastes would be intensified. Further, since the state implementation plans (SIP) were the assumed abatement schedule, there is probably a much larger solid waste due to scrubbers on electric utilities—a good example of intermedia transfers for pollutants.

The ORBES region, as the western part of the United States industrial heartland, currently shows a high level of pollutant loadings into the environment and a relatively lower level of environmental quality. The ORBES region currently has a high proportion of the areas of high emission density and high SOX concentrations. The choice of a high energy use business-as-usual scenario as against a conservation-oriented FTF scenario will lead to a significant worsening of the environment in this region.

4.4 Concluding Comments

This analysis of the implications of the two scenarios must be viewed as an illustration of economic and environmental assessment of alternative energy development scenarios through the use of SEAS. SEAS provides a tool in which different sets of assumptions about the future economy, environment, and energy demand and supply may be consistently compared and a comprehensive accounting of the results can be assessed. Such a system can also be useful as a screening method for proposed policies and help modify policy to achieve their intended results more efficiently.

Certain limitations of the SEAS must be emphasized. The regional impact estimates are not currently adequately addressed by the SEAS system.[8]

Environmental quality and energy costs in a region have become important factors in regional location of industries and households. Yet most current analyses of regional locations of firms and households (including SEAS) fail to incorporate them. We believe that environmental and energy factors need to be and can be incorporated in the analysis of regional economic growth. When such a regional module is incorporated in SEAS, the regional impacts estimated will provide some indication of where beneficial and adverse effects occur, both in the national and regional economies.[9] Such information can be useful for suggesting areas for more detailed analysis.

Another area that has not been addressed in this paper is the distributional income implications of energy development. It is quite likely that the energy developments over two or three decades could affect different individuals and regions quite differently. This limitation must be kept in mind, particularly if our exercise had considered different regions of the country.

Indeed, the major utility of SEAS is as an integrated strategic screening device of major proposed policies, whose comprehensive effects on the economy-energy-environment milieu can be assessed. Such a screening should help spotlight areas for further detailed inquiry and specific policy recommendations.

5. NOTES

1. Since these models do not disaggregate the world either in terms of economic sectors or by geography, there is chronic underspecification. Further, the use of systems dynamics, which has proved to be successful in correctly and completely specified microsystems, in the context of an incompletely specified macrosystem of the world, has posed problems (Carter [1974]).

2. For instance, Forrester assumes, without reference to a demographic literature, that world population grows with increased availability of food per capita and affluence — a relationship at variance with the experience of both affluent and low-income countries. Again, the use of the notion of costs as a function of resources for all industry means that even for non-extractive industries, there is no substitution between resource and nonresource inputs (Nordhaus [1975a]).

3. The Herrera-Scolnik model — known also as the Bariloche model — is somewhat different from the rest. It is an optimizing model that, instead of projecting future trends, attempts to maximize the imaginative objective function of meeting the "basic needs" of the poor in the developing world. For an interpretive survey of the model see Nordhaus [1975b].

There are other models, such as the Tinbergen-Linneman model — that attempts to meet minimum standards of living, reduce income disparities, conserve nonrenewable resources, and protect the environment — and the University of California at Davis models — that address issues such as fossil fuel consumption, heat radiation, heat balance, CO_2 emission, and so on — all of which address a broader range of global "survival" issues.

4. In the case of the PILOT model, this is possible to some degree since it uses twenty-three I-O sectors.

5. A select list of these individuals include T. R. Lakshmanan, Peter House, Ted Williams, Richard Ball, Roger Shull, Phil Patterson, Sam Ratick, Ron Ridker, William Watson, A. Shapanka, N. Dossani, S. Krishnamurthi, R. Meyer, R. Doggett, M. Kramer, M. Stern, R. Anderson, B. Wing, E. Lake, R. Ubico, and Peter Kroll.

6. See Almon et al. [1974].

7. Ridker, Watson, and Shapanka [1977].

8. This was also the conclusion reached by the National Scientific Advisory Panel headed by W. Leontief. See Leontief, Crocker, et al. [1976].

9. See Lakshmanan, July 1977.

6. REFERENCES

Almon, Clopper, M.R. Buckler, L.M. Horowitz, and T.C. Reimbold. *1985: Interindustry Forecasts of the American Economy.* Lexington, Mass.: D.C. Heath, 1974.

Behling, David J., Jr., William Marcuse, J. Lukachinski, and Robert Dullien. The Long-term Economic and Environmental Consequences of Phasing Out Nuclear Electricity. *Modeling Energy-Economy Interactions: Five Approaches.* Edited by Charles J. Hitch. Washington, D.C.: Resources for the Future, 1977.

Carter, Nicholas G. *Population, Environment and Natural Resources: A Critical Review of Recent Models.* World Bank Staff Working Paper No. 174, April 1974.

Cole, H.S.D., et al. *Models of Doom.* New York: Universe Books, 1973.

Dantzig, G.B., and S.C. Parikh. On a PILOT Linear Programming Model for Assessing Physical Impact on the Economy of a Changing Energy Picture. *Energy: Mathematics and Models.* Edited by Fred S. Roberts. Proceedings of SIMS Conference on Energy, pp. 1–23. Salt Lake City, Utah, July 1975.

Forrester, Jay W. *World Dynamics.* Cambridge, Mass.: Wright-Allen Press, 1971.

Glickman, Norman J. Son of Specification of Regional Econometric Models. *Papers and Proceedings of the Regional Science Association,* 1974.

Greenberger, Martin. Closing the Circuit between Modelers and Decision Makers. *EPRI Journal,* October 1977, pp. 6–13.

Harris, Curtis C. *Urban Economies: A Multi-Regional, Multi-Industry Forecasting Model.* Lexington, Mass.: D.C. Heath, 1973.

Herrera, Amilcar O., Hugo D. Scolnik, et al. *Catastrophe or New Society: A Latin American World Model.* Buenos Aires: The Bariloche Foundation, IDRC-064, 1974.

Hogan, William W., and S. Parikh. *Comparison of Models of Energy and the Economy.* Stanford Energy Modelling Forum Working Paper EMF 1.4, February 1977.

Hogan, William W., and Alan S. Manne. Energy-Economy Interactions: The Fable of the Elephant and the Rabbit? *Modeling Energy-Economy Interactions: Five Approaches.* Edited by Charles J. Hitch. Washington, D.C.: Resources for the Future, 1977.

House, Peter. *Trading Off Environment, Economics and Energy.* Lexington, Mass.: D.C. Heath, 1977.

Hudson, E.A., and D.W. Jorgenson. U.S. Energy Policy and Economic Growth. *The Bell Journal of Economics and Management Science*, Fall 1974, pp. 461–514.

Klein, L.R., and W.F. Finan. The Structure of the Wharton Annual Energy Model. Paper presented for the Energy Modeling Forum Meeting, Washington, D.C., October 1971.

Lakshmanan, T.R. A Model of Multi-Regional Economy and Energy Demand (MREED). The Johns Hopkins University Center for Metropolitan Research, July 1977.

Lakshmanan, T.R., and S. Krishnamurthi. *The SEAS Test Model: Design and Implementation*. Washington, D.C.: U.S. Environmental Protection Agency, 1973.

Lakshmanan, T.R., and Sam Ratick. The Economic and Environmental Effects of Energy Development Scenarios: A Strategic Assessment. Paper presented at the Soviet-American Seminar on Urban Environments, Northwestern University, Evanston, Ill., May 1977.

Lakshmanan, T.R., P. Kroll, M. Pappas, L. Chatterjee, and B. Barron. *The SEAS REGION Model: An Assessment of Current Status and Prospects*. Washington, D.C.: U.S. Environmental Protection Agency, 1979.

Landsberg, Hans H., John J. Schanz, Jr., Sam H. Schurr, and Grant P. Thompson. *Energy and the Social Sciences*. Washington, D.C.: Resources for the Future, 1974.

Leontief, Wassily. *The Future of the World Economy*. Oxford: The Oxford University Press, 1976.

Leontief, W., Thomas Crocker, et al. *Report of SEAS Evaluation Panel*. Reports, U.S. EPA, 1976.

Manne, Alan S., and E.T.A. Macro: A Model of Energy Economy Interactions. *Modeling Energy-Economy Interactions: Five Approaches*. Edited by Charles J. Hitch. Washington, D.C.: Resources for the Future, 1977.

Marcuse, W., L. Bodin, E.A. Cherniavsky, and Y. Sanborn. A Dynamic Time-Dependent Model for the Analysis of Alternative Energy Policies. Brookhaven National Laboratory, Report No. 19400, 1974.

Meadows, D.H., and D.L. Meadows. *The Limits to Growth*. New York: Universe Books, 1972.

Mesarovic, M., and E. Pestel. *Mankind at the Turning Point*. New York: E.P. Dutton, 1974.

Meyer, Richard, R. Doggett, M. Heller, and D. Cooper. *Impacts of Energy Development in the Ohio River Basin: Final Report*. I.R. & T. Prepared for OEMI, U.S. Environmental Protection Agency, September 12, 1977.

Nordhaus, W. World Modelling from the Bottom Up. IIASA Research Memorandum RM-75-10, Schloss Laxenburg, Austria, March 1975a.

Nordhaus, W. World Dynamics: Measurement without Data. *Economic Journal* 83(332), December 1975b, pp. 1156–83.

OBERS. U.S. Water Resources Council, *Concepts, Methodology, and Summary Data*, Vol. 1, 1972, OBERS Projections of Economic Activity, April 1974.

Okita, S., and Y. Kaya. *On the Future Japan and the World: A Model Approach.* Tokyo: Japan Techno-economics Society, 1973. (Mimeograph)

Ridker, Ron, W. Watson, and A. Shapanka. Economic, Energy and Environmental Consequences of Alternative Energy Regimes: An Application of RFF/SEAS Modelling System. *Modeling Energy-Economy Interactions: Five Approaches.* Edited by Charles J. Hitch. Washington, D.C.: Resources for the Future, 1977.

Searl, Milton F., ed. *Energy Modelling.* Washington, D.C.: Resources for the Future, March 1973.

U.S. Environmental Protection Agency (EPA), *The SEAS Model.* Washington, D.C.: EPA, 1975.

World Bank, *Report of the Special Task Force on the Limits to Growth.* Washington, D.C., September 1972, 94 pp. (Mimeograph)

2 OPERATIONAL METHODS FOR STRATEGIC ENVIRONMENTAL AND ENERGY POLICIES

P.J.J. Lesuis and F. Muller, *Erasmus University, Rotterdam*;
P. Nijkamp, *Free University, Amsterdam*

1. INTRODUCTION

The growing scarcity of exhaustible resources (energy, raw materials, clean air, and so forth) has claimed increased attention of economics. A wide variety of studies has been published about optimal environmental policies that call for prevention of the depletion of exhaustible resources (see among others Baumol and Oates [1975], Chatterji and van Rompuy [1976], MacAvoy and Pindyck [1975], Muller [1978], Nijkamp [1977], Smith [1977], and WAES [1977]).

Many analyses of optimal environmental management and preservation are of a static nature, so that long-term effects such as the impact of pricing policies and of technological changes cannot be integrated in an adequate manner. Consequently, substitution effects can hardly be dealt with.

In the present paper an attempt will be made to provide a comprehensive systematic analysis of energy and pollution problems by developing a decision model that is interconnected with the economic structure by means of an integrated input-output model. In this way the interactions between economic processes and environmental policies can be investigated and assessed.

The paper starts with the presentation of a formal input-output model extended with the energy and pollution sector. This model constitutes the basic ingredient of a policy model for optimal environmental management (section 2).

This model is extended in several ways, inter alia by incorporating price effects of inputs via demand relationships for these inputs (especially energy) and by introducing simultaneously shifts in technology via variable input-output coefficients (section 3).

Next, the policy aspects will be taken into account by assuming the existence of multiple diverging (or even conflicting) political options such as the search for maximum employment, minimum pollution, and moderate use of scarce resources. Furthermore, different exogenous developments will be considered; for example, the growth of world trade. The successive policy options and the exogenous developments will be integrated via a set of composite scenarios (section 4).

On the basis of the models developed in the foregoing sections, an attempt will be made to make a long-term prediction of production, pollution, and energy use in the Netherlands for each composite scenario. These predictions will not be given as point predictions, but rather as a band width for the predicted variables (see section 5).

The paper will be concluded with an outline of further future research.

2. AN INTEGRATED INPUT-OUTPUT MODEL WITH ENERGY AND POLLUTION

Several mathematical techniques are available for analyzing energy problems. A rather simple method departs from the demand equation for energy by estimating price or income elasticities. Examples of this can be found in Schweizer [1974] and Houthakker and Kennedy [1974a]. Other studies examine the supply equation of energy (Odell and Rosing [1975]).

In those cases were the number of variables increases and also interdependencies frequently occur, simulation models have been applied successfully. These models may be static or dynamic. Among the simulation models we mention input-output studies (see Tintner [1971]; Perry [1974]; Lesuis and Muller [1976]), network analysis and system analysis (Debanné [1973]; Oshima [1974]; Neu [1975]) as well as demand and supply models (Houthakker and Kennedy [1974b]; Jorgenson [1976]). Many of these models have also been optimized by mathematical programming techniques (Hoffman [1972]; Dean et al. [1973]; Muller [1978]).

Because a large part of energy consumption takes place in an intermediate form, input-output analysis seems a suitable method for studying energy-economic problems. This approach has the additional advantage in that environmental problems can also be integrated in a direct way, as we will see later.

According to the input-output method the relationship between various sectors in the economy can be presented by a matrix of intermediate deliveries, so that

$$x = Xi + f \tag{2.1}$$

where

x vector of gross production levels
X matrix of intermediate deliveries
f final demand vector
i unit vector.

If a linear relationship may be assumed between the level of production and the consumption of intermediate products, we get in case of constant prices

$$x = Ax + f \tag{2.2}$$

with A the matrix of technical coefficients ($A = X\hat{x}^{-1}$; $\hat{x}$ being the diagonal matrix of x).

From (2.2) it follows that

$$x = (I - A)^{-1} f. \tag{2.3}$$

This expression gives the relationship between final demand and total production. Projections of final demand then also allow us to predict x.

A limitation of the input-output approach is that the technical coefficients are assumed to be constant. This implies that each sector has only one average technique at its disposal. However, in practice often a choice can be made out of different production processes, implying substitution between different inputs. The choice of inputs is then determined by relative prices. The possibility of variable technical coefficients will be described in section 3.

Energy analysis makes it desirable to identify and separate the energy sectors in the input-output table as far as possible. This implies the partitioning of x, X, and f. Denoting the energy sectors by superscript e and the non-energy sectors by superscript n we get

$$\begin{bmatrix} x^n \\ x^e \end{bmatrix} = \begin{bmatrix} X^{nn} & X^{ne} \\ X^{en} & X^{ee} \end{bmatrix} i + \begin{bmatrix} f^n \\ f^e \end{bmatrix} \tag{2.4}$$

The outputs of the energy industry in this case may be expressed in energy units, e.g., coal equivalents or joules. A corresponding partitioning of the A-matrix results in

$$
\begin{bmatrix} x^n \\ x^e \end{bmatrix} = \begin{bmatrix} A^{nn} & A^{ne} \\ A^{en} & A^{ee} \end{bmatrix} \begin{bmatrix} x^n \\ x^e \end{bmatrix} + \begin{bmatrix} f^n \\ f^e \end{bmatrix}
\tag{2.5}
$$

The energy sectors in this expression are sufficiently detailed, so that the energy system itself is also representing an input-output system (X^{ee}). In case of a closed economy the lower part of equation (2.4) corresponds with the energy balance:

$$
x^e = X^{en} i + X^{ee} i + f^e
\tag{2.6}
$$

If different processes of energy production and energy consumption would be available, the coefficients of A^{en} and A^{ee} might change whenever changes in relative prices occur. The possibilities of energy substitution are investigated in section 3.

The integration of environmental pollution in the input-output framework is straightforward (c.f., Cumberland [1966]; Daly [1968]; Ayres and Kneese [1969]; Isard [1969]; Leontief [1970]; Muller [1973]). In view of the subject of the present study we will pay attention especially to pollution caused by energy consumption.

Differences in production techniques have the consequence that the emission rates are not the same for all sectors, even if energy consumption would be the same. If v_r^{kl} is the emission of pollutant r caused by the consumption of energy source k in sector l we get

$$
v_r^{kl} = q_r^{kl}(a^{kl} x^l + m^{kl})
\tag{2.7}
$$

In this equation the emission of pollutant r is related to energy inputs originating from the country itself ($a^{kl} x^l$) or from abroad (m^{kl}); q_r^{kl} is called emission factor, i.e., the emission rate per unit of energy consumption.

Let v_r^e and v_r^n be emissions per unit of product resulting from other sources than energy consumption, caused by energy sectors and nonenergy sectors respectively. If we also pay attention to pollution caused by final demand, total pollution becomes

$$
v_r = i' \begin{bmatrix} v_r^{kl} \end{bmatrix} i + \begin{bmatrix} v_r^n & v_r^e \end{bmatrix} \begin{bmatrix} x^n \\ x^e \end{bmatrix} + \begin{bmatrix} v_r^{fn} & v_r^{fe} \end{bmatrix} \begin{bmatrix} f^n + m^{fn} \\ f^e & m^{fe} \end{bmatrix}
\tag{2.8}
$$

Also for the final demand sector a distinction is made between pollution caused by energy consumption (v_r^{fe}) and pollution from other sources (v_r^{fn});

the imports of the final demand sector have been accounted for by m^{fe} and m^{fn}.

From equation (2.7) it appears that constant input coefficients and constant emission factors give rise to a fixed proportionate relationship between production and pollution, so in this case the emission coefficients (i.e., the pollution per unit production) remain constant. If the input-output coefficients or the emission factors happen to vary, however, the emission rates v_r^{kl} are also influenced. As the interindustry model describes the energy flows between productive sectors, it turns out to be possible to derive a matrix of physical energy flows. Assuming a constant technology in pollution abatement, these flows can be related to emission factors, which results in emission per type of pollutant. Considering a variable pollution abatement technology explicitly would require a specification of the relationship between the cost of emission reduction and the effect on emission factors. In the next section, a reduction in emission is obtained via substitution processes induced by relative energy prices (including abatement costs).

3. PRICE EFFECTS AND TECHNOLOGY SHIFTS

In the input-output system of the previous section the technology of each sector was taken as fixed at any time. This approach can be applied to energy in a consistent way only if the same constancy is assumed with respect to energy consumption. This section seeks to integrate the possibilities of input substitution in the analysis, taking system (2.5) as a starting point.

One way to introduce a variable production structure is to model trends in input-output coefficients without treating them as part of the model of producer behaviour (Leontief [1953]; Almon et al. [1974]). Another approach, discussed by Samuelson [1966], is to include input-output coefficients into the model of producer behaviour by treating them as endogenous variables dependant on prices rather than exogenously given parameters.

Recently many empirical studies of producer behaviour have been published including energy as one of the substitutable inputs. Examples applied to total manufacturing are the studies by Berndt and Wood [1975], based on time series data, and Fuss [1977], using a combined time series cross-section data set, while Griffin and Gregory [1976] made use of pooled international data. More detailed sectors, using cross-section data, have been studied by Halversen [1977]. Interfuel substitution is explicitly considered a.o. by Griffin [1977]. Hudson and Jorgenson [1976] analyze producer behaviour to derive an input-output matrix which contains the possibility of interfuel substitution and substitution for other inputs. All these studies analyze producer behaviour on the basis of duality between the production function and a unit cost function. This approach makes it possible to derive systems of relative factor demand equations by differentiating a unit cost function, as opposed to solving explicitly a constrained optimization problem (Diewert [1974]). The advantage of this approach is the fact that the solution contains the optimum cost shares needed to produce the output at minimum costs. From these cost shares the computation of input-output coefficients is straightforward.

Models of producer behaviour can be derived from the price possibility frontier of each sector:

$$P_r^{n\,,e} = f_r \ (P_1^n \ . \ . \ . \ P_M^n, \ P_{M+1}^e \ . \ . \ . \ P_{M+K}^e, \ PK_r, \ PL_r, \ PM_r^n, \ PM_r^e) \qquad (3.1)$$

where

P_r^n is output price of nonenergy sector, $r = 1,M$
P_r^e is output price of energy sector, $r = M+1,M+K$
PK_r is price of capital services in sector r
PL_r is price of labor services in sector r
PM_r^n is import price of material inputs in sector r
PM_r^e is import price of energy inputs in sector r.

Producer behaviour may be represented by several functional forms, such as the Generalized Leontief, the General Cobb-Douglas or the translog function as developed by Christensen, Jorgenson and Lau [1973]. From a theoretical viewpoint there is no preference for a specific choice. These general functional forms can be viewed as local second order approximations to any arbitrary twice differentiable cost function. They allow considerable generality, placing no restrictions on the Allen partial elasticities of substitution.

Application of the translog function to the many input case is hampered by the fact that the equations are usually linear in simple monotonic functions of inputs or prices and are plagued by multicollinearity problems, arising from lack in variation in input and factor price data, which is especially common in time series analysis. In addition, the application of flexible functional forms can be computationally cumbersome when many inputs are involved in the simultaneous estimation of the parameters.

Following the procedure adopted by Hudson and Jorgenson [1976] we may reduce multicollinearity and computational problems by imposing the a priori restriction that the production structure (3.1) is weakly separable in major categories as capital, labor, energy, and materials, which is consistent with the partitioning of input structure (2.5). The cost function (3.1) is (weakly) separable in these categories if it can be written as:

$$P_r^{n,e} = f_r \big(PN_r \ (P_1^n \ \dots \ P_M^n), \ PE_r(P_{M+1}^e \ \dots \ P_{M+K}^e), \ PK_r, \ PL_r, \ PM_r^n, \ PM_r^e \big) \tag{3.2}$$

where $PN_r(P_1^n \ \dots \ P_M^n)$ and $PE_r(P_{M+1}^e \ \dots \ P_{M+K}^e)$ are aggregator functions of the aggregate price indices PN_r and PE_r. Other input prices are already assumed to be aggregate price indices for simplicity reasons.

A sufficient condition for the price possibility frontier to be defined in the prices of the aggregates is that the overall price possibility frontier is separable and homogeneous in the aggregates. Moreover, the price possibility frontier is separable in the commodities within each aggregate if and only if the marginal rate of substitution between commodities within the aggregate only depends on prices within the aggregate (Leontief [1947]).

Imposition of the separability constraint yields two important simplifying results. First, only under weak separability conditions do aggregates exist (Fuss [1977]). This justifies the separate construction of submodels in the aggregates. Second, the existence of aggregates which are homothetic in their components implies an underlying two-stage optimization procedure consisting of optimizing the mix of components within each aggregate first, and then optimizing the level of each aggregate, justifying the construction of a model in the aggregates alone.[1]

Concerning the aggregator functions, it is common practice in empirical implementation of translog cost functions to use approximate Divisia aggregation (see Hulten [1973]; Diewert [1976]), since simple weighting of averages of the composite parts of the aggregates only provides an appropriate index in case of perfect substitutes or complements. To obtain consistent estimates for the submodel and the aggregate model, Fuss [1977] shows that the estimate of the aggregate price index from each submodel can serve as an instrumental variable in the estimation procedure of the aggregate model.

The aggregators PN_r and PE_r represent the cost price per unit to the optimizing agent. This cost can be specified by a unit cost function that under these separability conditions can be written in separate submodels for each sector r in translog form as follows:

The energy submodel:
$$\ln PE_r = \ln \beta_0^r + \sum_i \beta_i^r \ln P_{M+i}^e + \tfrac{1}{2} \sum_{ij} \sum \beta_{ij}^r \ln P_{M+i}^e \ln P_{M+j}^e \tag{3.3}$$

for all $i = j = 1, K$ energy inputs with prices P_{M+i}^e (energy imports may be included). The price possibility frontier for the materials submodel is specified as:

$$\ln PN_r = \ln \gamma_0^r + \sum_i \gamma_i^r \ln P_i^n + \tfrac{1}{2} \sum_{ij} \sum \gamma_{ij}^r \ln P_i^n \ln P_j^n \tag{3.4}$$

for all $i = j = 1$, M nonenergy inputs with prices P_i^n (nonenergy imports may be included).

Finally, the frontier for the inputs in aggregates of capital, labor, energy, and material inputs takes the form:

$$\ln P_r^{n,e} = \ln \alpha_0^r + \sum_i \alpha^r \ln P_i + \sum_{ij} \alpha_{ij}^r \ln P_i \ln P_j \qquad (3.5)$$

for both energy and nonenergy sectors and for all $i = j = 1,4$ aggregate inputs, with prices P_i, P_j equal to PK_r, PL_r, PE_r, PN_r.

Demand functions in each of the submodels are obtained by logarithmic differentiation of (3.3), (3.4), and (3.5) and read:

$$S_{i,r}^e = \beta_i^r + \sum_j \beta_{ij}^r \ln P_{M+j}^e \qquad i,j = 1 \ldots K \text{ energy sectors} \qquad (3.6)$$

$$S_{i,r}^n = \gamma_i^r + \sum_j \gamma_{ij}^r \ln P_j^n \qquad i,j = 1 \ldots M \text{ nonenergy sectors} \qquad (3.7)$$

$$S_{i,r} = \alpha_i^r + \sum_j \alpha_{ij}^r \ln P_j \qquad i,j = 1,4 \text{ aggregate input prices} \qquad (3.8)$$

The S_i expressions represent the optimum cost shares in virtue of Shephard's lemma.[2] As an example, for the energy submodel the optimum input quantity E_i in total input quantity E_r follows as

$$\frac{\delta PE_r}{\delta P_{M+i}^e} = \frac{E_i}{E_r} \qquad (3.9)$$

Combining (3.9) with the linear homogeneity of the cost function in prices, by Euler's theorem $PE_r E_r = \sum_j P_{M+j}^e E_j$, so

$$S_{i,r}^e = \frac{\delta \ln PE_r}{\delta \ln P_{M+i}^e} = \frac{\delta PE_r}{\delta P_{M+i}^e} \cdot \frac{P_{M+i}}{PE_r} = \frac{P_{M+i}^e E_i}{\sum_j P_{M+j}^e E_j} \qquad (3.10)$$

In the same way the optimum energy cost share in the aggregate model (3.5) is given by

$$S_{i,r} = \frac{PE_r \, E_r}{P_r^{n,e} \, X_r^{n,e}} \qquad (3.11)$$

$X_r^{n,e}$ being the output quantity and $P_r^{n,e}$ the output price of sector r of nonenergy sectors and energy sectors.

Homogeneity of the price possibility frontiers is implied by the symmetry restrictions and restrictions following from the accounting identity between value of input and output in each of the submodels.

Thus, (3.3), (3.6) is completed by the restrictions:

$$\sum_i \beta_i^r = 1$$

$$\sum_i \beta_{ij}^r = 0 \tag{3.12}$$

$$\beta_{ij}^r = \beta_{ji}^r \quad , \ i \neq j$$

In the same way (3.4) and (3.7) share the restrictions

$$\sum_i \gamma_i^r = 1$$

$$\sum_i \gamma_{ij}^r = 0 \tag{3.13}$$

$$\gamma_{ij}^r = \gamma_{ji}^r \quad , \ i \neq j$$

Finally, in the aggregate model (3.5), (3.8)

$$\sum_i \alpha_i^r = 1$$

$$\sum_i \alpha_{ij}^r = 0 \tag{3.13}$$

$$\alpha_{ij}^r = \alpha_{ji}^r , \qquad i \neq j$$

Prices are obtained by simultaneously solving the sectoral price possibility frontiers (3.3), (3.4), and (3.5) for all sectors. Some empirical results, based on estimations of the coefficients of the price frontier, are contained in section 5. Then, by means of cost-share expressions (3.6), (3.7), and (3.8), using the results of (3.10) and (3.11), input-output coefficients can be calculated in two stages. First, by dividing in the aggregate model the corresponding value share by the ratio of the input price to the output price, the input-output coefficients in the aggregates result (3.11). By multiplying these coefficients with the input-output coefficients from the submodels for the energy and nonenergy sectors respectively, the coefficients required in the interindustry system are obtained, as can easily be seen from (3.10) and (3.11). We get input-output coefficients for capital services, labor services, different energy inputs, material inputs by type, and imports of materials and energy, depending on their relative prices.

Another feature of the cost shares is their part in the calculation of substitution and price elasticities. The Allen partial elasticities of substitution (AES) between inputs i and j have been derived by Uzawa [1962] (see Berndt and Wood [1975]) as

$$\tau_{ii} = \frac{\alpha_{ii} + S_i^2 - S_i}{S_i^2} \quad \text{and}$$

$$\tau_{ji} = \tau_{ij} = \frac{\alpha_{ij} + S_i \ S_j}{S_i \ S_j} \quad , \qquad i \neq j \tag{3.14}$$

These elasticities are not constrained to be constant, but may vary with the value of the cost shares. The price elasticity of demand of factors

$$\epsilon_{ij} = \frac{\delta \ln x_i}{\delta \ln p_j} \qquad (3.15)$$

can be related to the AES as

$$\epsilon_{ij} = S_j \ \tau_{ij} \qquad (3.16)$$

Hence, even though $\tau_{ij} = \tau_{ji}$, in general $\epsilon_{ij} \neq \epsilon_{ji}$.

The model solution at this point consists of the simultaneous determination of the pattern of economic interactions that result from a given specification of the economic environment. The behaviour of the energy sectors is one component of this determination, and the simulated performance of the energy sector includes also its interrelationships with the rest of the economic system.

The energy characteristics of the economy should be expressed in terms of physical units rather than monetary terms. Energy prices are part of the solution of the energy model in terms of price indices, the conversion to price levels just being a matter of scaling. Thus, as the price index of each type of energy is known, a conversion from monetary terms into physical units can be made.

Given projections of the temporal evolution of the vectors of final demand and prices of the primary inputs PK_r, PL_r, PM_r^e and PM_r^n on the basis of given producer behaviour, projections of a future development can be made. This development can be judged by the policymaker, to find a balance with divergent objectives, such as employment, energy use, economic growth, and environmental deterioration, which may be conflicting in nature. In this respect multiple-criteria analysis may be a useful tool, as will be discussed in the next section.

Finally, it should be noted that a full-fledged integration of price and substitution effects would require a complete dynamic model for long-term projections. For the moment, however, only a comparative static framework will be dealt with.

4. COMPOSITE SCENARIOS FOR LONG-TERM ENVIRONMENTAL AND ENERGY POLICIES

Environmental management does not take place in a wonderland of no other political dimensions. Therefore, a single high priority objective such as minimizing costs or maximizing resources is less relevant in the actual decision process. In recent years the insight has grown that economic and environmental decision making has to be placed in a broader framework of multiple objectives. This new view has induced the development of *multi-objective decision-making tools* (see among others Blair [1978] and van Delft and Nijkamp [1977]).

Multiobjective decision models arise from the need to take into account the presence of a wide variety of conflicting priorities or political options (such as maximum employment, minimum pollution, and maximum availability of energy resources). Sometimes these conflicting priorities or options can be associated with certain interest groups (such as industry, environmentalists, and consumers). The basic problem related to the existence of multiple objectives is the fact that decisions are normally interdependent, so that any production decision has its impact on employment, pollution emission, and energy consumption, and vice versa. The intricate relationships between all relevant variables in an economic-environmental system have been described in more detail in sections 2 and 3 by means of system process functions.

Given this set of system process functions, a method has to be devised that relates the various objectives of policy-making interests to these functions. It will be shown in this section that the method of *displaced ideals* will be a useful instrument to attain compromise solutions from conflicting objectives.

The next step to the analysis will be the introduction of uncertainty in the system process function. External developments such as the growth of world trade, the supply of oil, or the occurrence of environmental disasters will affect the results of the above-mentioned decision model for economic-environmental policy. This problem will be investigated by assuming a set of alternative reasonable future *scenarios*. By combining these future scenarios with the successive political options, a *composite scenario* may be created which constitutes the basis for making a set of predictions about the future development of economic and environmental variables.

The existence of multiple objectives or multiple actors leads to a *multi-objective policy problem*, which can be formalized in general terms as:

$$\max_{x \, \epsilon \, k} w \, (x) \tag{4.1}$$

where

w is $J \times 1$ vector of objective functions w_j,
x is an $M \times 1$ vector of decision variables x_m, and
K   is the feasible area for the set of decision variables.

It is clear that, in case of a *linear* multiobjective model, (4.1) passes into

$$\max \ w \ (x) = C \, x$$
$$B \, x \leq b \tag{4.2}$$

where

C is a J×M matrix with coefficients related to the successive objectives,

B is a N×M matrix with coefficients related to the constraint set, and

b is a N×1 vector with coefficients related to the level of the constraints.

The common feature of multiobjective models is that the maximization of a single objective function will prevent the remaining objective functions from attaining their successive maxima. This conflict involves a double choice problem, viz., the choice of optimal values for both the successive *objective functions* and the successive *decision variables*. This problem has been studied quite extensively in the literature on multiobjective optimization (see for a survey Nijkamp [1977]).

A principal concept in multiobjective methodology is a *Pareto solution*. This solution reflects the conflicting nature of multiple objectives: any further increase of one objective function from a point on the possibility frontier onward will have a negative impact on the values of the others (when the objective functions are maximized simultaneously). Formally, a Pareto solution related to (4.1) can be defined as follows: a Pareto solution is a vector x^* for which no other feasible solution vector x does exist such that

$$w \ (x) \geq w \ (x^*) \qquad , \text{ and}$$
$$w_j \ (x) \neq w_j \ (x^*) \qquad , \text{ for at least one j.} \tag{4.3}$$

It can be proved that the set of Pareto solutions can be related to a parametric programming model: a feasible solution is a Pareto solution x^*, if and only if a vector of parameters (weights) λ does exist (with $i'\lambda = 1$[3] and $\lambda \geq 0$), such that x^* is the optimal solution of the following unidimensional program:

$$\max \ \varphi = \lambda' \ \{w \ (x)\}$$
$$x \ \epsilon \ K \tag{4.4}$$

Any solution of a multiobjective model should be a Pareto solution, because all other feasible solutions will always be dominated by the set of Pareto solutions. Therefore, the weights λ can be associated with any compromise solution in a multiobjective system, although there is not necessarily a one-to-one relationship between a final equilibrium solution and λ. The parametric model (4.4) can, in principle, be used to identify the whole set of Pareto solutions, although this appears to be a rather time-consuming matter in practice.

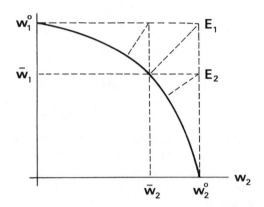

Figure 2.1. The Space of the Pareto Set of Two Objectives

The notion of a Pareto solution may be clarified for a two-dimensional objective problem as follows. Assume that there are two political options, viz., maximization of employment and maximization of environmental quality. Then the Pareto set (efficiency frontier) of these objectives can be sketched as in Figure 2.1. This Pareto set reflects the fact that a further increase in employment (w_1) will affect environmental quality (w_2) and vice versa. On the other hand, it is clear that a certain optimal compromise solution should always be located on the edge of the Pareto frontier.

A compromise solution between conflicting objectives can be attained in several ways. In the present paper the method of displaced ideals will be employed, as this method is rather manageable in many practical decision situations (see among others van Delft and Nijkamp [1977] and Zeleny [1976]).

The method of displaced ideals uses the ideal point of a multiobjective model as a reference point. An ideal point w_j^o can be defined as the maximum feasible value of one objective function, i.e.,

$$w_j^o = \max \; w_j \; (x) \; , \qquad \forall j \tag{4.5}$$

The ideal point of all objective functions together is indicated by point E in Figure 2.1. Given this ideal point, a best compromise can be attained by selecting a point on the Pareto frontier that has a minimum distance with respect to the ideal point. This requires the solution of the following program (assuming a general Minkowski distance metric):

$$\min \psi = \left\{ \sum_{j=1}^{J} (1-\hat{w}_j)^p \right\}^{1/p} \quad , \qquad p \geq 1$$

$$\hat{w}_j = \frac{w_j(x) - w_j^{min}}{w_j^o - w_j^{min}} \qquad , \qquad Aj \qquad\qquad (4.6)$$

$$x \in K$$

where

$\hat{w}$ represents the standardized objective function w_j, and
w_j^{min} corresponds to the minimum feasible value of the jth objective function.

The easiest way to solve (4.6) is to put p equal to 1, since in that case the goal function is a linear transformation of the original objective functions. If p = 2, a quadratic form of the goal function emerges. The solution of (4.6) will be denoted by $\overline{w}_j$ (j=1,...J).

If necessary, this solution can be used as an intermediate step in an *interactive procedure*. In that case, the decision maker has to indicate whether or not the first compromise solution is satisfactory. In other words, he has to indicate which objective functions have to be increased in value or at least to remain equal. Denote this set of indices j' related to these objective functions by S. Then the following program has to be solved:

$$\max w_j(x) \qquad\qquad , \quad \forall j$$

$$x \in K \qquad\qquad\qquad (4.7)$$

$$w_j,(x) \geq \overline{w}_j, \qquad , \quad \forall J' \in S$$

This gives rise to a new ideal point, e.g., E_2 (hence the name *displaced ideal*). Then the minimum distance procedure of (4.6) may again be repeated, etc., until a final converging compromise solution is attained (cf. Fandel [1972]).

In the context of our comprehensive economic-environmental model, it is reasonable to assume at least three different conflicting political options, viz., maximization of employment, minimization of pollution, and minimization of energy consumption. This set of three political scenarios gives rise to the following successive objective functions: max w_1, min w_2, and min w_3. The solutions of w_1, w_2, and w_3 associated with the ideal solution can be calculated in a straightforward manner. The same holds true for the compromise solution $\overline{w}$. These solutions can be represented in Table 2.1.

Table 2.1.   Results of the Various Scenarios

	w_1	w_2	w_3
Employment scenario			
Environmental scenario			
Energy scenario			
Compromise scenario			

By assuming a certain tolerance area around the results of these scenarios (say 5 percent), a prediction of the *band width* of objectives and decision variables may be made for each political scenario. It should be noted that a scenario as such is not a forecast of the future; it only presents a picture of a plausible future based on reasonable political choices or on reasonable exogenous circumstances. Similarly, a stochastic approach might be employed.

It should be noted that the ultimate result is co-determined by relative political priorities for the objectives concerned. In this way the interactive approach via displaced ideals may be very useful. An alternative way of accessing political priorities in the case of three objectives may be the use of a so-called *viewpoint triangle* (see Figure 2.2), in which the decision maker has to indicate his relative weights w_j (j = 1,2,3; $w_1 + w_2 + w_3 = 1$) for the three objectives (see also Pantell [1976]):

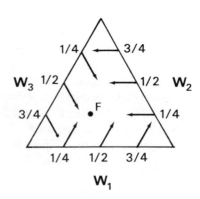

Figure 2.2.   A Viewpoint Triangle

Each point F in the triangle corresponds in a one-to-one relationship to the relative weights attached to the objective functions, while the triangle guarantees the additivity conditions for the weights. These weights may then be used as parameters in the model (4.4).

In addition to political scenarios, one may distinguish *exogenous scenarios*, which are not under the control of the decision maker but which have a significant impact on the values of the system process functions. Examples of such exogenous data are the development of world trade, the possible imports of energy resources, the international environmental jurisdiction, and others. Each of these scenarios influences the economic-environmental system, for example, through the final demand sector, the price sector, and through the constraint levels. Several of these scenarios can be translated into scenarios describing the rate of growth in economic systems. For example, Cumberland [1976] has made a forecast of energy requirements and environmental impacts based on three scenarios, viz., a high growth trend scenario, a moderate growth scenario with price effects, and a low growth scenario with energy conservation and management policies.

All relevant scenarios s_l ($l = 1 \ldots L$) can be incorporated in the system process model (either as shifts in constraint levels or as shifts in parameters) and next can be used in the multiobjective framework. This implies that each exogenous scenario gives rise to a certain solution, which is in turn determined by the political scenario at hand. This can be illustrated by means of Table 2.2, which reflects all combinations of political and exogenous scenarios.

Each combination of political and exogenous scenarios will be called hereafter a *composite scenario*; thus, the total number of composite scenarios is equal to $4L$.

It should be noted that each exogenous scenario has its own Pareto frontier with respect to the three objective functions. This implies that for each political scenario an *expansion curve* can be identified over all exogenous scenarios.

Table 2.2. Combinations of Political and Exogenous Scenarios

s_1 .... s_L
Employment scenario
Environmental scenario
Energy scenario
Composite scenario

Table 2.3. Input-Output Table for the Netherlands (1972)[a]

		(1)	(2)	(3)	(4)	(5)	(6)	
1	Agriculture	881	17	0	3	9808	3	
2	Chemicals	318	995	167	475	673	79	
3	Metallurgy and metals	115	175	6042	1388	1822	89	
4	Building	176	121	173	1623	452	99	9
5	Remaining industry	4213	504	558	3045	9693	439	
6	Transport	31	62	50	72	315	418	
7	Housing	0	0	0	0	0	0	
8	Services	982	983	1018	1668	4415	1289	
9	Coal	2	72	97	1	3	0	
10	Natural gas et al.	46.2	170.5	34.9	30.5	250.1	10.2	
11	Oil refinery	167	666	204	422	395	379	
12	Public utilities	41.8	338.5	251.1	117.5	554.9	113.8	
13	Imports	497	2781	3940	3597	16458	2119	
14	Labor services	5267	2876	5425	9457	16660	5450	
15	Capital services	2754	2811	2327	1271	6726	2253	50
16	Total production	15491	12572	20287	23170	68225	12741	60

[a]Millions of guilders
[b]Competitive imports are incorporated in the deliveries of sectors 9, 10, and 11; all other imp
appear in row 13.

For the exogenous scenarios, again, a tolerance area of say 5 percent may be assumed, and this leads to a forecast based on a band width instead of on discrete points.

Finally, it is clear that the foregoing approach can be dynamized in a straightforward way. Recursive programming techniques can be used here to derive an intertemporal equilibrium forecast. The basic idea is, however, similar for dynamic models, although normally the degree of freedom and of computational complexity increases.

(8)	(9)	(10)	(11)	(12)	Competi- tive imports[b]	Final Demand	
						Domes- tic	Foreign
66	2	0	0	0	0	1727	2984
343	2	4	151	26	0	1003	8255
463	8	8	96	86	0	2719	7262
417	5	4	63	60	0	18520	551
2686	6	8	41	132	0	22080	24820
3775	2	9	32	8	0	1429	6538
0	0	0	0	0	0	6015	0
5385	26	50	171	212	0	38994	10195
13	1	0	68	40	−235	48	217
80.4	7.9	8.6	0.3	233.4	0	250	897
667	8	11	326	214	−1042	1729	5138
488.6	32.1	15.4	64.7	364.6	0	2358	35
6956	19	5	5082	52			
34836	191	97	815	1219			
9297	17	1773	2374	2129			
65473	327	1993	9284	4776			

5. APPLICATIONS

The models described in sections 2–4 will not be illustrated by an empirical application for the Netherlands, with 1972 as a reference year. As a consequence, the conversion factors between input-output data, energy data, and emission data are also based on figures from this year. Thus, the validity of the results of the model depends heavily on the accuracy and reliability of the economic, environmental, and energy data. Adding labor, it is in principle possible to specify a static model including objective functions for employment, environmental pollution, and energy consumption in a comprehensive way, which makes it possible to apply the multiobjective policy approach exposed in section 4.

Table 2.3 shows the input-output relationships for the Dutch economy in 1972. A special feature of interest is that competitive imports of energy products are allocated to the domestic energy sectors; as a consequence, total competitive energy imports also appear in the energy rows with a minus sign. The main reason for this is that pollution not only arises from domestically produced energy sources but also from the import of energy products.

Next, energy consumption data by sector are shown in Table 2.4. Apart from domestic consumption of coal (including cokes), natural gas, and oil, also exports abroad are reported because these exports draw on domestic availability of energy sources. The consumption of electricity is not shown explicitly, but is contained in the output row of the public utility sector. More detailed information about the energy sectors is given by Lesuis and Muller [1976].

As to the emission of air pollutants, we confine ourselves in the present study to the emissions caused by burning fuels for heating or automotive purposes. The pollutants distinguished are carbon monoxide (CO), nitrogen oxides (NO_x), sulfurdioxide (SO_2), aerosols, aldehydes (COH) and hydrocarbons ($C_x H_y$). The emissions are related to the specific consumption of

Table 2.4. Use of Energy (Netherlands, 1972)

		Coal, Cokes[a]	Natural Gas[b]	Oil Products[a]
1	Agriculture	252	1,290	340
2	Chemicals	227	5,899	5,220
3	Metallurgy and metals	2,259	1,394	760
4	Building	0	18	1,002
5	Remaining industry	60	3,604	894
6	Transport	8	410	2,127
7	Housing	0	0	0
8	Services	65	3,017	4,484
9	Coal	382	316	243
10	Natural gas	0	342	0
11	Oil refinery	379	12	3,862
12	Public utilities	391	9,337	2,601
	Private consumption	399	8,650	7,140
	Exports	1,701	24,317	37,547
	TOTAL	6,123	58,606	66,220

[a]Thousands of metric tons
[b]Millions of m³

energy; the emissions originating from burning coal, natural gas, and oil are shown in Table 2.5. Due to assumed intensive antipollution investments, pollution in industrial sectors is relatively low.

Regarding the consumption of material inputs, labor inputs, pollution, and energy restrictions are formulated in a linear programming model. Because of the substitutability of energy sources only *total* energy consumption, expressed in calories, has been restricted. In contrast, the emission of each pollutant has been constrained separately. A complicating factor of the model is that final energy demand has to be divided between domestic consumption and exports, because these categories lead to different amounts of pollution.

By solving the linear programming model, an ideal point can be calculated according to equation (4.5). As objective function we maximize total labor and minimize total energy consumption and total pollution. For this purpose pollution has been expressed in *pollution units*, i.e., the amount of pollution weighed by appropriate pollution standards. The level of activities is constrained by imposing both a minimum and maximum amount of final demand; also labor use, pollution, and energy consumption have been restricted. The results from these optimizations are given in Table 2.6, while the ideal point appears from Table 2.7.

Because of the direct relationship between pollution and energy consumption, minimization of these objectives leads to more or less the same results. It is clear, however, that in the case of pollution emissions that are independent of energy consumption, the results of a minimum energy problem and a minimum pollution problem will be different.

Next, two compromise solutions have been calculated according to (4.6), assuming $p = 1$. These results are also included in Table 2.7. The first compromise solution reaches the imposed level of maximum employment, with a slightly lower amount of pollution. Because of the linear structure of the model together with the assumption that $p = 1$ and the maximum level of employment imposed, the solution attains the same level of employment. It has been assumed that the policy maker wishes the pollution level to be at least 10 percent less. This second compromise solution implies a lower level of pollution at the cost of less employment. Other solutions can be calculated in further iterations until a solution has been reached that satisfies the policy maker.

As a last example we now intend to give some insight into the functioning of the substitution process induced by exogenous developments. Based on input-output data and corresponding sectoral price indices, a preliminary estimate of the parameters of the translog price frontier can be made. Sectoral capital prices were derived from the price of investment goods, depreciation rates by type of investment and interest rates, while labor price

Table 2.5. Emission of Pollutants Caused by Energy Consumption (Netherlands, 1972)[a]

		From coal							
		CO	NO_x	SO_2	Aero-sols	COH	C_xH_y	CO	N
1	Agriculture	0.00	0.00	0.00	0.00	0.00	0.00	0	3
2	Chemicals	0.36	1.52	3.33	0.56	0.00	0.00	0	11
3	Metallurgy, metals	1.70	7.44	12.83	4.37	0.47	0.50	0	3
4	Building	0.00	0.00	0.00	0.00	0.00	0.00	0	0
5	Remaining industry	0.13	0.45	1.02	0.42	0.02	0.02	0	10.
6	Transport	1.32	0.01	0.12	0.12	0.00	0.15	0	0.
7	Housing	0.00	0.00	0.00	0.00	0.00	0.00	0	0.
8	Services	10.73	0.08	0.96	0.99	0.00	1.23	0	3.
9	Coal	0.14	3.74	6.13	4.90	0.00	0.03	0	0.
10	Natural gas et al.	0.00	0.00	0.00	0.00	0.00	0.00	0	0.
11	Oil refinery	0.28	0.93	2.52	1.28	0.04	0.05	0	0.
12	Public utilities	0.20	6.80	8.84	7.68	0.34	0.38	0	34.
	Private Consumption	65.83	0.52	5.87	6.06	0.00	7.54	0	10.
TOTAL		80.69	21.49	41.62	26.38	0.87	9.90	0	80.

[a]Thousands of metric tons

indices were obtained by dividing total labor input value by the number of man-years. For each of the submodels parameters of the translog function were estimated simultaneously, applying the method of Zellner's minimum distance estimator (see Malinvaud [1970], esp. pp. 325–375), based on an iterative procedure available in TSP (Time Series Processor developed at Harvard/MIT). From these the development in price indices may be determined. Taking 1972 as a reference year we propose two alternative scenarios for exogenous developments. In the first scenario we assume an increase in exogenous import prices of oil of 200 percent and a price increase of coal of 25 percent. In the second scenario this assumption is combined with an increase of 25 percent in sectoral capital input prices and 50 percent in labor input prices. The effects on endogenous prices are shown in Table 2.8. Due to the low share of energy inputs and possible substitution processes,

| From natural gas | | | | | | From oil | | | |
SO$_2$	Aero-sols	COH	C$_x$H$_y$	CO	NO$_x$	SO$_2$	Aero-sols	COH	C$_x$H$_y$
0	0.03	0	0	39.96	4.75	5.41	1.19	0.16	4.91
0	0.10	0	0	16.06	5.48	15.85	1.12	0.16	1.30
0	0.03	0	0	46.32	5.19	25.13	1.35	0.11	2.59
0	0.00	0	0	107.07	4.88	4.70	0.68	0.08	5.81
0	0.09	0	0	187.80	11.87	34.52	2.42	0.20	10.42
0	0.01	0	0	165.12	64.96	18.65	5.21	0.92	23.77
0	0.00	0	0	1.60	0.05	0.01	0.01	0.00	0.08
0	0.08	0	0	430.14	17.11	10.18	2.34	0.14	22.28
0	0.01	0	0	1.60	1.08	0.90	0.16	0.03	0.22
0	0.00	0	0	1.80	0.09	0.02	0.01	0.00	0.10
0	0.00	0	0	1.71	18.47	164.10	4.81	0.54	1.50
0	0.23	0	0	9.11	19.13	80.67	2.32	0.30	1.17
0	0.21	0	0	991.13	40.00	47.66	4.65	1.12	87.47
0	0.79	0	0	1999.42	193.06	407.80	26.27	3.76	161.62

the total effects of an increase in energy prices are mitigated. Price effects are substantially higher if, in addition, price increases in the primary inputs of labor and capital occur, as is the case in scenario 2.

Using both prices and the parameters of the translog price possibility frontier, we are able to determine the input coefficients in 1963 prices for each alternative. This gives us some impression about the consequences of alternative developments on substitution processes (see Table 2.9). Detailed results from the estimation procedure are reported in the Appendix.

6. CONCLUSIONS

This study presents a rather detailed description of the interrelationships between economic structure, energy consumption, and pollution, with an

Table 2.6. Results from Optimization

		1972		Max. Labor		Min. Pollution	
		Prod.[a]	Final Demand	Prod.[a]	Final Demand	Prod.[a]	Final Demand
1	Agriculture	15491	4711	22658	7065	8441	2355
2	Chemicals	12572	9258	18080	13887	6858	4629
3	Metallurgy, metals	20287	9971	27901	14293	11765	4990
4	Building	23170	19071	24606	20000	22150	18520
5	Other industry	68225	46900	98778	70350	38347	23450
6	Transport	12741	7967	9301	3983	9133	3983
7	Housing	6015	6015	6015	6015	6015	6015
8	Services	65473	49189	73464	53590	77909	39854
9	Coal	327	0	0	0	0	0
10	Natural gas	1993	1147	1896	800	1297	700
11	Oil refinery	9284	6867	7159	3555	5935	3555
12	Public utilities	4776	2393	4798	1914	3687	1914

[a]Millions of guilders

Table 2.7. The Ideal Point and Compromise Solutions

	w_1 Employment[a]	w_2 Energy[b]	w_3 Pollution[c]
Employment scenario	4898	983	1774
Environmental scenario	3674	755	1462
Energy scenario	3674	755	1462
First compromise	4898	983	1722
Second compromise	4261	983	1550

[a]Thousands of man-years
[b]10^{15} cal
[c]Pollution units

application to the Dutch economy. Using a static approach, the interrelationships between various sectors of the economy were analyzed in an
input-output framework, making a distinction between energy-producing
and energy-consuming sectors. This approach was integrated with the energy

Table 2.8. Price Effects under Alternative Scenarios (1963=100)

		Energy Prices (PE)		Materials Prices (PN)			Sector Prices (P)		
		1972	Sc.1	Sc.2	1972	Sc.1	Sc.2	1972	Sc.1	Sc.2
1	Agriculture	104.4	151.8	181.2	131.1	133.0	189.2	134.2	135.9	193.4
2	Chemicals	118.8	160.7	198.6	120.6	125.4	174.0	106.1	111.8	152.8
3	Metallurgy	121.6	147.8	189.2	132.1	134.0	190.0	126.2	128.0	181.2
4	Building	103.5	143.7	178.2	144.6	146.8	210.4	162.1	164.8	238.9
5	Other industry	104.3	130.2	161.8	127.8	129.5	184.1	116.6	118.0	167.7
6	Transport	101.5	151.7	182.5	148.1	150.4	214.5	133.4	136.9	193.6
7	Services	104.6	138.3	172.1	153.0	155.5	221.9	206.0	207.9	299.7
8	Coal	126.2	148.7	171.7	155.2	157.4	225.1	213.5	220.5	310.8
9	Natural gas	104.6	119.4	153.0	149.1	151.4	215.9	109.0	109.6	142.0
10	Oil refining	94.6	238.3	254.7	132.8	136.5	192.2	101.8	172.0	200.0
11	Public utilities	123.2	149.8	185.5	149.8	152.0	217.1	99.5	104.1	138.0

Table 2.9. Aggregate Capital, Labor, Energy, and Materials Input Coefficients (1963 Prices)

	Capital			Labor			Energy			Materials		
	1972	Sc.1	Sc.2	1972	Sc.1	Sc.2	1972	Sc.1	Sc.2	1972	Sc.1	Sc.2
1 Agriculture	.127	.122	.095	.264	.272	.271	.025	.020	.026	.616	.616	.650
2 Chemicals	.181	.163	.105	.110	.117	.108	.128	.134	.146	.620	.621	.610
3 Metallurgy	.104	.105	.124	.155	.157	.150	.040	.035	.039	.750	.749	.735
4 Building	.048	.040	.026	.263	.270	.273	.046	.037	.048	.685	.688	.687
5 Other industry	.082	.085	.100	.154	.155	.153	.027	.023	.024	.777	.775	.759
6 Transport	.226	.224	.207	.377	.387	.386	.095	.078	.088	.327	.328	.338
7 Services	.175	.179	.140	.440	.443	.465	.044	.034	.037	.364	.361	.361
8 Coal	.070	.035		.494	.532	.491	.298	.257	.377	.192	.207	.216
9 Natural gas	.692	.684	.593	.096	.112	.135	.043	.048	.051	.109	.103	.200
10 Oil refining	.215	.396	.354	.035	.045	.043	.734	.515	.548	.060	.051	.055
11 Public utilities	.365	.382	.403	.179	.179	.167	.337	.312	.313	.147	.144	.140

64

balance in physical terms in a consistent way. The emission of pollutants could be calculated directly from energy consumption in physical terms.

By specifying a number of objectives to the performance of the economy, the linear programming solution to each program contains interesting information to a policy maker concerning the changes occurring within the economy due to changes in objectives, without explicitly specifying the instruments available to reach them. Combining these objectives, a multi-objective policy problem can be formulated, which can be solved by the concept of displaced ideals.

One is interested, however, not only in the static case but also in future developments. A static approach would deny the possibility of different out-comes due to substitution processes arising from changes in technology and relative prices. In the variable input-output structure of section 3 the technical coefficients are determined by relative prices. The results obtained from our estimations seem to produce encouraging results.

A possible extension to our analysis would be to give more explicit consideration to the supply side of the input-output model; e.g., the production of capital goods. This includes consideration of production techniques including the abatement of pollution, which in the present model can only be reduced by substitution between energy sources. It might also be useful to include a lag structure in the model to account for the time needed to adapt to external developments and wishes.

The model may also be used as a tool in scenario analysis by assuming different policy options and exogenous developments. Finally, the regional repercussions of policy issues might be studied in more detail by means of a regionalization of the foregoing model. This will be the subject of further research.

7. APPENDIX: PRELIMINARY ESTIMATES OF THE PARAMETERS OF THE TRANSLOG PRICE POSSIBILITY FRONTIER

In Tables 2.10, 2.11, and 2.12 the estimated parameters are reported. For the energy submodel the domestic sectors coal and oil refinery are extended to account for imports of coal and oil. All energy imports by material sectors are assumed to be delivered through domestic energy sectors. In the same way material imports by energy sectors are obtained from the domestic material sectors. Due to the symmetry conditions $coeff_{ij} = coeff_{ji}$; these coefficients are reported only once. Throughout a uniform price structure has been assumed for sectoral deliveries. The results should be regarded as preliminary.

Table 2.10. Preliminary Estimates of Parameters of the Translog Price Possibility Frontier for the Energy Submodel of the Dutch Economy[a]

		Agri-cul-ture	Chemi-cals	Metals	Build-ing	Other Ind.	Trans-port	Servi-ces	Coal	Natu-ral Gas	Oil Refin-ery	Public Utili-ties
1.	Coal											
	β 1	.054	.428	.312	.049	.065	.004	.087	.095	.004	.029	.432
	β 11	-.072	-.604	-.173	-.065	-.098	-.004	-.116	-.003	-.001	-.004	-.492
	β 12	.157	.144	.104	-.064	.164	.016	.083	.027	.027	-.051	.081
	β 13	-.214	.287	-.048	.121	-.188	-.014	.048	.101	.004	.024	-.139
	β 14	.131	.174	.119	.009	.125	.005	-.013	.042	-.028	-.000	.552
	β 15	—	—	—	—	—	—	—	—	—	.035	—
	β 16	—	—	—	—	—	—	—	-.164	—	—	—
2.	Natural gas											
	β 2	.036	.042	-.006	.116	.085	.000	.005	.000	.429	.069	.263
	β 22	.067	-.076	-.058	-.521	-.014	-.002	.051	-.031	.421	-.157	-1.833
	β 23	-.050	.120	-.029	.515	.008	.054	.104	-.241	-.458	.022	1.048
	β 24	-.172	-.187	-.014	.071	-.156	-.066	-.237	.023	.011	.016	.705
	β 25	—	—	—	—	—	—	—	.225	—	.172	—
	β 26	—	—	—	—	—	—	—	—	—	—	—
3.	Oil refinery											
	β 3	.803	.353	.350	.632	.470	.771	.485	-.002	.257	.036	.265
	β 33	.277	-.097	.042	-.594	.219	-.066	-.122	-.056	-.057	-.026	.456
	β 34	.039	-.308	.036	-.040	-.038	.028	-.028	-.000	.513	.006	-1.364
	β 35	—	—	—	—	—	—	—	.199	—	—	—
	β 36	—	—	—	—	—	—	—	—	—	-.024	—

		.107	.177	.346	.202	.380	.224	.424	.036	.311	.008	.040
4. Public util.	β 4	.107	.177	.346	.202	.380	.224	.424	.036	.311	.008	.040
	β 44	.003	.322	-.139	-.039	.071	.034	.280	-1.031	-.493	.007	.109
	β 45	—	—	—	—	—	—	—	.968	—	—	—
	β 46	—	—	—	—	—	—	—	—	—	-.027	—
5. Coal import	β 5	—	—	—	—	—	—	—	.871	—	—	—
	β 55	—	—	—	—	—	—	—	-1.226	—	—	—
	β 56	—	—	—	—	—	—	—	—	—	—	—
6. Oil import	β 6	—	—	—	—	—	—	—	—	—	.858	—
	β 66	—	—	—	—	—	—	—	—	—	-.153	—

[a]Italic figures significant at the 5 percent level; (–) entries not estimated

Table 2.11. Preliminary Estimates of Parameters of the Translog Price Possibility Frontier for the Materials Submodel of the Dutch Economy[a]

		Agri-culture	Chemi-cals	Metals	Build-ing	Other Ind.	Trans-port	Servi-ces	Coal	Natu-ral Gas	Oil Refin-ery	Public Utili-ties
1. Agriculture	γ 1	.237	.000	—	.002	.208	.003	.007	.061	—	—	—
	γ 11	.126	-.005	—	-.009	.045	.006	.001	-.257	—	—	—
	γ 12	.053	.010	—	.019	-.031	.001	-.005	.351	—	—	—
	γ 13	-.011	-.011	—	.004	-.015	-.001	.025	.189	—	—	—
	γ 14	-.016	-.011	—	.000	-.006	.012	-.009	.111	—	—	—
	γ 15	.064	.010	—	-.020	.000	.003	.013	-.409	—	—	—
	γ 16	.003	-.005	—	.006	-.002	-.010	-.024	.029	—	—	—
	γ 17	-.215	.016	—	.001	.013	-.007	.002	-.011	—	—	—
2. Chemicals	γ 2	.074	.649	.015	.032	.020	.025	.025	.100	.071	.442	.077
	γ 22	.053	-.164	.016	-.013	.022	-.015	.048	.146	.272	.449	.332
	γ 23	-.046	-.028	-.015	-.013	-.056	.032	-.027	-.732	.118	-.251	-.099
	γ 24	-.000	.030	.027	-.024	.008	-.028	.037	-.385	-.030	.084	-.024
	γ 25	-.012	.148	-.018	.023	.045	.030	-.079	.717	-.097	-.087	-.273
	γ 26	.001	.013	.003	-.007	.001	-.041	.043	-.381	-.340	-.145	.038
	γ 27	-.044	-.007	-.010	.019	.013	.024	-.013	.286	.079	-.048	.030
3. Metals	γ 3	.010	.034	.768	.110	.050	.039	.019	.172	.173	.188	.221
	γ 33	.079	.063	-.183	.080	.009	.081	-.056	1.019	-.396	.246	.573
	γ 34	.037	.046	.002	.208	.022	.034	.031	.247	-.101	.076	.111
	γ 35	-.029	-.035	.087	-.171	.063	-.118	-.019	-.095	.603	.066	-.281
	γ 36	-.000	.013	-.004	.000	.008	-.003	.084	-.090	-.360	.030	-.016
	γ 37	-.025	-.043	.115	-.106	-.029	-.020	-.034	-.533	.137	-.166	-.284

4. Building	γ 4	.021	.022	.016	.393	.008	.024	.033	.069	.041	.101	.119
	γ 44	.016	.017	-.007	-.057	.013	.018	.039	-.367	-.066	.073	-.050
	γ 45	-.026	-.056	-.028	-.163	-.028	.027	-.065	.214	.101	-.092	-.043
	γ 46	-.003	-.019	.002	-.009	-.003	-.069	-.013	.069	.038	-.150	-.007
	γ 47	-.003	-.003	.005	.049	-.002	.009	-.015	.112	.061	.011	.016
5. Other Ind.	γ 5	.528	.155	.081	.332	.610	.357	.254	.249	.275	.089	.249
	γ 55	-.125	-.022	-.004	.289	-.080	.625	.393	-.532	-.974	-.032	.604
	γ 56	.004	.005	.007	.022	.007	-.554	-.231	.281	.750	.149	-.092
	γ 57	.128	-.045	-.040	.023	-.005	-.009	-.006	-.172	-.380	-.000	.090
6. Transport	γ 6	.004	.010	.006	.007	.007	.244	.311	.024	.102	.011	.015
	γ 66	-.006	-.024	-.006	-.015	-.012	.845	.239	.227	-.148	.019	.090
	γ 67	.004	.019	-.000	.005	.005	-.161	-.094	-.133	.062	.098	-.007
7. Services	γ 7	.126	.129	.115	.124	.097	.308	.351	.326	.337	.170	.318
	γ 77	.157	.067	-.065	.010	.009	.168	.164	.454	.042	.107	.157

[a]Italic figures significant at the 5 percent level; (−) entries not estimated.

Table 2.12. Preliminary Estimates of Parameters of the Translog Price Possibility Frontier for the Aggregate Submodel of the Dutch Economy[a]

		Agriculture	Chemicals	Metals	Building	Other Ind.	Transport	Services	Coal	Natural Gas	Oil Refinery	Public Utilities
1. Materials	α 1	.487	.540	.598	.542	.626	.258	.262	.201	.287	.055	.108
	α 11	.025	.105	-.008	.003	-.032	.067	.033	.165	.573	.043	.030
	α 12	.001	-.032	-.000	.007	-.002	-.007	-.002	.038	-.095	-.033	-.028
	α 13	.128	-.067	-.048	-.041	-.042	.005	-.036	-.054	.135	-.001	.003
	α 14	-.153	-.003	.059	.033	.079	-.063	.007	-.147	-.612	-.006	-.004
2. Energy	α 2	.019	.120	.031	.023	.020	.063	.021	.128	.068	.574	.267
	α 22	.005	.113	.007	.008	.003	.024	.001	-.021	.061	.028	.086
	α 23	.011	.016	.000	.011	-.003	-.000	-.003	.163	.069	-.021	-.056
	α 24	-.016	-.095	-.004	-.025	.004	-.014	.007	-.179	-.033	.028	.000
3. Labor	α 3	.407	.178	.232	.334	.212	.436	.442	.638	.196	.036	.211
	α 33	.009	.049	.062	.143	.084	.157	.325	.051	.065	.063	.064
	α 34	-.147	.003	-.012	-.112	-.037	-.160	-.283	-.158	-.268	-.039	-.010
4. Capital	α 4	.088	.162	.138	.101	.142	.244	.275	.033	.448	.335	.414
	α 44	.319	.098	-.040	.106	-.044	.240	.270	.487	.916	.019	.016

[a]Cursive figures significant at the 5 percent level.

8. NOTES

1. Homotheticity is a necessary and sufficient condition for the validity of a two-stage procedure; the restriction of linear homogeneity in the submodel is required to ensure that the product of the aggregate price and quantity indices equals total costs of the components; see Fuss [1977]. It should be noted that the model concerned has an aggregate character, so that individual actions and decisions at the firm level (such as risk aversion) cannot be analyzed.
2. For further discussion see Diewert [1974].
3. i is a summation vector with unit elements.

9. REFERENCES

Almon, C., M.R. Buckler, L.M. Horowitz, and T.C. Reimbold (1974), *1985: Inter-industry Forecasts of the American Economy,* D.C. Heath, Lexington, Mass.

Ayres, R.U., and A.V. Kneese (1969), Production, Consumption and Externalities, *The American Economic Review,* vol. LIX, pp. 282-297.

Baumol, W.J., and W.E. Oates (1975), *The Theory of Environmental Policy,* Prentice-Hall, Englewood Cliffs, N.J.

Berndt, E.R., and D.O. Wood (1975), Technology, Prices and the Derived Demand for Energy, *The Review of Economics and Statistics,* vol. 57, nr. 3, pp. 259-268.

Blair, P., (1978), *Multi-Objective Regional Energy Planning,* Martinus Nijhoff, Leiden.

Chatterji, M., and P. van Rompuy (1976), Lecture Notes in Economics and Mathematical Systems, vol. 126, *Energy, Regional Science and Public Policy,* Springer Verlag, Berlin.

Christensen, L.R., D.W. Jorgenson, and L.J. Lau (1973), Transcendental Logarithmic Production Frontiers, *The Review of Economics and Statistics,* vol. 55, pp. 28-46.

Cumberland, J.H., (1966), A Regional Inter-Industry Model for Analysis of Development Objectives, *Regional Science Association Papers,* vol. 17, pp. 65-95.

Cumberland, J.H., (1976), Forecasting Alternative Regional Electric Energy Requirements and Environmental Impacts for Maryland, 1970-1990, *Energy, Regional Science and Public Policy* (Chatterji/van Rompuy [1976]).

Daly, H.E., (1968), On Economics as Life Science, *The Journal of Political Economy,* vol. 76, pp. 392-406.

Dean, R.J., et al. (1973), *World Energy Modelling: Concepts and Methods,* Energy Research Unit, Queen Mary College, London.

Debanné, J.G., (1973), A Pollution and Technology Sensitive Model for Energy Supply-Distribution Studies; in M.S. Searl (ed.), *Energy Modelling,* Resources for the Future, Washington, D.C.

van Delft, A., and P. Nijkamp (1977), *Multi Criteria Analysis and Regional Decision Making,* Martinus Nijhoff, Leiden.

Diewert, W.E., (1974), Applications in Duality Theory; in M.D. Intrilligator and D.A. Kendrick (eds.), *Frontiers of Quantitative Economics,* vol. II, North Holland Publishing Company, Amsterdam.

Diewert, W.E., (1976), Exact and Superlative Index Numbers, *Journal of Econometrics*, vol. 4, pp. 115-146.

Fandel, G., (1972), *Optimale Entscheidung bei mehrfacher Zielsetzung*, Springer Verlag, Berlin.

Fuss, M.A., (1977), The Demand for Energy in Canadian Manufacturing, *Journal of Econometrics*, vol. 5, pp. 86-116.

Griffin, J.M., and P.A. Gregory (1976), An Intercountry Translog Model of Energy Substitution Responses, *The American Economic Review*, vol. 66, pp. 845-857.

Griffin, J.M., (1977), Interfuel-Substitution Possibilities: A Translog Application to Intercountry Data, *International Economic Review*, vol. 18, pp. 755-770.

Halversen, R., (1977), Energy Substitution in U.S. Manufacturing, *The Review of Economics and Statistics*, vol. 59, nr. 4, pp. 381-388.

Hoffman, K.C., (1972), A Unified Planning Framework for Energy System Planning, Ph.D. Thesis, Polytechnic Institute of Brooklyn, N.Y.

Houthakker, H., and M. Kennedy (1974a), *Demand for Energy as a Function of Price*, Harvard University, Cambridge, Mass.

Houthakker, H., and M. Kennedy (1974b), *The World Petroleum Model — Overview*, Harvard University, Cambridge, Mass.

Hudson, E.A., and D.W. Jorgenson (1976), Tax Policy and Energy Conservation: in D.W. Jorgenson (ed.), *Econometric Studies of U.S. Energy Policy*, North Holland Publishing Company, Amsterdam.

Hulten, C.R., (1973), Divisia Index Numbers, *Econometrica*, vol. 41, pp. 1017-1026.

Isard, W., (1969), Some Notes on the Linkage of the Ecologic and Economic Systems, *Papers Regional Science Association*, vol. XXII.

Jorgenson, D.W. (ed.), (1976), *Econometric Studies of U.S. Energy Policy*, North Holland Publishing Company, Amsterdam.

Leontief, W.W., (1947), Introduction in the Theory of the Internal Structure of Functional Relationships, Econometrica, vol. 15, pp. 361-373.

Leontief, W.W., (1953), *Studies in the Structure of the American Economy*, Oxford University Press, New York.

Leontief, W.W., (1970), Environmental Repercussions and the Economic Structure: An Input-Output Approach, *The Review of Economics and Statistics*, vol. 52, pp. 262-271.

Lesuis, P.J.J., and F. Muller (1976), Perspectives on Short Term Energy Shortages in The Netherlands; in M. Chatterji and P. van Rompuy (eds.), Lecture Notes in Economics and Mathematical Systems, vol. 126, *Energy, Regional Science and Public Policy*, pp. 104-118, Springer Verlag, Berlin.

MacAvoy, P.W., and R.S. Pindyck (1975), *The Economics of Natural Gas Shortage (1960-1980)*, North Holland Publishing Company, Amsterdam.

Malinvaud, E., (1970), *Statistical Methods of Econometrics*, Second Edition, North Holland Publishing Company, Amsterdam.

Muller, F., (1973), An Operational Mathematical Programming Model for the Planning of Economic Activities in Relation to the Environment, *Socioeconomic Planning Sciences*, vol. 7, pp. 123-138.

Muller, F., (1978), *Energy and Environment in Interregional Input-Output Models*, Studies in Applied Regional Science, Martinus Nijhoff, Boston/Leiden.

Neu, H., (1975), *A Dynamic Model for Simulating Fictive Energy Demand and Supply in the European Communities: Scenarios for the Year 2000 and Beyond*, Euratom Report.

Nijkamp, P., (1977), *Theory and Application of Environmental Economics*, North Holland Publishing Company, Amsterdam.

Odell, P.R., and K.E. Rosing (1975), *The North Sea Oil Province, An Attempt to Simulate Its Development and Exploration, 1969-2029*, Erasmus University, Rotterdam.

Oshima, K., (1974), *A Model for Assessing Energy Utilization in the Future*, Industrial Research Institute, Tokyo.

Pantell, R.H., (1976), *Techniques of Environmental Systems Analysis*, Wiley, New York.

Perry, B.W., (1974), The Short-run Consequences of Increased Energy Costs: An Input-Output Approach, *Energy Systems and Policy*.

Samuelson, P.A., (1966), Non-Substitution Theorems; in I. Stiglitz (ed.), *The Collected Scientific Papers of P.A. Samuelson*, vol. I, MIT Press, Cambridge, Mass., pp. 513-536.

Schweizer, P.G., et al. (1974), *A Regional Energy Model for Examining New Policy and Technology Changes*, Pittsburgh, Pa.

Smith, V.L. (ed.), (1977), *Economics of Natural and Environmental Resources*, Gordon & Breach, New York.

Tintner, G., (1971), *A Study of the Consequences of a Possible Energy Crisis in Austria*, Technische Hochschule, Vienna.

Uzawa, H., (1962), Production Functions with Constant Elasticities of Substitution, *The Review of Economic Studies*, vol. 29, pp. 291-299.

WAES, (1977), *Energy: Global Prospects 1985-2000*, McGraw-Hill, New York.

Zeleny, M. (ed.), (1976), *The Theory of Displaced Ideal*, Multiple Criteria Decision Making, Springer Verlag, Berlin.

3 COSTS AND BENEFITS OF WATER POLLUTION CONTROL

William D. Watson, Jr., *U.S. Geological Survey*

1. INTRODUCTION

The United States Congress, in amending the Federal Water Pollution Control Act in 1972, tied the control of water pollution to the application of pollution control technology. By 1977 all major point sources of water pollution were to have "best practicable control technology" (BPT) in place followed by the application in 1983 of "best available control technology" (BAT). The specific levels of discharges and technology for their achievement are being described in industry "development documents" issued by the U.S. Environmental Protection Agency (EPA). [1]

In passing this law Congress deviated from past approaches in two significant ways. First, control is to be based upon technological requirements, not upon water quality standards as it had been in prior legislation. Second, controls for specific sources are to be more or less uniform across the nation and vast authority has been given to EPA, a federal bureaucracy, to oversee their implementation. These deviations reflected disenchantment by Congress with prior legislation, whereby States had nearly autonomous authority to establish and enforce water quality standards.

Some Congressional members recognized that the 1972 act was based upon incomplete information, and that it could substantially accelerate pollution control expenditures, and were concerned that the 1983 BAT requirement might be too costly. Therefore, a provision was incorporated in the legislation to establish a National Commission on Water Quality (NCWQ) to study costs of and progress toward cleaner water with primary emphasis to be given to investigating "all aspects of the total economic, social, and environmental effects of achieving or not achieving, the effluent limitations and goals set forth for 1983 (FWPCA Amendments [1972], p. 60)." The findings of the NCWQ were to provide the bases for any "mid-course corrections" in the 1972 legislation.

The National Commission was, in fact, established in 1973, spent $17 million over a two-and-a-half-year period and in 1976 issued a final staff report (NCWQ [1976a]) and a report with recommendations to Congress (NCWQ [1976b]). Its main recommendation was that "Congress postpone the deadline by which municipal, agricultural and industrial discharges shall be required to meet the 1983 requirements from July 1, 1983, to a date not less than five and no more than ten years after 1983 (NCWQ [1976b], p. 7)." This recommendation was based upon several different findings and assertions that are challenged by the analysis in this paper.

The Commission found that costs to meet the 1983 BAT requirements, while substantial, would be less than costs to meet the 1977 BPT requirements but that expected benefits (of unstated magnitude) would nonetheless be less than the 1983 cost increment. However, the Commission's benefit findings consisted almost entirely of inferred benefits from reducing biochemical oxygen demand (BOD) and suspended solids (SS). BOD and SS do contribute significantly to water pollution damages. As analysis in this paper will show, there is substantial reduction in BOD and SS by implementing the 1977 BPT standards with somewhat smaller incremental reductions in BOD and SS when the 1983 BAT standards are implemented. But what is more important, other types of water pollutants, such as chemical oxygen demand and dissolved solids, will be substantially reduced by implementation of BAT standards. And, consequently, contrary to the NCWQ findings, it will be shown that avoided damages or benefits from controlling these other pollutants, as well as benefits from further incremental reductions in BOD and SS, make the benefits of the 1983 BAT requirement larger than its costs for industrial point sources.

The Commission has also asserted that mining, agriculture, and urban nonpoint sources are large contributors to waste loads and water pollution damages. Thus, according to the Commission, application of high control levels to industrial point sources and municipal sewage plants, as required by

the application of BAT by 1983, may leave a large amount of pollution un-
touched and provide little improvement in water quality. The Commission's
observation that nonpoint sources may be important contributors to water
pollution damages is valid. However, one cannot automatically infer from
this that high control levels are therefore not required for industrial sources
and municipal sewage plants. What is required is empirical analysis demon-
strating this. Unfortunately, neither the staff report nor the report to Congress contains such analysis. Analysis in this paper will confirm the
Commission's assertion that damage from nonpoint source pollution is
substantial but that high control levels for industrial sources, even to BAT
levels by 1984, are likely to generate benefits that will exceed control costs.[2]

Dynamics is a third area which was covered only in a partial way by the
National Commission. The Commission states that its recommendations do
consider population and economic growth over time. Here again, however,
no specific analysis is provided to show that the recommended delay in the
1983 BAT requirement holds up when values-at-risk increase over time as
the population and the economy grow. Analysis in this paper will show that
timing is crucial. By examining control costs and damage costs over the
period from 1975 to 2025, both in terms of year-by-year values and discounted values, it will be shown that, compared to the 1983 BAT requirement, a policy to delay implementation could have higher control and
damage costs. As an example, for industrial sources, the analysis in this
paper indicates that in 1975 BPT control costs are lower than the costs of
BAT controls. However, by 1984 this analysis also shows that BAT controls
will generate control plus damage costs that are then lower than those of a
BPT policy. Further, there are perhaps even better control levels intermediate between BPT and BAT controls where total control and damage costs
would be minimized. Compared to BAT controls, these intermediate controls would be superior because of their lower costs but inferior because they
would carry a higher risk of high environmental damages; thus, they may
not necessarily be better than BAT controls when account is taken of both
cost and risk. An important point here is that dynamic considerations which
are likely to be important, as in the case of industrial point sources, can only
be taken into consideration by performing dynamic analysis. Comparisons
of alternative policies in a single year cannot generally identify superior
policies for all subsequent years.

The National Commission also devoted some attention to the issue of
flexibility by pointing to the need for more data and analysis for revising
control decisions. However, its recommendations are so general that they are
probably of little help. One approach to this problem is to assign probabilities to various states of events and then determine expected cost savings as

though decisions are tailored to each of these states rather than to the perceived state of events underlying current policy. These alternative states could cover different distributions of damage costs and control costs and different growth rates for population and the economy. Analysis of this kind, to be presented in this paper, will indicate that there is likely to be substantial expected costs savings from gathering additional data of certain kinds and revising control accordingly.

The analysis and report of the National Commission is very broad in scope, going much beyond the confines of examining the 1983 BAT requirement. In this context, one wonders why the Commission did not address more completely the issue of effective and efficient incentives for enforcing water pollution control regulations. One approach, which economists regard as being very efficient and effective, is to levy effluent charges. The level of unit charges and total revenues for various control policies are estimated in Ridker and Watson [1978] but not presented here in order to reduce length.

On the whole, the National Commission report to Congress arrives at major recommendations that are only partially substantiated by its studies. This is unfortunate. If the Commission's recommendations on delaying the 1983 BAT requirements are adopted, there is a high probability that this could lead to environmental damage costs for industrial point sources that would far exceed the control costs that would be saved by delay.

The next section provides a brief description of methods. Following sections present analyses of control and damage costs for alternative controls and expected cost savings from gathering additional information. The final section draws policy implications and conclusions.

2. METHODS[3]

The estimation of pollution control benefits and costs and damage costs involves four steps: projections of national economic activity, abatement costs,[4] and pollution residuals; assignment of national point source residuals to regions; estimation of regional transportation residuals and urban runoff; and estimation of regional air and water pollution damages as a function of regional ambient conditions.

Estimates of national economic activity are derived using the national components of the Resources for the Future/Strategic Environmental Assessment System (RFF/SEAS). This is a system of interlinked models, the core of which is a dynamic input-output model of the United States economy developed by Clopper Almon at the University of Maryland (Almon et al. [1974]). Its national economic accounting structure consists of 185 sectors delivering commodities to each other and to various final consumers (households, investors in fixed capital and inventories, government, and net exports). In addition, there are 364 side equations dealing with product and technology mixes within these sectors. The purpose of these side equations is to provide more detail for projecting energy use, residuals, and abatement costs. All coefficients linking producing sectors with each other and with consumers are subject to change over time, some on the basis of econometrically fitted equations with time trends or lagged variables, but most on the basis of exogenously specified changes in technology, tastes, relative prices, supply constraints, and so on, determined on the basis of special studies. In the case of technology, the assumption was made that such changes will occur in evolutionary ways: best practice slowly becomes average practice, processes and products now at the pilot or demonstration stage become commercial and begin being used, and techniques still in the laboratory or experimental stage are brought on stream with appropriate time lags. Six main areas were emphasized: the substitution of concrete for lumber and steel in construction, increasing use of plastics and aluminum, improved efficiency of transportation equipment and the introduction of electric cars in significant numbers after 2000, process changes in primary metals production (which tend on net to improve efficiency and reduce residuals), extensive development of communications and its partial substitution for some types of transportation, and energy supply and conversion technology. Coefficient change and technology forecasts are, of course, essential ingredients of any attempt to make long-term forecasts.[5]

ABATE, another submodel within this system, estimates the investment and operating and maintenance costs associated with the control of pollution for 131 abating sectors. The costs calculated by ABATE for a given year create a demand for resources that is reflected through feedbacks which modify the output levels from the affected economic sectors. In turn, these changed output levels result in different sector growth rates from which the abatement costs are calculated during the next year.

National gross pollution residuals for point sources are calculated by applying gross pollution coefficients (units of gross pollution per unit of output) to output and side equation values (including the household sector and municipal waste water treatment plants). In any given year, more than 900 calculations are made. Net emissions are calculated as the product of gross emissions and the percentage not controlled. These percentages correspond directly with the control levels and timing used in calculating abatement costs. National residuals are assigned to regions using employment shares from U.S. Water Resources Council [1974a] and special industry location studies (Watson [1977]).

In addition to point source residuals, RFF/SEAS also calculates residuals for nonpoint sources: transportation, agriculture, mining, construction, forestry, and urban runoff.[6]

A model developed by Heaney et al. [1977], is used to estimate urban runoff and runoff control costs. Calculations are performed for 248 separate urbanized areas. Urban runoff depends upon acres and population density in three different zones — areas with combined sewers, those with storm sewers, and unsewered areas — and upon four types of activity within these zones — residential, commercial, industrial, and other. Costs of controlling runoff depend upon the mix of the different sewered zones and upon cost tradeoffs between size of treatment facility and storage for delayed treatment. Estimates for future years are made by assuming that gross runoff and control costs are proportional to population growth in each urbanized area. Population growth by urbanized area is based upon U.S. Water Resources Council [1974c].

The procedures used to estimate regional air and water pollution damages are outlined in Figure 3.1. Regional residuals are transformed into ambient concentrations using dispersion models with appropriate source-receptor transfer coefficients for each region; per capita average damages in dollars are calculated as a function of average per capita exposure; and per capita damages (adjusted by income-environment elasticities) are multiplied by regional population and summed to obtain national damages for the sources and pollutants indicated in Figure 3.1. National damages and control costs are added to obtain total environmental costs. Total national costs over a range of controls are obtained by changing assumed national control levels.

Six scenarios covering the years 1975–2025 have been simulated in the RFF/SEAS system. A brief description of each is provided in Table 3.1.

Both pollution control costs and damages are uncertain because of the incomplete state of information, measurement error, random error, and other factors. But uncertainty can be quantified, and by so doing one can estimate trade-offs between total *expected* costs and risk avoidance, and also savings in expected costs that result when an improved state of information leads to better decisions. The resulting trade-off between total expected costs and risk avoidance is illustrated by Figure 3.2. Risk avoidance is defined as the probability that the damages associated with a given control level will not exceed the 1975 damage level in a given year. By this definition, control levels smaller than j* such as A and B are inefficient since a move to j* would reduce expected total costs *and* risk. On the other hand, the control levels on EE are efficient. A northeast move along EE raises total expected costs but reduces the probability of exceeding 1975 damage levels. Thus, if society chooses controls like j* that minimize expected total costs, over a

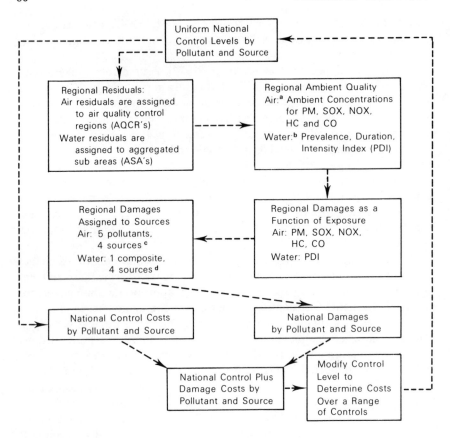

[a]Air pollutants include particulate matter (PM), sulfur oxides (SOX), nitrogen oxides (NOX), hydrocarbons (HC), and carbon monoxide (CO).

[b]Ambient water quality is measured by the prevalence, duration, intensity index.

[c]Air Pollution Sources: Electric Utilities, Industry, Residential and Commercial Sources, Transportation.

[d]Water Pollution Sources: Electric Utilities, Industry, Municipal Waste Water Treatment Plants, Urban Non-Point Sources, Agricultural Runoff, Mining and Milling, Other Non-Point Sources (Sediment from Mining, Non-Urban Construction, and Forestry).

Figure 3.1. Method for Estimating Regional Damage Costs

long period of time its pollution control and associated damage costs will be minimized. But in some years it may experience damage costs that are very high, so high that society is willing to pay something extra in terms of control costs in order to reduce the frequency with which high damage levels

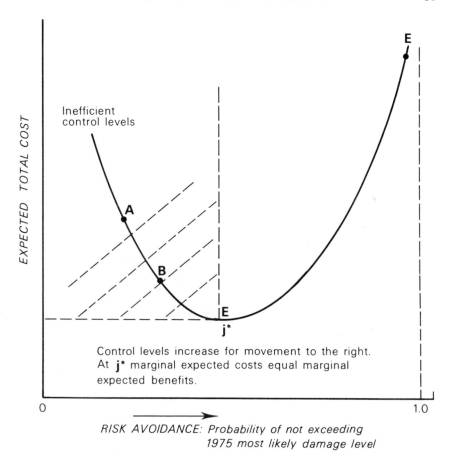

Figure 3.2.   Expected Total Costs and Risk Avoidance for Alternative
Control Levels

may be experienced. Thus, the control level that minimizes expected total
cost is not necessarily the optimal one to choose. It would certainly not be
anything less than this level,[7] but it could be something greater, depending
on the cost society is willing to pay to reduce the risks of high damage levels.
The empirical analysis that follows will investigate whether simulated EPA
controls are efficient in this sense.

Three alternative national pollution control policies are simulated: BPT,
BAT, and a cost-minimizing policy. Both the BPT and BAT policies are
fully implemented beginning in 1975. This allows easy comparison with a
cost-minimizing policy and allows one to see the years when BAT is less

Table 3.1. Scenarios for the National Economy

Scenarios	Characteristics
DH (Difficult case)	Population series D, high productivity growth rate; import restrictions and subsidies to develop domestic substitutes for imported energy, and stockpiling; strict pollution control policy, including no breeder; high oil prices; expansion of agricultural exports.
DL (Low economic growth)	Same as DH except low productivity series is used.
FH (Low population)	Same as DH except population series F is used.
FL (Low population and economic growth)	Same as DH except population series F and low productivity series are used.
DHNU (Nuclear phaseout)	Same as DH except that nuclear power is phased out.
DHOP (Oil price decline)	Same as DH except that oil prices decline and subsidies for domestic energy production are removed.

costly than BPT. It is also useful to identify efficient policies. These start with BPT and BAT controls. Where control is already efficient (that is, at a level like those on locus EE in Figure 3.2) it is unchanged, but for sources and pollutants where control is inefficient (like A and B in Figure 3.2), it is brought up to the just-efficient level (like j* in the figure).

The methods described here have a number of shortcomings. There is no attempt to identify pollutants that may become increasingly harmful in the future. Instead the focus is on well-known water pollutants. The aggregation of all water pollutants to estimate damages probably muddies important interactions. Uniform national controls are emphasized because that is the context in which policy decisions are currently being made. But it is quite likely that the appropriate level of control varies substantially among regions and if applied would reduce aggregate control plus damage costs significantly below the levels reported in this paper. Estimates of exposures are derived from simple models that almost certainly do not adequately capture all the nuances of interdependent transport interactions and microscale exposure variations. Existing estimates of damage costs and functions have many limitations. There is no attempt in this study to improve on these; they are used in their current condition. Estimated pollution control costs exclude enforcement costs, such as legal fees, monitoring costs, and other administrative costs incurred in implementing and enforcing environmental regulations. In some instances data required for the analysis did not exist. These gaps were filled by assigning data based upon subjective evaluation of known and similar circumstances. Obviously, use of better, more refined data would be desirable.

The empirical analysis and implications that follow should, of course, be viewed in light of these shortcomings.

3. RESULTS

3.1. Emissions and Regional Damages[8]

We begin in Table 3.2 with estimates of national water pollution emissions for scenario DH for each of our three different control policies—best practicable technology (BPT), best available technology (BAT), and cost-minimizing control (M). The three control policies for point sources and urban runoff are fully implemented beginning in 1975. This allows us to examine cost switchovers between BPT and BAT policies over time and to identify the years where one policy becomes less costly than the other. By definition, a cost-minimizing policy—M—provides the lowest costs (sum of expected control and damage costs) of any of the three policies, but its emissions can be the same, higher, or lower in comparison with BPT and BAT emissions. In most cases, as shown by the estimates in Table 3.2, point source and urban runoff emissions under policy M are higher than BPT and BAT emissions. Later, when these aggregate estimates are broken down by major source category (electric utilities, industrial, municipal waste water treatment, urban runoff, agriculture, mining, and other nonpoint sources), we will see that this reflects two opposing forces, namely, cost-minimizing emissions for municipal waste water treatment are above both the BPT and BAT levels, whereas for the other sources they are usually below BPT levels but never as small as BAT emissions. Thus, the policy M emissions for municipal waste water treatment tend to keep the aggregate policy M emissions above BAT and BPT levels, while for the other sources policy M emissions tend to position the aggregate M estimate between the BPT and BAT levels. Obviously, the first of these impacts outweighs the second in the aggregate estimate of policy M emissions.

As stated earlier, in this study we do not analyze the costs and benefits of control policies for agriculture, mining, and other nonpoint sources. However, it is still necessary to include these emissions at some convenient levels, because total pollution damages are a function of exposure from all emis-

Table 3.2. National Water Pollution Emissions for Alternative Policies, Scenario DH (million tons)

	1975		1985		2000		2025	
	Point Sources and Urban Runoff[a]	Agriculture, Mining, and Other Nonpoint Sources[b]	Point Sources and Urban Runoff	Agriculture, Mining, and Other Nonpoint Sources	Point Sources and Urban Runoff	Agriculture, Mining, and Other Nonpoint Sources	Point Sources and Urban Runoff	Agriculture, Mining, and Other Nonpoint Sources
Biochemical Oxygen Demand (BOD)								
Gross[c]	15.6	4.3	20.2	3.7	27.0	4.6	47.2	7.1
Net BPT	3.3	3.2	4.0	2.3	4.9	2.3	5.0	3.1
BAT	2.0	3.2	1.7	2.3	.9	2.3	.6	3.1
M	5.2	3.2	5.3	2.3	4.9	2.3	6.9	3.1
Actual (this study)	4.4							
Actual (Gianessi & Peskin)[d]	7.7	14.3						
Chemical Oxygen Demand (COD)								
Gross	15.7	n.e.	20.9	n.e.	30.0	n.e.	55.2	n.e.
Net BPT	4.5	—	5.7	—	6.6	—	7.5	—
BAT	2.4	—	2.8	—	2.5	—	2.6	—
M	4.3		3.8		4.7		7.8	
Actual (this study)	7.2							
Suspended Solids (SS)								
Gross	67.5	666.3	103.0	586.9	147.9	731.5	284.7	1133.4
Net BPT	12.9	501.3	18.5	337.3	24.4	346.9	28.6	467.9
BAT	4.0	501.3	4.1	337.3	2.7	346.9	1.8	467.9

M	15.2	501.3	12.2	337.3	15.1	346.9	31.3	467.9
Actual (this study)	16.7	501.3						
Actual (Gianessi & Peskin)	21.8	2064.0						
Dissolved Solids (DS)								
Gross	36	331.3	43.7	318.4	52.0	424.6	88.7	711.1
Net BPT	15.6	260.6	18.7	146.7	18.4	150.5	21.3	204.1
BAT	12.5	260.6	14.4	146.7	12.2	150.5	13.4	204.1
M	17.3	260.6	18.9	146.7	18.7	150.5	24.5	204.1
Actual (this study)	26.1	260.6						
Actual (Gianessi & Peskin)	118.9	946.4						
Nutrients								
Gross	2.4	6.0	2.9	5.4	3.6	5.9	5.3	7.5
Net BPT	1.4	4.1	1.5	3.5	1.6	3.7	1.0	4.4
BAT	1.3	4.1	1.3	3.5	1.2	3.7	0.5	4.4
M	1.5	4.1	1.6	3.5	1.7	3.7	1.4	4.4
Actual (this study)	1.6	4.1						
Actual (Gianessi & Peskin)	0.6	4.4						
Other[e,f]								
Gross	2.5	3.4	3.6	3.7	5.4	4.5	10.5	6.7
Net BPT	0.4 (1.5)	3.4	0.6	1.8	0.9	1.2	1.0	1.8
BAT	0.1	3.4	0.1	1.8	0.1	1.2	0.1	1.8
M	0.4	3.4	0.7	1.8	0.4	1.2	1.0	1.8
Actual (this study)	1.5	3.4						
Actual (Gianessi & Peskin)	1.1	15.4						

[a] Includes emissions from electric utilities, industrial point sources, municipal waste water treatment plants, and urban runoff sources.

(Table 3.2 continued)

[b]Includes point emissions and sediment runoff from minerals, ore, and coal mining and milling, and sediment runoff from nonurban construction, forestry, acid coal mine drainage, and agriculture.

[c]Gross emissions from mining and nonpoint sources (other than agriculture) are calculated as emissions that would have occurred assuming 1975 control levels in every year after 1975. Gross emissions for agricultural nonpoint sources are emissions that would have occurred if erosion control measures in effect in 1975 and subsequent years were to be removed. Gross emissions for point sources and urban runoff are discharges assuming no control in any year.

[d]Source is Gianessi and Peskin (1978). Their estimates are for 1972 and include discharges from man-originated as well as natural sources. Their estimated discharges from natural sources are (in million tons):

Biochemical Oxygen Demand	3.5
Suspended Solids	522.0
Dissolved Solids	231.0
Nutrients	1.1
Other	3.8

These estimates should be subtracted from the agriculture, mining, and other nonpoint source estimate to obtain their estimate of man-originated discharges in that category. This allows their estimates to be directly compared with this study's estimates, which include only man-originated discharges.

Gianessi and Peskin's estimates of discharges from point sources and urban runoff are all man originated. In this category, except for dissolved solids, there is reasonable agreement between the estimate of this study and their estimates, considering the differences in base years and data sources.

In the mining and other nonpoint source category, a substantial part of the difference between the two sets of estimates is due to use of different data sources for sediment runoff from nonirrigated agriculture. Gianessi and Peskin use an estimate from a report prepared by the Midwest Research Institute [1975]. That report estimated sediment delivered to water from nonirrigated agriculture as 1.8 billion tons. Gianessi and Peskin then applied fixed coefficients to this number to obtain estimates of various pollutant loadings from nonirrigated agriculture. In comparison, this study uses data from a U.S. Department of Agriculture [1975] study to obtain an estimate of 517 million tons of sediment discharged to water from irrigated and nonirrigated agriculture in 1972. As a third point of comparison, a study by Wade and Heady [1976] estimates that gross erosion from all agriculture, only a part of which gets into water, amounted to about 1.5 billion tons in the early 1970s. This difference in base sediment estimates makes the Gianessi and Peskin man-originated estimates (under the category of agriculture, mining, and other nonpoint source discharges) about 3.5 times larger than this study's estimates. Thus, when this study's estimates in the agriculture, mining, and other nonpoint source category are multiplied by 3.5 and the Gianessi and Peskin natural source estimates (from above) are added, there would be reasonable agreement except for nutrients between the two studies.

[e]Includes emissions of acids, bases, oil, grease, pesticides, and heavy metals (all entries except Gianessi and Peskin).
[f]Includes phosphorus and heavy metals.

sions, irrespective of the sources of the emissions. Further, so that we may correctly analyze costs and benefits for point sources and urban runoff, we must be able to separate damages for these sources from total damages. We do this by calculating total damages as a function of total exposures from all sources and then we assign a part of these damages to point sources and urban runoff in proportion to their share in total exposures where exposures are a linear function of emissions.

To project emissions from agriculture, mining, and other nonpoint sources, we have used the following convenient assumptions. For ore, coal, and minerals milling and mining, it is assumed that all facilities meet BPT standards by 1980 and BAT standards by 1985. The per unit sediment runoff from ore, coal, and minerals mining is assumed to be reduced to about one-half of its current level by 1985. Sediment runoff from nonurban construction and forestry (per unit of activity) is assumed to be one-half and one-fourth current levels by 1985 and 2000, respectively. Acid mine drainage from abandoned coal mines is assumed to be one-half and one-fourth current levels by 1985 and 2000, respectively. Sediment runoff from agriculture on a per unit basis is assumed to be about two-thirds of its pre-1970 level beginning in 1975. Our objective in using these assumptions is to generate estimates of emissions for agriculture, mining, and other nonpoint sources that will be close to actual practice.

Another useful way of characterizing the emissions estimates in Table 3.2 is in terms of source-receptor relationships. Point source and urban runoff emissions occur mainly in areas where people reside and where the assimilative capacity of receiving waters may be limited insofar as this affects the possibilities for damage because of the nearness of the emissions sources and the affected population. In contrast, agriculture, mining, and the sources in our other nonpoint category are dispersed over relatively large areas where population density is relatively low and where the assimilative capacity of receiving waters may be large enough so that emissions cause little damage. Therefore, even though, as shown in Table 3.2, emissions from agriculture, mining, and nonpoint sources are far larger than emissions from point sources and urban runoff, their pollution damages are likely to be relatively modest.

In devising economically efficient pollution control policies, it is important to distinguish between emissions and the damages they cause. The estimates in Table 3.2 could lead to too little emphasis on controlling pollution from point sources and urban runoff. A narrow objective that emphasized reduction in emissions would probably concentrate on agriculture, mining, and nonpoint sources because of the sheer bulk of the discharges from these sources. However, as we will see, because point source emissions and urban runoff occur where population is relatively dense and consequently where damages are relatively higher, it is economically efficient to have relatively high controls for these sources, even though the reductions in their discharges are small compared to emissions from agriculture, mining, and other nonpoint sources.[9]

The percentage share of emissions from each of the major water pollution sources is shown by the estimates in Table 3.3. Again, it is useful to think of emissions as falling into two general categories: nondispersed and dispersed discharges where nondispersed discharges are those occurring in relatively densely populated areas, whereas dispersed emissions occur over wide regions with relatively large amounts of assimilative capacity being available in receiving waters. In Table 3.3 nondispersed emissions are those from electric utilities, industrial point sources, municipal waste water treatment plants, and urban runoff; dispersed emissions are those from agriculture, mining, and other nonpoint sources. In terms of shares, it is clear from the estimates in Table 3.3 that discharges from dispersed sources represent the bulk of emissions except for chemical oxygen demand (COD) in some years.[10] Nonetheless, to repeat an earlier point, until one transforms these emissions into damages it is difficult to say anything on the basis of these numbers alone about economically efficient control levels for any source.

In the real world, pollution damages take place at the regional level and that is where they are measured in this analysis. Figures 3.3, 3.4, and 3.5 show water pollution damages by ASA at constant 1975 levels, BPT levels, BAT levels, and cost-minimizing levels in the years 1985, 2000, and 2025, respectively. These are damages due to emissions from all the sources covered in this analysis. For BPT, BAT, and cost-minimizing controls, these damages are those that result from the net emissions reported in Table 3.2. In 1975, most damages according to this study's estimates were concentrated east of the Mississippi, principally in Florida, the Middle Atlantic ASAs, the Great Lakes region, the Ohio River basin, the lower Mississippi River basin, and also in the San Francisco Bay area, Southern California, and the Houston-Galveston Bay area. Over time with controls kept constant at 1975 levels, regional damages would increase, especially in Florida, the Middle Atlantic ASAs, and in the Ohio and Mississippi River drainage basins. Under BAT controls, damages would be reduced substantially in these otherwise heavily damaged regions. In terms of the regional distribution of damages, BPT and cost-minimizing controls are in between damages at constant 1975 levels and BAT damages. Compared to BAT controls, they allow somewhat higher damage levels in Florida, the Middle Atlantic ASAs, and the Ohio and Mississippi River drainage basins, but their damages never reach the levels given by constant 1975 controls.

Table 3.4 shows this study's estimates of national damages by major source category. The residuals and damages for agriculture, mining, and other nonpoint sources, in any given year, are kept approximately constant as different control policies are applied to the other point sources and urban runoff. Damages from industrial point sources are particularly sensitive to changes in control levels because industrial point sources, for the most part, are located near population and because there is a relatively large amount of residuals that can be discharged by industrial point sources.

It is important at this point for better understanding to take note of some specific assumptions that were made in calculating damages from agriculture, mining, and other nonpoint sources.

Wade and Heady [1976] report that damages from agriculture sediment discharges are likely to be in a range from $250 to $500 million per year. We used this range of estimates and one other assumption to normalize our damage estimates in the base year. The additional assumption is that sediment discharges from mining and other nonpoint sources are widely dispersed like those from agriculture and hence they contribute to damages in proportion to their loadings relative to agricultural sediment loadings. Armed with this, we ran our damage estimating model for 1971 until we found a factor which, when applied to agricultural sediment, caused the model to assign about $350 million of damages to agricultural sediment. This weight was then used for mining and other nonpoint source sediment in keeping with the proportionate assumption above. In terms of specific pollutants, this procedure was applied only to suspended solids and dissolved solids since they are the bulk of pollutants derived from sediment runoff. The other pollutants from agriculture, mining, and other nonpoint sources are treated exactly like pollutants from any other source. That is, they enter the damage-estimating model unweighted and compete one-to-one with pollutants from other sources in the determination of damages. We hope our procedure for weighting suspended and dissolved solids correctly adjusts discharges to account for the wide dispersion, remoteness, and relative accessibility of agriculture, mining, and other nonpoint sources to substantial amounts of assimilative capacity. But to be somewhat conservative we have left some of the discharges from these sources unweighted and have thus assigned more damages to these sources and therefore less damages to point sources and urban runoff. We did this on purpose so that, if anything, our analysis of the costs and benefits of controlling discharges from point sources and urban runoff would be biased in the direction of lower cost-minimizing controls.

3.2. Control Costs, Damage Costs, and Benefits

Expected cost-risk curves (of the type illustrated by Figure 3.2) have been estimated for water pollution discharges from each of the three major point

Table 3.3. Sources of Water Pollution Emissions, Scenario DH

	1975[a]	1985		2000		2025	
		BPT	BAT	BPT	BAT	BPT	BAT
Biochemical oxygen demand, percent							
Industrial point sources	31.4	30.8	11.2	38.4	12.8	41.0	11.9
Mun. sewage treatment	21.7	29.0	26.7	26.8	12.1	18.4	1.8
Urban runoff	4.7	3.8	4.1	2.7	3.8	2.4	2.6
Agriculture	29.0	26.9	42.9	25.1	55.9	25.9	56.7
Mining & other nonpoint sources[b]	13.2	9.5	15.1	7.0	15.4	12.3	27.0
Net discharges (10^6 tons)	7.6	6.3	4.0	7.2	3.2	8.1	3.7
Chemical oxygen demand, percent							
Industrial point sources	54.3	60.8	47.1	72.9	55.1	76.5	65.5
Urban runoff	45.7	39.2	52.9	27.1	44.9	23.5	34.5
Net discharges (10^6 tons)	7.2	5.7	2.8	6.6	2.5	7.5	2.6
Suspended solids, percent							
Electric utilities	0	0.3	0	0.2	0	0.3	0
Industrial point sources	1.7	3.2	0.1	4.9	0.1	4.6	0.1
Mun. sewage treatment	0.3	0.6	0.3	0.6	0.1	0.3	0
Urban runoff	1.1	1.1	0.8	0.9	0.6	0.6	0.3
Agriculture	63.7	70.0	73.0	71.8	76.3	62.3	65.9
Mining & other nonpoint sources	33.2	24.8	25.8	21.6	22.9	31.9	33.7
Net discharges (10^6 tons)	518.0	355.8	341.4	371.3	349.6	496.5	469.7

Dissolved solids, percent

Electric utilities	0.8	1.8	1.7	1.1	0.9	1.3	1.1
Industrial point sources	3.7	2.5	1.1	3.3	1.4	3.7	1.9
Mun. sewage treatment	3.3	5.5	5.1	5.3	4.4	3.5	2.6
Urban runoff	1.3	1.6	1.1	1.2	0.8	0.9	0.5
Agriculture	49.3	64.5	66.3	67.7	70.3	58.8	61.0
Mining & other nonpoint sources	41.6	24.1	24.7	21.4	22.2	31.8	32.9
Net discharges (10^6 tons)	286.7	165.4	161.1	168.9	162.7	255.4	217.5

Nutrients, percent

Industrial point sources	1.7	3.3	0.8	4.3	0.9	5.0	1.4
Mun. sewage treatment	24.7	26.2	26.0	25.3	23.9	12.7	8.4
Urban runoff	1.2	0.9	0.7	0.7	0.5	0.7	0.4
Agriculture	67.1	65.6	68.4	65.9	70.7	76.0	83.7
Mining & other nonpoint sources	5.3	4.0	4.1	3.8	4.0	5.6	6.1
Net discharges (10^6 tons)	5.7	5.0	4.8	5.3	4.9	5.4	4.9

Other[c], percent

Industrial point sources	28.9	22.0	2.8	38.7	4.8	32.8	5.1
Urban runoff	1.7	2.4	2.0	2.2	2.2	1.6	1.1
Agriculture	0.2	0.7	0.8	1.0	1.5	0.9	1.3
Mining & other nonpoint sources	69.2	74.9	94.4	58.1	91.5	64.7	92.5
Net discharges (10^6 tons)	4.9	2.4	1.9	2.1	1.3	2.8	1.9

[a] Actual 1975 emissions and shares as estimated by this study.
[b] Includes point emissions and sediment runoff from minerals, ore and coal mining and milling, and sediment runoff from nonurban construction, forestry, acid coal mine drainage, and agriculture.
[c] Includes acids, bases, oil, grease, pesticides, and heavy metals.

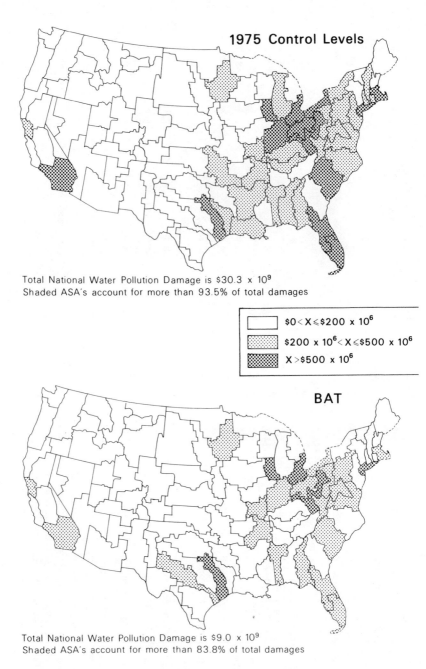

1975 Control Levels

Total National Water Pollution Damage is 30.3×10^9
Shaded ASA's account for more than 93.5% of total damages

☐	$0 < X \leqslant 200 \times 10^6$
▨	$200 \times 10^6 < X \leqslant 500 \times 10^6$
▩	$X > 500 \times 10^6$

BAT

Total National Water Pollution Damage is 9.0×10^9
Shaded ASA's account for more than 83.8% of total damages

Figure 3.3. Regional Water Pollution Damages, Scenario DH, 1985

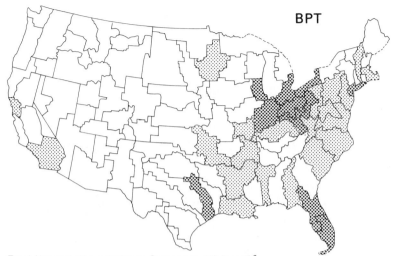

BPT

Total National Water Pollution Damage is 19.0×10^9
Shaded ASA's account for more than 90.3% of total damages.

X is water pollution damage
per year in 1971$

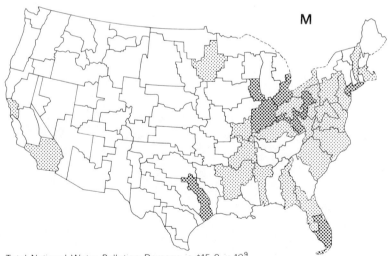

M

Total National Water Pollution Damage is 15.8×10^9
Shaded ASA's account for more than 88.5% of total damages

93

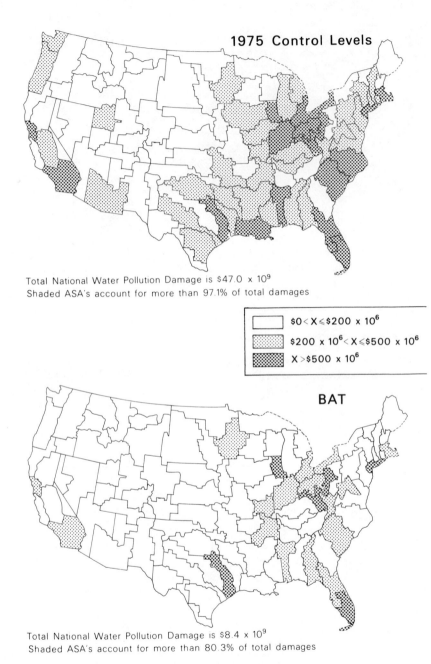

1975 Control Levels

Total National Water Pollution Damage is $47.0 x 10^9
Shaded ASA's account for more than 97.1% of total damages

$0 < X \leqslant 200×10^6
$200 \times 10^6 < X \leqslant 500×10^6
$X > 500×10^6

BAT

Total National Water Pollution Damage is 8.4×10^9
Shaded ASA's account for more than 80.3% of total damages

Figure 3.4. Regional Water Pollution Damages, Scenario DH, 2000

94

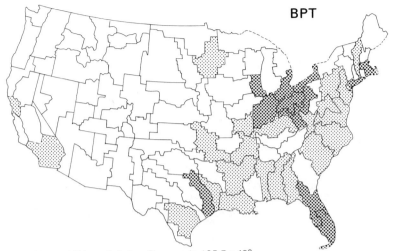

BPT

Total National Water Pollution Damage is $25.7 × 10^9
Shaded ASA's account for more than 92.0% of total damages

X is water pollution damage
per year in 1971$

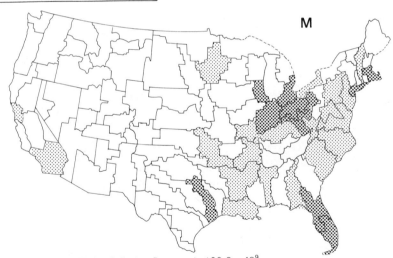

M

Total National Water Pollution Damage is $20.3 × 10^9
Shaded ASA's account for more than 90.1% of total damages.

95

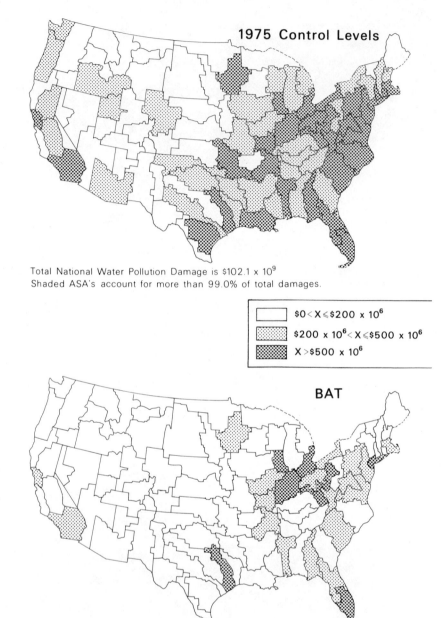

1975 Control Levels

Total National Water Pollution Damage is $102.1 x 10^9$
Shaded ASA's account for more than 99.0% of total damages.

☐	$0 < X \leqslant $200 x 10^6$
▨	$200 x 10^6 < X \leqslant $500 x 10^6$
▩	$X > $500 x 10^6$

BAT

Total National Water Pollution Damage is $10.3 x 10^9$
Shaded ASA's account for more than 83.5% of total damages.

Figure 3.5.   Regional Water Pollution Damages, Scenario DH, 2025

96

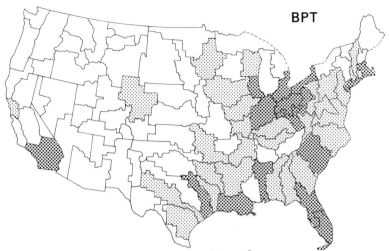

Total National Water Pollution Damage is $35.3 × 10^9$
Shaded ASA's account for more than 95.4% of total damages.

X is water pollution damage
per year in 1971$

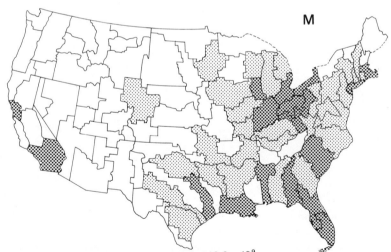

Total National Water Pollution Damage is $40.0 × 10^9$
Shaded ASA's account for more than 96.2% of total damages.

Table 3.4. National Water Pollution Damages for Alternative Controls,
Scenario DH (millions of 1971 dollars)

	1975 Controls	BPT	BAT	M
	1975			
Electric utilities	.4	.3	.2	.4
Industrial point sources	5.4	2.6	.4	2.6
Municipal sewage treatment	2.5	2.2	1.9	3.5
Urban runoff	2.9	1.6	1.0	1.4
Agriculture	.9	.9	.9	.9
Mining & other nonpoint sources	1.0	1.0	1.0	1.0
Total	13.1	8.6	5.4	9.8
	1985			
Electric utilities	1.3	1.1	.7	.9
Industrial point sources	14.9	7.6	1.0	3.0
Municipal sewage treatment	5.6	4.5	3.0	7.1
Urban runoff	6.3	3.6	2.1	2.6
Agriculture	1.3	1.3	1.3	1.3
Mining and other nonpoint sources	.9	.9	.9	.9
Total	30.3	19.0	9.0	15.8
	2000			
Electric utilities	1.0	.9	.4	.9
Industrial point sources	26.7	13.9	1.3	5.1
Municipal sewage treatment	7.8	5.2	2.7	7.7
Urban runoff	9.1	3.3	1.6	4.2
Agriculture	1.6	1.6	1.6	1.6
Mining and other nonpoint sources	.8	.8	.8	.8
Total	47.0	25.7	8.4	20.3
	2025			
Electric utilities	2.3	1.8	.8	1.8
Industrial point sources	67.9	20.6	2.1	20.6
Municipal sewage treatment	12.9	5.2	2.0	9.1
Urban runoff	15.3	4.0	1.7	4.8
Agriculture	2.2	2.2	2.2	2.2
Mining and other nonpoint sources	1.5	1.5	1.5	1.5
Total	102.1	35.3	10.3	40.0

sources and urban runoff sources. These are used below to present the principal implications of alternative national water pollution control policies.

Figure 3.6 shows the expected total cost-risk curves for controlling water pollution from electric utility plants. For the year 1985, BPT controls are on the inefficient part of the trade-off curve. For all other years, both the BPT and BAT controls are efficient. The data in panel A of Table 3.6 indicate in the period 1975–2025 that BAT controls, compared to BPT and minimum cost (M) controls, would raise expected *control costs* by $38.7 to $33.6 billion but lower expected *damage costs* by $28.3 to $21.9 billion for a total overall cost increase of $10.4 to $11.7 billion. These extra costs of BAT in comparison with minimum costs can be thought of as insurance to reduce the probability of incurring very large unanticipated environmental damages in the future. Thus, BAT controls are economically efficient; but whether or not we want to incur these extra insurance costs depends, of course, upon social preferences concerning trade-offs between costs and risk.

The next sources to be considered are industrial point sources. The NCWQ (1976b) has argued that best practicable technology (BPT) standards are relatively cheap to meet and remove enough pollution so that pollution damages will be substantially reduced and that going beyond BPT to BAT standards for industrial point sources would move firms into a range of control where costs are high but would produce relatively few additional benefits since BAT requirements would work on the margin of pollution not removed under BPT standards. The analysis in this study disagrees with these arguments in three important respects. First, as shown by the estimates in Table 3.5, discharges of chemical oxygen demand, suspended solids, and dissolved solids are substantially reduced when BAT technology is applied in comparison with BPT technology. Second, compared to BPT, the incremental costs of BAT by 1984 are less than its incremental benefits. This is shown in Figure 3.7, panel A, by the crossover of the BAT and BPT cost schedules. Prior to 1984, BPT has lower costs; this agrees with the studies of the National Commission on Water Quality. However, by 1984, population and gross residuals have grown enough so that the higher control levels of BAT are less costly in terms of control and damage costs. Figure 3.8 indicates that it is only in 1975 and again near the year 2025 that a BPT strategy for industrial sources would be economically efficient. This illustrates the importance of dynamic analysis. The third way in which this analysis of industrial point sources disagrees with the NCWQ recommendations has to do with the implications of cost-effectiveness analysis versus cost-benefit analysis. Because of the sheer magnitude of residuals from agriculture, mining, and other nonpoint sources, it is relatively inexpensive at the margin to control these residuals. Thus, on the basis of cost-effectiveness consider-

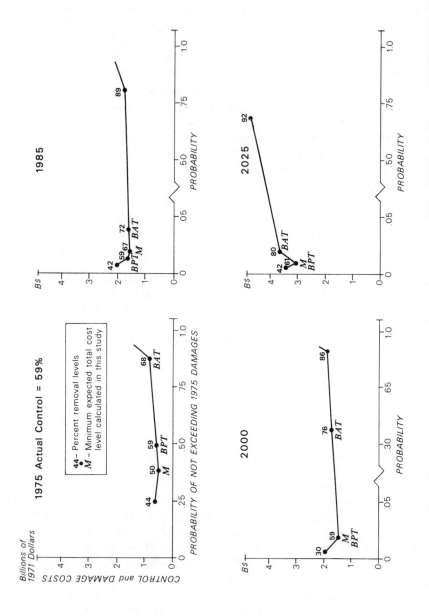

Figure 3.6. Expected Total Costs and Risks Associated with Different Control Levels for Water Pollution Discharges from Electric Utilities, Scenario DH

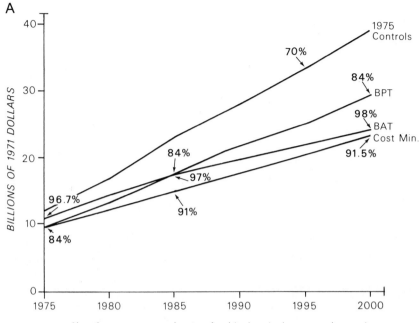

% = Average removal rates for biochemical oxygen demand,
chemical oxygen demand, suspended solids, dissolved solids,
nutrients, oil and grease, acids, and bases.

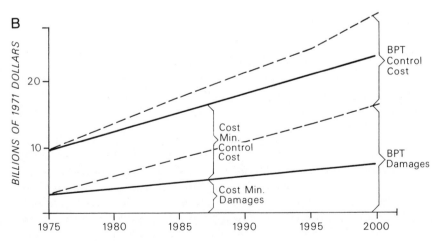

Figure 3.7. Water Pollution Control Costs for Industrial Sources,
            Scenario DH

Table 3.5.   Net Discharges of Water Pollution from Industrial Sources, Scenario DH (million tons)

	1985	2000	2025
Biochemical oxygen demand			
BPT	2.0	2.8	3.3
BAT	.4	.4	.4
M	.9	1.2	3.3
Chemical oxygen demand			
BPT	3.5	4.8	5.7
BAT	1.3	1.4	1.7
M	2.1	2.5	5.7
Suspended solids			
BPT	11.5	18.1	22.1
BAT	.3	2.4	.2
M	4.1	6.2	22.1
Dissolved solids			
BPT	4.2	5.5	8.5
BAT	1.8	2.2	4.2
M	2.6	3.3	8.5
Nutrients			
BPT	.2	.2	.3
BAT	.04	.04	.07
M	.08	.1	.3
Other[a]			
BPT	.5	.8	.9
BAT	.05	.06	.1
M	.2	.2	.9

[a]Includes acids, bases, oil, grease, pesticides, and heavy metals.

ations, one might be lead in the direction of reducing these residuals to a relatively great extent and industrial point residuals to a much smaller extent, especially when considering controls beyond BPT levels. However, as shown in Figure 3.7 (panel B) and Figure 3.8, in the period from 1976 to 2020, the incremental benefits of controls beyond BPT levels exceed incremental control costs up to the cost-minimizing level, M, a level about midway between BPT and BAT controls.[11] It is clear from this cost-benefit analysis that BPT controls are not economically efficient; by moving at

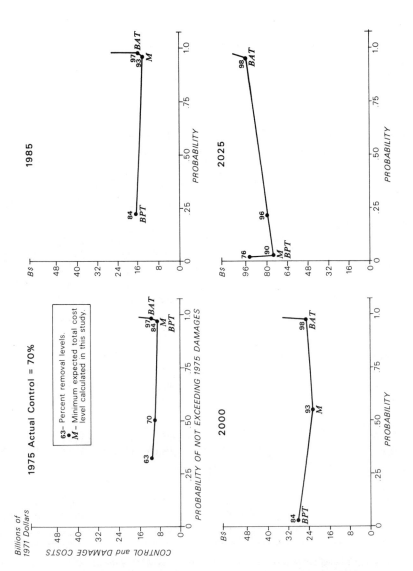

Figure 3.8. Expected Total Costs and Risks Associated with Different Control Levels for Water Pollution Discharges from Industrial Sources, Scenario DH

least to cost-minimizing controls it is possible to reduce both expected costs and risk (see panel B of Table 3.6). On the other hand, BAT policy is economically efficient. In the period from 1975 to 2025, its expected costs are higher than minimum costs by $275 billion, but it has a higher weighted probability that future damages will *not exceed* 1975 damages — .99 compared to .59.

The NCWQ report to Congress (1976b) states that it is not critical to move beyond BPT controls for industrial point sources very soon and that

Table 3.6.   Cumulative Expected Water Pollution Control Benefits and Costs, 1975–2025, Scenario DH (billions of 1971 $)

Policy[a]	Control Costs	Damage Costs	Total Costs	Benefits	B/C	X^b
A. Electric Utilities						
BPT	30.4	58.3	88.7	119.5	3.9	.08
BAT	69.1	30.0	99.1	149.2	2.2	.29
M	35.5	51.9	87.4	125.8	3.5	.06
B. Industrial Point Sources						
BPT	1019.2	702.8	1722.0	5827.7	5.7	.18
BAT	1790.9	69.3	1860.2	6483.4	3.6	.99
M	1214.5	370.9	1585.3	6168.8	5.1	.59
C. Municipal Sewage Treatment						
BPT	440.6	253.3	693.9	753.1	1.7	.13
BAT	801.2	143.5	944.7	855.9	1.1	.50
M	202.8	388.2	591.0	620.5	3.1	.04
D. Urban Runoff[c]						
BPT	141.5	205.3	346.8	404.6	2.9	.43
BAT	267.1	103.0	370.1	504.6	1.9	.75
M	160.1	178.9	339.0	431.3	2.7	.51
E. All of the Above Sources						
BPT	1631.7	1219.7	2851.4	7104.9	4.4	.21
BAT	2928.3	345.8	3274.1	7993.1	2.7	.63
M	1612.9	989.9	2602.7	7346.4	4.6	.30

[a]Costs and benefits are total and not incremental, that is, they include amounts that would have occurred without the policy plus any additional amounts that result because the policy is in place.

[b]Weighted probability of not exceeding 1975, most likely damages.

[c]Includes combined sewer overflows.

we ought to take additional time to determine cost effective strategies. In contrast, this analysis indicates that we ought to move fairly soon beyond BPT controls at least to controls where costs are minimized. Perhaps it is useful to think of ways to remain flexible in our control efforts on the chance that additional data will indicate more preferred strategies.[12] But for the present, this study indicates that both costs and risks will be substantially larger under continuation of BPT controls. While BAT controls can be correctly characterized as being economically efficient, that is not very useful for policy. Compared to minimum cost controls, BAT controls have a smaller risk of incurring unanticipated large environmental damages, but they also have larger control costs. The preferred trade-off between cost and risk depends upon social preferences, and we do not know whether or not BAT controls are consistent with these preferences. It is also unlikely that the NCWQ knew the preferred trade-off. In general, on economic grounds alone, it is impossible to know which of the infinite number of efficient controls, among which BAT controls number, is the socially preferred one. But one thing is certain, BPT controls for industrial point sources cannot be in this choice subset because on economic grounds they are inefficient from a national viewpoint.[13]

Municipal sewage treatment plants are the third source to be considered. The cost-risk trade-off curves in Figure 3.9 indicate that both BPT and BAT controls are efficient in the period 1975–2025. BAT control has total expected costs that are $250.8 billion higher than the costs of BPT, but BAT has less risk than BPT since its weighted probability of not exceeding 1975 damages is .50 compared to .13 for BPT control. This is the only source where the analysis of this study agrees with the recommendation of the NCWQ. That is, BPT controls are found to be efficient in all years.

However, it should be realized that the lower cost of BPT control comes at the expense of exposure to a higher probability of large damage costs at some future date.

The fourth major source of water pollution is urban nonpoint sources, including combined sewer overflows. The Federal Water Pollution Control Act requires urban jurisdictions to provide for control of runoff residuals. In agreement with the NCWQ studies, we find that urban runoff loadings are not insignificant. By our estimates they typically represent 15 to 30 percent of the mass loadings in urban areas. According to Figure 3.10, BPT controls at the indicated levels would be inefficient in all years except for the period from 1990 to 2010. BAT controls would be efficient and would have controls exceeding those of a minimum cost policy (M). As shown by the estimates in panel D of Table 3.6, BAT compared to M would have control costs that are $107 billion larger and damage costs that are $76 billion smaller in the period

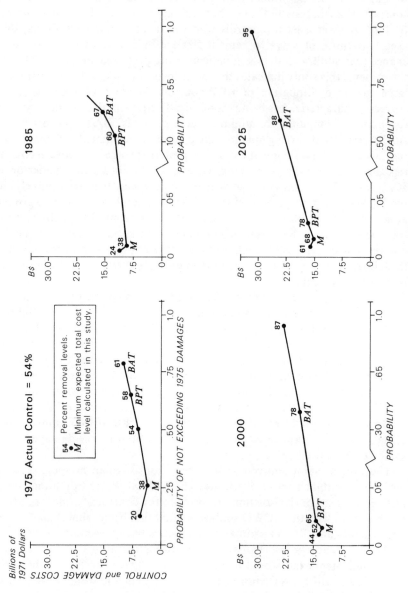

Figure 3.9.   Expected Total Costs and Risks Associated with Different
              Control Levels for Water Pollution Discharges from Municipal
              Sewage Plants, Scenario DH

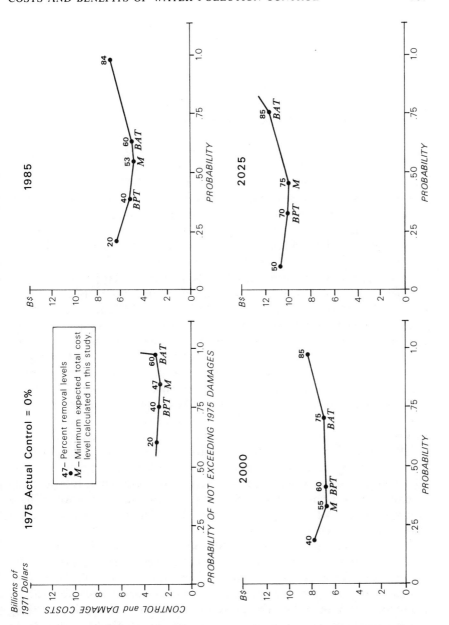

Figure 3.10. Expected Total Costs and Risks Associated with Different Control Levels for Runoff from Urban Non-Point Sources, Scenario DH$_a$.

1975 through 2025. Overall, BAT is more costly than M but it does provide less risk of high damages as indicated by its higher weighted probability of not exceeding 1975 damage levels.

The NCWQ report to Congress [1976b] asserts that urban runoff, including combined sewer overflows, is a relatively important source of water pollution and, as a consequence, going beyond BPT controls by 1984 for industrial point sources may do little to improve water quality. This analysis agrees that urban runoff is a relatively important source of water pollution but disagrees on the other point. On the basis of explicit benefit-cost comparisons we find that controls above BPT levels for industrial sources by 1984 are economically justified. The basis for the NCWQ assertions on the role of urban runoff versus other sources of pollution is unclear. At best, it seems to be based upon some tenuous estimates of loadings from urban runoff and not upon any systematic analysis of benefits and costs for all sources.

Panel E of Table 3.6 contains estimates of benefits, costs, and benefit-cost ratios for all sources for alternative control policies. The *cumulative average* benefit-cost ratios under all of the policies are larger than 1. From the perspective of maximizing net benefits or minimizing total expected costs, policy M is, of course, superior to BPT and BAT. It has controls at levels for which, year-by-year, *marginal* control costs just equal *marginal* benefits. This superiority is reflected in the total cost estimates: a move from policy BPT to M, or BAT to M, would provide cumulative cost savings of 249 or 671 billion dollars respectively in the period 1975 to 2025. In the aggregate, BPT is inferior to M, it has both higher costs and risk, whereas BAT compared to M has higher costs but lower risk. But, as before, in the absence of a social trade-off function between cost and risk it is not possible to know whether controls at level M or BAT are preferred.

BPT for all four sources and all years is not inefficient. Therefore, an alternative comparison is to calculate the cost difference between BPT and BPT adjusted so that when it would otherwise be inefficient it is brought up to minimum cost control levels. Such an adjusted BPT policy would have accumulated costs for the period 1975 to 2025 that are $145.4 billion less than an unadjusted BPT policy.

An additional set of expected cost and benefit estimates are shown in Table 3.7. These have been discounted and summed in the usual fashion for the indicated years. Discounted pollution control costs are calculated using estimates of actual capital expenditure rather than annualized capital requirements as in Table 3.6. Discounting, of course, applies declining weights over time so that these estimates are smaller than the cumulative estimates shown in Table 3.6. The cumulative estimates are neutral with respect to vantage point since they use annualized capital control costs and

Table 3.7. Discounted Expected Water Pollution Control Benefits and Costs, Discount Rate = 9%, Scenario DH (billions of 1971 $)

Discounted to 1975 for the Period 1975–2000

Policy[a]	Control Costs	Damage Costs	Total Costs	Benefits	B/C	X[b]
A. Electric Utilities						
BPT	3.5	9.2	12.7	17.6	5.0	.08
BAT	8.2	5.7	13.9	20.9	2.5	.29
M	3.8	8.0	11.8	18.7	4.9	.06
B. Industrial Point Sources						
BPT	86.4	74.1	160.5	507.8	5.9	.18
BAT	145.5	9.0	154.5	577.7	4.0	.99
M	105.4	35.9	141.3	548.0	5.2	.59
C. Municipal Sewage Treatment						
BPT	42.3	41.7	84.0	85.9	2.0	.13
BAT	81.4	30.1	111.5	94.4	1.2	.50
M	6.4	66.4	72.8	59.4	9.3	.04
D. Urban Runoff						
BPT	11.8	35.6	47.4	37.9	3.2	.43
BAT	27.6	20.9	48.5	52.7	1.9	.75
M	15.7	29.7	45.4	44.1	2.8	.51
E. All of the Above Sources						
BPT	144.0	160.6	304.6	649.2	4.5	.21
BAT	262.7	65.7	328.4	745.7	2.8	.63
M	131.3	140.0	271.3	670.2	5.1	.30

[a]Costs and benefits are total and not incremental, that is, they include amounts that would have occurred without the policy plus any additional amounts that result because the policy is in place.

[b]Weighted probability of not exceeding 1975, most likely damages.

apply the same unitary weight to the costs of each year. The discounted estimates, on the other hand, are meant to reflect trade-offs as perceived by individuals attempting to optimize *their* present discounted values in the year 1975. In the aggregate, a move from BPT or BAT controls to cost minimizing controls (M) would provide expected cost savings discounted to the year 1975 of 33 or 57 billion dollars respectively for the period from 1975 to 2000.[14]

4. THE GAINS FROM ADDITIONAL INFORMATION

It is sometimes argued that there is little point in attempting to set pollution controls at cost-minimizing or efficient levels because we can have so little confidence in our estimates of avoided damage or benefits that, as a consequence, it would be better to establish controls consistent with broad goals like "protection of human health and welfare" until such time as adequate information is available for setting controls closer to efficient levels with a high degree of confidence. The analytic framework developed here can be applied to indicate that such a strategy might be very wasteful, that it would be better to set controls at what we believe today to be efficient levels and revise them as additional information becomes available. To demonstrate this, it is necessary to make a number of assumptions about the way in which new information might reduce uncertainty and alter the assessment of appropriate control levels and about how much it might cost to acquire. Needless to say, all such assumptions must be fairly arbitrary—there is obviously no precise way to know in advance what the benefits and costs of acquiring more information are likely to be—but if the magnitudes are anywhere near correct, the argument will have been made.

The gains from improved information are assessed by comparing the expected total costs of least-cost control levels that were appropriate, given initial information, with the expected total costs of least-cost control levels appropriate given newer, additional information, using the *new* information to estimate expected costs in both cases. When the least-cost controls differ, the cost difference (costs at old levels minus costs at new levels) will be positive and will measure the gain (or cost savings) of choosing least-cost controls. These cost differences are then weighted by subjective probabilities of occurrence to derive expected gains from collecting more information. Three ways in which additional information could change least-cost controls are: the confidence ranges for damages and costs could be narrowed or widened; the entire distribution of damages could be shifted to either higher or lower values; and the future, instead of being like scenario DH, could be like any of the other scenarios described in Table 3.1.

Cost savings from additional information have been estimated for each of these cases, based on the assumptions indicated below. The estimates are reported in Table 3.8.

Cost savings associated with changes in confidence limits assume a 15 percent probability that confidence ranges will be narrowed by 20 percent, a 15 percent probability that they will be widened by 20 percent, and a 70 percent probability that they will be unchanged by new information.

Cost savings associated with shifts in the distribution of damages assume the following shift factors and (in parentheses) probabilities: .5 (.05), .8 (.25),

1.0 (.35), 1.2 (.25), 1.5 (.1). In each case, the most likely damage estimate is multiplied by the shift factor and the new distribution of damages centered around this value. Expected cost savings are estimated as the sum of probability weighted differences between total expected costs for each scenario at the least cost control levels from DH and expected total costs at its own least cost control levels.

The estimates in columns 2 and 3 of Table 3.8 indicate that new information on confidence limits is likely not to provide very large cost savings. In contrast, new information on damage distributions may provide immediate and substantial gains. New information on the course of the future is likely to provide only small gains for the period 1975 to 1985. This is not surprising; the passage of time is too brief for different economic conditions and population growth to have much impact. Beyond 1985, the course of the future can make a larger difference.

To determine economically efficient expenditure levels for gathering information it is assumed that marginal gains from new information equal expected marginal costs of collecting and utilizing the information when associated costs are about one-half of the expected gains and the gains are between one-half and two-thirds of their reported levels. Thus, economically efficient gathering, analyses, and use of new data would entail the levels of effort reported in Table 3.9. Total expected gains are also shown. Revision of control using new information would generate expected cumulative costs savings (net of extra information and transactions costs) of $10.0 to $13.4 billion for the period 1975 to 2025. Annual net savings would be about $60 million in 1980 and rise to about $400 million by 2025. If these net savings

Table 3.8.   Expected Gross Savings from Using Additional Information to Revise Water Pollution Controls (millions of 1971 $)

	Confidence Limits		Damage Distributions		Course of the Future	
Period	Cumulative Savings	Savings per Year	Cumulative Savings	Savings per Year	Cumulative Savings	Savings per Year
1975–1985	8.8	0.8	1365.4	124.1	868.3	78.9
1985–2000	254.5	17.0	4833.7	322.2	3698.0	246.5
2000–2010	255.4	25.5	5138.8	513.9	3428.5	342.9
2010–2025	224.5	15.0	11486.5	765.8	8715.9	581.1
Total savings 1975–2025	743.2		22824.4		16710.7	

Table 3.9. Expenditure for and Payoff from Additional Information
(millions of 1971 $)[a]

Efficient Expenditure Levels (5-year Lag Assumed)			
Period	Expenditure Level per Year		
1975–1980			
Damages information	$31	to	$42
Futures information	20	to	26
Total	51	to	68
1980–1995			
Damages information	85	to	113
Futures information	62	to	82
Total	147	to	195
1995–2005			
Damages information	135	to	180
Futures information	86	to	114
Total	221	to	294
2005–2025			
Damages information	195	to	260
Futures information	145	to	194
Total	340	to	454

Expected Net Savings from Revised Control Based on New Information			
1975–1985	$ 561	to	$ 748
1985–2000	2197	to	2929
2000–2010	2206	to	2941
2010–2025	5107	to	6809
Total	10071	to	13427

[a]Developed from Table 3.8.

are to be captured, the new information must be used to revise control toward efficient levels. There would be little point in collecting the information if decision makers are legally constrained or otherwise do not plan under any circumstances to revise control.

We now have enough data to make our point. Earlier, it was shown that a move from BPT controls to cost-minimizing controls for these sources and years when BPT would otherwise be inefficient would reduce expected total costs (as determined with highly uncertain estimates of control and damage costs) by \$145 billion in the period 1975 to 2025. It has been shown that with new information (and control revised accordingly), additional net expected cost savings of about \$12 billion can be achieved in the period 1975 to 2025. Clearly, the first step, a move to efficient control, provides a much larger expected payoff even though it is based upon incomplete damages and future information. New data and revised control also increase gains but by much less than this initial gain. This result should not necessarily be surprising; even information collection and analyses are subject to diminishing returns.

5. IMPLICATIONS AND CONCLUSIONS

We are going to make very little progress in solving the problem of water pollution until we recognize it for what it is: primarily an economic problem, best understood in terms of economic benefits and costs. In sponsoring many studies that assessed aspects of benefits and costs, the National Commission seems to have recognized this principle, but it also seems clear that it went well beyond the findings of its studies in making recommendations to Congress.

Even though many of the Commission's studies assessed aspects of benefits and costs, there was no concerted effort to estimate systematically benefits and costs for any one point in time or over time. In spite of this, the Commission's recommendations to Congress imply that the costs of moving beyond BPT controls by 1984 are greater than the associated benefits.

The analysis in this paper agrees with many of the key specifics of the National Commission's studies. But when these specifics are made part of a dynamic analysis of benefits and costs, this study arrives at somewhat different conclusions.[15] The fact that some of our findings differ from those of the National Commission, while interesting, is perhaps not the most important result of this analysis. Rather, it is that the methods of this analysis allow for systematic investigation of costs and benefits over time and thereby permit straightforward economic evaluations of alternative control policies. Shortcuts to this procedure, which look only at trade-offs in a single year and only at cost-effectiveness measures, are not likely to lead to very good policy choices.

6. NOTES

1. The 1972 amendments also established a tentative objective of elimination of all pollution discharges by 1985. This has now come to be regarded as a symbolic indication of commitment to cleaner water rather than a practical objective.

2. The analysis in this paper is comprehensive in its coverage of residuals. Residuals discharged by both point and nonpoint sources are used to determine water pollution damages. However, benefit cost analyses of pollution control are done only for point sources (electric utilities, industry including feedlots and dairies, and municipal sewage plants) and for urban runoff. For these sources, control benefits are calculated as avoided damages when residuals from the indicated sources are changed while residuals from other sources are kept at a given constant level.

3. The more general discussion given here describes methods used to derive results for both air and water pollution. More detailed methods in the appendix cover water pollution only. Specific methods for estimating air pollution costs and benefits are to be found in Ridker and Watson (1978).

4. The estimates of abatement costs reported in this analysis are annualized costs unless otherwise noted.

5. A more complete discussion of all assumptions is to be found in Ridker and Watson [1978]; Ridker, Watson, and Shapanka [1977]; and Shapanka [1977].

6. The methods for estimating transportation, agricultural, mining, and other nonpoint source residuals are described in Ridker and Watson [1978].

7. So long as society is not concerned with reducing the risk of experiencing very large control costs.

8. To reduce length, estimates of ambient water quality are not presented in this paper. Estimates of ambient water quality by ASA are to be found in Ridker and Watson [1978].

9. Stated in slightly different terms, a control policy that minimizes the cost of reducing emissions to some given level may be vastly inferior to a control policy that maximizes net benefits. That is, cost-effectiveness analysis may be a poor substitute for cost-benefit analysis. The National Commission on Water Quality, in making recommendations to Congress, relied mostly on cost effectiveness considerations.

10. Owing to data limitations, no estimates of COD were made for dispersed sources; therefore, we cannot calculate comprehensive shares for the pollutant. The data that are available would seem to indicate that COD emissions from dispersed sources are somewhat smaller than emissions from non-dispersed sources.

11. From 1974 to 2020, control plus damage costs for policy M are less than those of BPT, which indicates that the benefits of moving from policy BPT to M (that is, the additional avoided damages of such a move) are greater than the additional control costs.

12. In a later section we will present estimates of cost savings from revising control policy as a result of having additional information on damages and the course of the future.

13. We are really dealing in the world of second best here. If policy allowed states or regions to set region-specific controls, then BPT controls could very well be economically efficient in some particular areas.

14. Similar results are obtained when costs are discounted to 2000 for the period 2000 to 2025. These comparisons and analyses for all major air pollutants are presented in Ridker and Watson [1978].

15. Statistical details of the comparison of the results of this study with earlier studies, as well as a detailed description of methods used in this study, are available from the author.

7. REFERENCES

Almon, C., Jr., M.D. Buckler, L.M. Horowitz, and T.C. Reimbold. 1974. *1985: Interindustry Forecasts of the American Economy* (Lexington, MA, D.C. Heath).

AWARE (Asociated Water and Air Resources Engineers, Inc.). 1973. *Estimating Water Pollution Control Costs from Selected Manufacturing Industries in the U.S. 1973-1977.* Report to the U.S. Environmental Protection Agency (Nashville, AWARE).

Cooper, B.S., and D.P. Rice. 1976. "The Economic Cost of Illness Revisited," Social Security Bulletin, Social Security Administration, DHEW Publication No. (SSA) 76-11703 (Washington, D.C., U.S. Government Printing Office).

Council on Environmental Quality. 1976. *Environmental Quality: 1976* (Washington, D.C., GPO).

Dornbusch, D.M. 1973. *Benefit of Water Pollution Control on Property Values.* Report to the U.S. Environmental Protection Agency (Washington, D.C.).

FWPCA Amendments. 1972. Federal Water Pollution Control Act Amendments, Public Law 92-500, 92nd Congress, S. 2770, October 18, 1972.

Gianessi, L.P., and H.M. Peskin. 1977. "Water Pollution Discharges: A Comparison of Recent National Estimates," Discussion Paper D-2 (Washington, D.C., Resources for the Future).

Gianessi, L.P., and H.M. Peskin. 1978. Work in progress under NSF grant SOC 77-15045 (Washington, D.C., Resources for the Future).

Harris, R.N.S., G.S. Tolley, and C. Harrell. 1968. "The Residence Site Choice," *The Review of Economics and Statistics*, vol. 60, pp. 241-247.

Heany, J.P., W.C. Huber, M.A. Medina, Jr., M.P. Murphy, S.J. Nix, and S.M. Hasan. 1977. *National Evaluation of Combined Sewer Overflows and Urban Stormwater Discharges* (EPA-600/2-77-064) (Cincinnati, OH, EPA).

Heintz, H.T., Jr., A. Hershaft, and G.C. Horak. 1976. *National Damages of Air and Water Pollution.* Report to the U.S. Environmental Protection Agency (Rockville, Md., Environmental Control, Inc.).

Lake, E., C. Blair, J. Hudson, and R. Tabors. 1976. *Classification of American Cities for Case Study Analysis*, vol. III. Report to the U.S. Environmental Protection Agency (Cambridge, MA, Urban Systems Research and Engineering, Inc.).

Luken, R.A., D.J. Basta, and E.H. Pechan. 1976. *The National Residents Discharge Inventory* (Washington, National Research Council).

Midwest Research Institute. 1975. *Cost and Effectiveness of Control of Pollution from Selected Non-point Sources* (Kansas City, MO, Midwest Research Institute).

NCWQ. 1976a. *Staff Report to the National Commission on Water Quality.* April 30, 1976 (Washington, D.C., GPO).

NCWQ. 1976b. *Report to the Congress by the National Commission on Water Quality.* March 18, 1976 (Washington, D.C., GPO).

Page, T., R.H. Harris, and S.S. Epstein. 1976. "Drinking Water and Cancer Mortality in Louisiana," *Science*, vol. 193, no. 4247, July 2, pp. 55-57.

Ridker, R.G., and W.D. Watson. 1978. *To Choose a Future: Resource and Environmental Problems of the U.S., A Long-Term Global Outlook,* manuscript in progress (Washington, D.C., Resources for the Future).

Ridker, R.G., W.D. Watson, Jr., and A. Shapanka. 1977. "Economic, Energy, and Environmental Consequences of Alternative Energy Regimes, an Application of the RFF/SEAS Modeling System" in C.J. Hitch, ed. *Modeling Energy-Economy Interactions: Five Approaches*, pp. 135–198 (Washington, D.C., Resources for the Future).

Shapanka, A. 1977. "Technological Assumptions and Their Use in Studying the Resource and Environmental Consequences of Population and Economic Growth in the U.S." (Washington, D.C., Resources for the Future).

Truitt, J.B., A.C. Johnson, W.D. Rowe, K.D. Feigner, and L.J. Manning. 1975. "Development of Water Quality Management Indices," *Water Resources Bulletin*, vol. 11, no. 3 (June).

U.S. Department of Agriculture. 1975. *Control of Water Pollution from Cropland*, vol. I (Washington, D.C., USDA, Agricultural Research Service).

U.S. Water Resources Council. 1974a. *1972 OBERS Projections, Regional Economic Activity in the U.S.*, vols. 2–7 (Washington, D.C., USDA Economic Research Service).

U.S. Water Resources Council. 1974b. *1972 OBERS Projections, Regional Economic Activity in the U.S.: Aggregated Subareas* (Washington, D.C., USDA Economic Research Service).

U.S. Water Resources Council. 1974c. *1972 OBERS Projections, Regional Economic Activity in the U.S.: Standard Metropolitan Statistical Areas* (Washington, D.C., USDA Economic Research Service).

Wade, J.D., and E.O. Heady. 1976. *A National Model of Sediment and Water Quality: Various Impacts on American Agriculture* (CARD Report 67), (Ames, Iowa, Center for Agricultural and Rural Development, Iowa State University).

Watson, W.D., Jr. 1977. "Models Used in Assessing Resource and Environmental Consequences of Population and Economic Growth in the U.S." (Washington, D.C., Resources for the Future).

4 LONG-RUN ENERGY POLICIES IN AN ECONOMIC SETTING

L.H. Klaassen and J.H.P. Paelinck,
Netherlands Economic Institute, Rotterdam

1. INTRODUCTION

Since the so-called "energy crisis" of December 1973, the authors have given thought to some economic principles that could possibly guide decision making in the energy and raw materials sectors.[1]

Following up their previous research, in this paper the authors first summarize and synthesize the main conclusions reached so far, and then go on to develop some new models that express their latest ideas.

As is patent from their previous publications, economic principles in a modern setting (differential game theory, optimal control) guide the authors' thoughts, and they are indeed convinced that *some sort* of economic rationality will *in the long run* be responsible for the—perhaps new—types of equilibrium that will emerge. It is believed too often that such forces as political whims or short-term windfalls have brought about the situations observed; in a world of short-term scarcity *and* long-term potentials, choices must be and *are* made all the time. Such choices belong typically to the realm of economic science and, as such, can be analyzed by the tools of the economist.

2. PRELIMINARY THOUGHTS

Recent developments on the market for energy-carrying raw materials, and more particular those on the crude-oil market, have made it clear how much oil-consuming countries (and most of all those in the Western World) depend on oil-producing countries. The energy crisis made that eminently clear, and subsequent price increases have made us wonder whether the time has not come for some large-scale adjustments as far as the consumption and production of energy-supplying raw materials in the Western World are concerned.

In our discussion we propose to leave out of account such phenomena as the boycott practised during the oil crisis. A boycott strategy cannot be profitable, for the oil-producing no more than for the oil-consuming countries, as will be demonstrated later on. Let us rather try to analyze other strategies, such as price and knowledge strategies, which can be continued in the long run.

But first let us look somewhat closer into the importance of energy as a factor in the economy.

2.1. Energy as a Production Factor

For a very long time the cost of energy hardly played a role in total production costs. For most branches of activity they did not count for more than 3 or 4 percent; only a few energy-intensive branches like the iron and steel industry, the chemical industry, the aluminum industry, and transport boasted higher figures. As a result it was generally assumed that fluctuations in the cost of energy hardly affected total production costs and hence had no influence to speak of on the price formation of products, or on sales. For, assuming that a product's final price is proportional to its total cost price, we may state that the elasticity of demand in respect to costs is the same as that in respect of price. If the energy represents, say, 4 percent of total production costs, a 10 percent rise in the energy price results in total costs increasing by 0.4 percent. At an elasticity of demand of 1.5, demand for the product involved would fall by 0.6 percent, not a very impressive figure.

However, it is easy to give several reasons why such an approach is to be considered incomplete and too simple; in fact, it was not even satisfactory under the circumstances in the past.

First, while the example is based on a 10 percent increase, the rises of the recent past amounted to multiples of a hundred percent. Price increases of that magnitude do, of course, raise the share of energy cost in total production costs considerably, and thus make total production costs much more sensitive to further rises of the energy price.

Second, the sensitivity of the final price of a certain product to a rise in the price of energy depends not only on the share of direct energy costs but also on that of the indirect energy costs, i.e., the price of the energy incorporated in inputs bought from other industries. If the energy quotas of these inputs are known, the direct and indirect energy costs can be calculated, with the help of an input-output table, as a proportion of total production costs. It has been done for the Netherlands with the help of the 1972 input-output table (*Energy Conservation, Ways and Means*), and the calculations have revealed striking differences between the direct and the cumulated energy consumption in some sectors. In the chemical industry the cumulated energy consumption exceeds direct consumption by nearly 30 percent; the corresponding percentage in the iron and steel industry is over 180, in agriculture 66, in the building industry 175, in the means-of-transportation industry 250, to mention a few.

In calculating the above figures of cumulated energy consumption, the energy content in imported goods was left out of account. Calculations made by Paelinck and Markey[2] with figures of 1959, in which the energy content of imported goods was to some degree taken into account, showed that this energy content makes quite a difference. They found that in the iron and steel industry the cumulated energy costs represented 26.19 percent of total production costs, in the building materials sector approximately 12 percent, and in chemical industry just over 10 percent. Referring to 1959, these figures are relatively low: if present energy prices were counted, and the energy content of imports fully accounted for, the outcome would be considerably higher.

A point not to be overlooked is that in the iron and steel industry, energy carriers serve not only to supply heat but also as a raw material in the production process.

But even if we took all the factors mentioned into consideration, we would not have complete insight into the economic significance of energy nor in the proportion of energy costs represented in total production costs. We still would have to add to the industry's energy consumption the amount of energy incorporated in the capital goods.

Obviously, establishing the definite long-term effects of the increased oil prices on the economy in general and the consumption of energy in particular will require intensive research and careful computation; we shall discuss this in detail later on. From what we know now, it may be assumed already that the long-term effects are likely to exceed by far the effects we have been able to observe at short delay. Attempts to develop more rational methods of energy consumption will certainly be stimulated by the higher prices but cannot be expected to be successful until after some lapse of time.

What makes the research so difficult is that for each empirical case the responses on the short, medium, and long term are different. It is known, e.g., that in the first few weeks after a price increase for the Métro in Paris the number of passengers decreases sharply; after that, demand will tend towards a new (medium-term) equilibrium, ceteris paribus on a somewhat lower level than the old one; the new level will then be adjusted once more owing to long-term substitution effects.

The reaction patterns initiated by a rise in the price of energy are even more complicated. The effects of the unique event of a sudden enormous increase in the price of oil manifest themselves in waves. The first refers to direct energy consumption, the second to indirect energy consumption, and the third —arriving much later— represents the rise in the prices of capital goods. Now, since the reactions to the successive waves, as they manifest themselves through time, will probably show quite different patterns, it is easy to understand that the whole process is extremely complicated and can only be analyzed in the long run; it has by no means come to an end yet.

The repercussions of the increase in energy prices on spatial behaviour present a clear example of a long-term adjustment process. Energy costs, as a considerable portion of transportation cost, form an important element of the costs of conveying individuals and groups from one place to another. Increased energy costs may, therefore, be expected to have a negative influence on the total number of moves or the average distance covered per move. Because the different modes of transport are affected differentially, there will be (lagged) relative price modifications, and shifts in modal split may ensue. Still later, locational shifts might follow, if the costs of home-to-work traffic rises to such a level that people prefer changing either their residence or their place of work.

Will the chain of reactions indicated above result in provisional or permanent adjustments? The question is all the more apt because all changes in price will instigate price compensations whose objective is to enable everybody to buy the same packet of goods and services as before, whatever the original cause of the price increase.

Models built for the purpose of helping to formulate an energy policy or, in more general terms, a policy associated with energy production and energy consumption, must take adequate account of the long-term effects of the increased energy price.

2.2. Energy Price and Level of Knowledge

One reason why the effects of changes in the price of energy-holding raw materials are so difficult to measure is that, as pointed out above, those very changes initiate substitution processes intended to save on energy. Two elements play a role: (1) demand decreases because the product has become more expensive; and (2) in the long run, more efficient production and consumption methods are introduced, made possible by the higher level of knowledge that the higher energy price has inspired.

Figure 4.1 shows a simplified representation of the role the level of knowledge plays within the process of price-building and consumption.

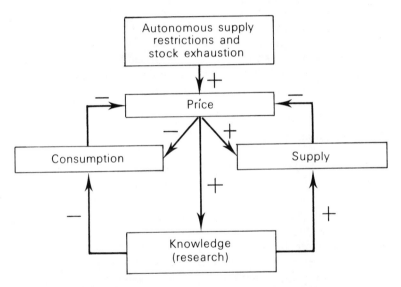

Figure 4.1.   The Direct and Indirect Influences of Autonomous Supply
Restrictions and Stock Exhaustion of Raw Materials

The scheme demonstrates that the demand for energy carriers does not depend on the price alone; even at constant prices, technical advance makes it possible to produce the same output with less energy. Steel production is a case in point. From data presented by Walter Isard[3] it appears that specific coal consumption per ton of steel was reduced to one third in a period of sixty years. Because it is very difficult to separate price-induced from autonomous technical progress, we prefer to state in general terms that in the course of time our level of knowledge will be raised, and that scarcity-induced price increases are likely to stimulate and accelerate technical advances that make for economies in specific consumption.

Technology apart, price increases will of course affect consumption anyhow. When petrol is expensive, people will tend to buy thriftier cars, adjust their thermostats downward, invest in better insulation of houses and other buildings, and so on.

If supplies are stimulated by the promise of higher profits as well as technical progress, while demand decreases because people try to save on energy *and* learn to use it to more effect, a situation might be created in which price reduction becomes once more possible. To such a development, growth of knowledge would be the main contributor.

Now it is impossible to establish a priori to what heights knowledge will rise; that is why in all models to be presented the level of knowledge will be introduced as a separate variable. In that way its influence can be taken into account through the whole process. An example is the following analytical model.

2.3. An Analytical Model

An analysis of possible world strategies can start with a model in which two groups of countries are included, viz., the developed, oil-consuming countries and the oil-producing developing countries. Developing countries that do not produce oil will provisionally be left out of the analysis, not because they are not considered important: on the contrary, they — or more generally, countries possessing neither raw materials nor kowledge — might well turn out to be the ones that have to pay the piper. The group is left out of account merely to avoid complications in the analysis of possible strategies of oil-producing and oil-consuming countries. The two groups of countries figuring in the analysis will be indicated as OPC (oil-producing developing countries) and OCC (oil-consuming countries).

With respect to oil-consuming countries, two relations are assumed:

a. Total production of OCC is divided among home consumption and investment in knowledge, the latter referring not only to abstract knowledge but also to means of production that are knowledge intensive and require high-class technology. This assumption is made to highlight the relative strength of the OCC in determining their strategic position towards the OPC. The OCC's strongest trump card is their knowledge tank and its possible expansion. Mark that this knowledge tank is inexhaustible: elements of it can be traded while the stock itself keeps intact.

b. The increase of production in OCC depends on the increase in the supply of energy-carrying raw materials as well as on the efficient use of that supply; for the latter element we shall again substitute the level of knowledge.

Assumption 2 implies that by limiting their consumption, OCC can raise the level of knowledge and thus the efficiency of energy consumption; the same level of production can then be maintained with less energy. So, the first strategy to be pursued by OCC would be that of developing techniques and adjustment processes that save on energy consumption and make the OCC less dependent on OPC. Raising the level of knowledge would also include searching for methods permitting the profitable exploitation of less scarce energy materials such as coal.

A logical second strategy would be to raise the price of knowledge (again including means of production that incorporate high-class technology) to be exported to OPC. The two strategies could also be combined, naturally.

For the OPC the situation is the following. The consumption level in OPC is determined by their own production volume and the volume of imports from OCC. Production increases in OPC depend on the knowledge acquired from OCC. Consumption goods and knowledge are paid for out of the receipts for oil supplied to OCC; for OPC, oil is important only as a medium of exchange.

Two strategies for OPC follow from this situation: (1) raising the price of oil and (2) decreasing the imports of consumption goods.

Energy imports by OCC can also be interpreted as increases in the stock of energy-carrying raw materials, so that dealing with the problem in full would call for at least a two-sector model. Substitution of raw materials is clearly different from substitution of energy sources; the former is attended by some specific problems in both the capital and the labor sphere.

To determine the future demand for energy inputs it will be necessary to know to what extent production will increase and the efficiency of energy use enhanced—distinguishing in this regard between *spontaneous* and *politically induced* growth and improvements.

Policy can help by stimulating research that may lead to saving on energy in consumption and production. Better insulation (perhaps combined with the use of nonchemical energy sources like the sun), recycling of certain energy-intensive raw materials (e.g., aluminium), searching for alternative low-energetic production processes, and so on, are possibilities to be considered. The research aspect, given only a side glance by most authors, is focused upon here; the Netherlands Economic Institute believes that developing an advanced quaternary sector is one of the main political issues of the future.

That such research should be technicoeconomic can be derived from the above argument: it would be illogical to substitute a production process (or a consumption process: insulation, for example) by another which directly and indirectly would cost more in the long run. That is why it is so urgent to try and quantify all the relations involved.

From the results obtained with a simple model using differential game theory[4], the following arguments can be derived.

- Simultaneous rise of prices in OCC and OPC is disadvantageous to OCC but has some advantages for OPC: when the energy price is raised, the total return on energy exports increases. Only part of that return is needed for the importation of knowledge, so the OPC can maintain and even expand the amount of knowledge they import.
- A rise in the level of knowledge in OCC attended by a rise in the price of oil will, of course, work out positively for OPC, while its effect on OCC depends on whether the level of knowledge rises more than the price of oil. If so, the efficiency of the use of oil will increase more than its price, and a benefit will have been achieved for both OCC and OPC. In the second, somewhat more elaborated, version of the model it is assumed that the rise of the knowledge level is in some way related to the rise of the energy price. That is indeed a very realistic assumption. It means that research activities aimed at saving energy will be intensified as the effective price level of energy is raised. For the moment we will leave this matter be, establishing merely that an adequate response to the price-raising strategy would be to raise the efficiency of energy consumption to a degree where the price increase has no real effect. Whether that is possible will evidently depend on how much energy prices rise. It is clear that a very steep rise can only be compensated in the *very* long run.
- The result of the third combination of strategies — a rise in the OCC price level and a cut in OPC imports — is uncertain and depends on the values the various quantities have actually adopted. Indeed, it seems improbable that a rise in the price of knowledge should not be followed by a rise in the price of energy-bearing materials.
- The fourth pair of strategies combines the raising of the level of knowledge in the OCC with a decrease in the imports of consumption goods into the OPC. The effect on developed countries is uncertain; it depends on the ratio between the increase of knowledge and the de-

crease of imports. For the OPC the combination promotes growth; it widens the prospects for the importation of technological knowledge and of knowledge incorporated in means of production.

Out of the four alternatives mentioned, the most desirable and also the most probable strategy seems that combination in which the OPC gradually raise their price level, the OCC responding with increased efficiency of their production as far as energy consumption is concerned, introduction of new methods for the efficient use of domestic raw materials (coal and gas), and substitution of less energy-intensive production processes. At any rate such an energy-saving strategy offers the best possibility of responding to the price-raising strategy on the part of the OPC if, and to the extent that, the price increase remains within certain limits.

From the foregoing it is evident that an essential part in the whole process is played by the price of energy in relation to the efficient use of energy. That is why, in the extention of the model now to be discussed, special attention is devoted to price and efficiency. Three hypotheses will be introduced.

a. It is assumed that energy consumption in OCC depends on the effective energy price, i.e., the price of a unit of energy in money, divided by the efficiency of its use. High efficiency means low specific energy consumption, hence low consumption per unit of product; low efficiency means high specific consumption. With efficiency 1.0 and money price 1, the effective price is the same as with efficiency 0.5 and money price 0.5. The price elasticity of the demand for energy thus introduced eliminates — for its higher values at any rate — the supposed limitative character of energy in production. In what follows, however, keeping reality in mind and taking into account that adjustment processes take a long time to work out, we shall assume that the price elasticity of demand for energy will not reach high values; on the other hand they will not be supposed to be negligible.

b. Here as before, it will be assumed that the level of knowledge in the OCC also depends on the effective price of energy as defined above. The philosophy behind that assumption is that efforts to carry through technical improvements and to accelerate adjustment processes (e.g., with respect to the volume of traffic as a function of the spatial structure) will be more intensive and stand a greater chance of success, according as the effective energy price is higher.

The two hypotheses combined imply that the actual elasticity of energy consumption in respect to the price of energy expressed in money is a fairly complicated figure, in which are incorporated the speed at which energy consumption reacts to changes in the effective price, as well as the price adopted by knowledge in response to the effective price of energy.

   c. A third realistic assumption can be made—that the price at which OPC can import consumption goods from OCC depends on the effective energy price. So, technology remaining on the same level, OPC will be confronted with the energy price they have set themselves, while on the other hand they will profit from increases in knowledge that result in a lower effective price of energy.

Adding these three hypotheses has made the model essentially more complicated, but the conclusions from the earlier, simple model remain valid for the more sophisticated version.

Once more it appears that for both groups of countries that combination of strategies is most profitable by which the OCC aim at a relative rise of their knowledge level[5] that keeps ahead of the relative price increases the OPC carry through regularly. Under the tentative assumption that the demand for energy is fairly price inelastic, and the energy quota in the OPC's consumption imports not too high, this strategy will be beneficial to the OPC too. The outcome of the other strategies is uncertain, with the exception of the one by which the OPC limit their imports while the OCC raise their knowledge level; however, that strategy is favorable to growth in the oil-producing countries.

Another possibility of extending the model, viz., with the limited absorption capacity of the OPC, has not been elaborated. Obviously, this limited capacity has an unfavorable influence on production in the OPC while favoring that in the OCC. Our conclusions will not be affected by such an extension, the less so if we may assume that the absorption capacity of OPC will steadily increase in the long run.

2.4. Provisional Conclusion: Testing of Raw Material Models Required

The models presented in the previous sections represent thinking schemes, helpful perhaps for determining tentative strategies, but not (yet) fit to be actually tested, for two reasons.

First, as repeatedly argued, we are dealing with adjustment processes and technical advances on the very long term, a term in fact that exceeds many times the period during which we have been confronted with a high energy price. We lack, in fact, any practical experience that could serve as a base for, say, estimations of price elasticity; at best, a few simulations with assumed elasticities can be carried out. Even so, it seems recommendable to disaggregate the model by a number of important sectors, and to that end it will be necessary to know the (cumulated) energy content of each sector. There is no essential obstacle, but in practice no attempts have yet been made to establish sectoral energy quotas. We just do not know them.

Second, there is the more fundamental and extremely difficult problem of how to measure the "level of knowledge." It is easy enough to represent this level by the symbol K in the model and just work with it as if it were measurable; to carry out the actual measurement is something else again! We do not think there is much against just proceeding with K in the model. For one thing, it is not at all unusual in economics to work with quantities that can be ranked but not measured (the utility concept is a case in point). For another, the level of knowledge—to be interpreted here as level of efficiency—is so essential in the tug-of-war for power now in progress that it would be a grave mistake to leave it out of the analysis because it is unmeasurable. The omission would weaken rather than enhance the quality of truth of the analysis.

Nevertheless, we should do our utmost to quantify at least those parts of the variable that are amenable to the operation. We have demonstrated in some detail how to cope with the problem of saving energy. *It is now for the economists to complete the model with behavioural relations*; the model should be *dynamic* and include short-, medium-, and long-term effects explicitly, especially of price differentials.

In what follows, some submodels will be developed in order to contribute to the progressive building up of a set of adequate analytical tools.

3. FURTHER INVESTIGATIONS[6]

It would be possible to develop exploratory models for countries with different characteristics. One could think of the scheme shown in Figure 4.2.

		T_1	T_2	T_3	T_4	T_5
Developed countries:	D	x	x	x	x	x
Developing countries:	DD	x	x	x	0	0

Figure 4.2.

Type 1 would be oil-producing countries; type 2, countries producing other raw materials; type 3 would be countries producing other sources of energy. Types 4 and 5 refer to high levels of industrialization and development of knowledge; the latter feature has been stressed in section 2 (the "quaternary" sector, the presence of a factor K).

Developed countries could possess all five characteristics, so that there could be $\sum_{i=1}^{5} \binom{5}{i} = 2^5 - 1 = 31$ possible types. Probably not all these types occur, but most developed countries do possess more than one type characteristic.

Three types of characteristics are possible among developing countries, plus the absence of any, leading to $\sum_{i=0}^{3} \binom{3}{0} = 2^3 = 8$ possible combinations.

It would be possible to set up a model for each category[7] and to combine them into strategy models like the differential game model referred to in section 2.

Hereafter we will develop two exploratory models for the case of developed countries wishing to reopen old sources of energy (coal mines, for example) or to invest in knowledge to open up new energy sources (e.g., the EEC JET project), considering also the transitory fission-fusion problem. In such developments stress will be laid on $D(T_3 - T_5)$ types.

3.1. Economics of Alternative Energy Sources

The substitution of oil for traditional sources of energy is well known; as soon as the long-term-trend price of oil-based calories sank below that of classical energy sources (especially coal), coal mines started being closed down, less productive ones first. Figure 4.3 illustrates that development.

$C' - C''$ is the long-term cost line of oil production; c_i, $i = 1, 2, 3$ are the production costs of three coal-mine fields, closed down at periods t_1, t_2, and t_3, respectively.

The regional consequences of this process have been studied elsewhere.[8] Moreover, they can be drastic when the region includes elements of type 2 (raw materials) and declining type 4 elements (heavy industry based on old technologies). Such was the case of Lorraine (France) some twenty years ago.

From point C'' on, the trend has recently changed, and it may induce countries to think of reopening closed coal mines or look for alternative forms of energy, the latter strategy being also inspired by environmental considerations ("clean" energy—solar or eolic—as opposed to sulphur

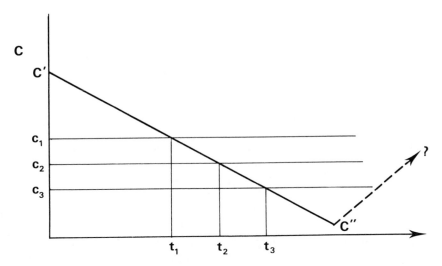

Figure 4.3.

dioxide-producing coal burning, which moreover has a low conversion coefficient).

The point is that both strategies involve starting-up costs; reopening mines is a costly procedure, and developing new technologies demands even heavier investment (in terms of capital sum and research time), with uncertain outcome. Figure 4.4 pictures the situation in the latter case.

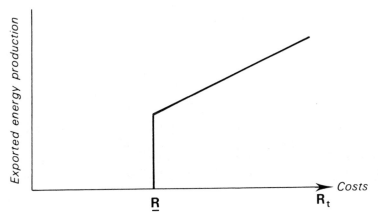

Figure 4.4.

A minimum sum has to be invested (R) to produce an expected energy return, and obviously the problem includes a step function leading to a $0-1$ solution, a well-known feature in mathematical programming.

As both problems (reopening old energy sources and developing new ones) are isomorph from this point of view, they will be merged in the same problem. To overcome the $0-1$ problem in a first investigation phase, two mathematical features will be introduced:

- we will use multistage linear programming, leading to possibly extreme (i.e., corner) solutions;
- we will define a time period long enough for, say, investment in knowledge to reach a sufficiently high level to surpass the threshold value R.[9]

The model will now be exposed and propositions developed.

3.2. A Simple Model

The following equations define the model.

$$U_t \equiv C_t + I_t + X_t \tag{3.1}$$

$$U_t \leq aK_t + bE_t \tag{3.2}$$

$$K_t \equiv cK_{t-1} + I_{1,\ t-1} \tag{3.3}$$

$$E_t \equiv M_t + N_t \tag{3.4}$$

$$N_t = d \sum_{0}^{t-1} I_{2\tau} \tag{3.5}$$

$$I_t \equiv I_{1t} + I_{2t} \tag{3.6}$$

The first equation is the product-expenditure identity, stating that the product is exhausted by consumption, investment, and exports consumption, investment, and exports.[10]

The second equation is a linear production frontier, limiting uses to a production dependent on capital and energy; as capital investment is not essential to the reasoning, it will be skipped in the simple version to be presented later, as will be equation (3.3), which is the capital-accumulation equation.

The fourth equation states that energy is provided by imports and new energy sources, the latter being proportional to accumulated research (3.5).

The last identity can also be skipped in a simpler version, so that the model now reads:

$$U_t = C_t + I_t + X_t \tag{3.7}$$

$$U_t \leq bE_t \tag{3.8}$$

$$E_t = M_t + N_t \tag{3.9}$$

$$N_t = d \sum_0^{t-1} I_{2\tau} \tag{3.10}$$

$I_{2\tau}$ in (3.10) is energy-oriented research investments.

3.3. A One-period Horizon Programming Model

Now let us examine the choice problem over two periods, the horizon being one period ahead. Again, long-term exploration is involved, as the unit period has been defined as relatively long in respect of the "maturation" of investment.

So, fixing $t = 1, 2$, we now have to introduce an objective function and additional constraints. The objective will be to maximize

$$\varphi = \sum_{t=1}^{2} e_t C_t \tag{3.11}$$

where e_t is a discount factor, $e_0 \equiv 1$.

The additional constraints read

$$\left. \begin{array}{l} X_t - p_t^* M_t \geq B_t^* \\[2mm] X_t \leq X_t^* \end{array} \right\} \qquad t = 12 \qquad \begin{array}{l} (3.12a) \\[2mm] (3.12b) \end{array}$$

All the variables are supposed to be expressed in values at constant prices; p_t^* is the *relative* import price of energy imports, relative to constant export prices. The balance-of-payments constraint (3.12a) has to be interpreted in that sense; the limitation of exports by the world market (3.12b) is of straightforward interpretation.

The complete two-period model now reads, for max $C_1 + e_2 C_2$:

$$C_1 + I_1 + X_1 \leq bM_1 \tag{3.13a}$$

$$C_2 + I_2 + X_2 \leq bM_2 + bdI_1 \tag{3.13b}$$

Putting $B_1^* = B_2^* = 0$, one can write (3.12) without loss of generality as:

$$M_1 \leq X_1 p_1^{*-1} \leq X_1^* p_1^{*-1} \tag{3.14a}$$

$$M_2 \leq X_2 p_2^{*-1} \leq X_2^* p_2^{*-1} \tag{3.14b}$$

all variables being nonnegative.

(3.13) and (3.14) represent in fact six constraints on the eight endogenous variables C_i, I_i, X_i, and M_i, $i = 1, 2$; that means that all but two of the decision variables can take nonzero values.

The dual system can be written[11]

$$1 - \lambda_1 \leq 0 \tag{3.15a}$$

$$c_2 - \lambda_2 \leq 0 \tag{3.15b}$$

$$-\lambda_1 + bd\lambda_2 \leq 0 \tag{3.15c}$$

$$-\lambda_2 \leq 0 \tag{3.15d}$$

$$-\lambda_1 - \mu_1 + \nu_1 \leq 0 \tag{3.15e}$$

$$-\lambda_2 - \mu_3 + \nu_2 \leq 0 \tag{3.15f}$$

$$b\lambda_1 - \gamma_1^* \nu_1 \leq 0 \tag{3.15g}$$

$$b\lambda_2 - \gamma_2^* \nu_2 \leq 0 \tag{3.15h}$$

From (3.15a), (3.15b), (3.15g), and (3.15h) it follows that constraints (3.13) and the left-hand side of (3.14) are exactly satisfied (dual variables strictly positive); from (3.15c) it can be inferred in addition that $I_2 = 0$ (Lagrangean derivate strictly negative).

That means that the system can be reduced by eliminating C_i and X_i to the following program.

$$\max \ (\delta - p_1^*)M_1 + (e_2 bd - 1)I_1 + (b - p_2^*)M_2 \tag{3.16}$$

s.t.

$$p_1^* M_1 \leq \alpha_1^* \tag{3.17a}$$

$$p_2^* M_2 \leq \alpha_2^* \tag{3.17b}$$

$$-(b - p_1^*)M_1 + I_1 \leq 0 \tag{3.17c}$$

$$-(b - p_2^*)M_2 - bdI_1 \leq 0 \tag{3.17d}$$

The last two constraints are imposed by $C_i \geq 0$ $(i = 1,2)$. Again, using dual variables ρ_i (3.17a,b) and σ_i (3.17c,d), one obtains

$$(b - p_1^*) - p_1^* \rho_1 + (b - p_1^*)\sigma_1 \leq 0 \tag{3.18a}$$

$$e_2(b - p_2^*) - p_2^* \sigma_1 + (b - p_2^*)\sigma_2 \leq 0 \tag{3.18b}$$

$$(e_2 bd - 1) - \sigma_1 + bd\sigma_2 \leq 0 \tag{3.18c}$$

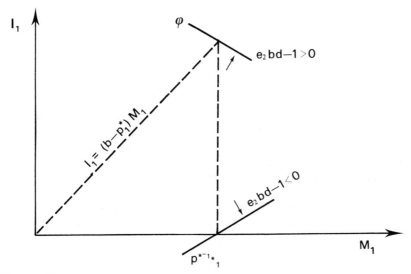

Figure 4.5.

High relative oil prices in period 2 ($b - p_2^* < 0$) automatically exclude oil import in period 2 (from (3.18b)). The solution to the remaining program is given in Figure 4.5 below, for the case $(b - p_1^*) > 0$.[12]

The choice between consumption and energy research is dependent on the inequality

$$e_2 bd \overset{>}{\underset{<}{}} 1 \qquad (3.19)$$

Three factors play an important part: the discount rate of future consumption (c_2), the product-energy ratio (b), and the expected efficiency of the research, d. If any of these factors is very weak, or if all three are relatively weak, little or no energy research will be planned.

3.4. A Two-period Transition Model

The choice to be made in favor of fission as a transitional source of energy, awaiting the fusion period, can be treated in the same vein. The relevant strategy problem can be set up as follows.

$$\max \ C_o + e_1 C_1 + c_2 P_2 - \tilde{e}_2 I_o \qquad (3.20)$$

$$\text{s.t.} \ \ C_o + I_o \leq P_o^* \qquad (3.21a)$$

$$C_1 + \tilde{I}_1 + k I_o \leq \tilde{\tilde{k}} \ \triangle M_1^* + \triangle P_o^* \qquad (3.21b)$$

$$P_2 - k I_o - \tilde{k}\tilde{I} \leq P_o^* + \tilde{\tilde{k}} \ (\triangle M_1^* + \triangle M_2^*) \qquad (3.21c)$$

P_i is productive capacity, P_o^* being given; $\triangle M_i^*$ are increases (decreases) in oil imports, exogenously given. k, $\tilde{k}$ and $\tilde{k}_o$ are the respective (expected) product-energy coefficients for fission investment, fusion research and investment, and oil inputs.

Again, the Lagrangean differentials show that constraints (3.21) are satisfied exactly (λ, μ, ν are the three relevant dual variables, partials being taken with respect to C_o, C_1, I_o, $\tilde{I}_1$, and P_2 successively).

$$1 - \lambda \leq 0 \qquad (3.22a)$$

$$e_1 - \mu \leq 0 \qquad (3.22b)$$

$$-e_2 - \lambda + k(\mu + \nu) \leq 0 \qquad (3.22c)$$

$$-\mu + k\nu \leq 0 \qquad (3.22d)$$

$$e_2 - \nu \leq 0 \qquad (3.22e)$$

This leads to the simplified system

$$\max \ [k(e_1 + e_2) - e_2 - 1]I_o + (e_2\tilde{k} - e_1)\tilde{I}_1 \qquad (3.23)$$

$$\text{s.t.}$$

$$I_o \leq P_o^* \qquad (3.24a)$$

$$\tilde{I}_1 \leq P_o^* + \tilde{k} \triangle M_1^* + k I_o \qquad (3.24b)$$

from the nonnegativity constraints on C_1, C_2.

Figure 4.6 shows the possible situations.

A and B represent the coefficients of I_o and $\tilde{I}_1$ in (3.23). Again the solution depends on efficiencies in transformation and time-discount rate. In (3.20), coefficient e_2 was introduced as a high negative discount rate on disposal of fissile material (nuclear waste);[13] a high value of $\tilde{e}_2$ might reduce (case A = 0) or suppress (A < 0) the I_o program. The $\tilde{I}_1$ program in turn is a function of its expected efficiency, $\tilde{k}$.

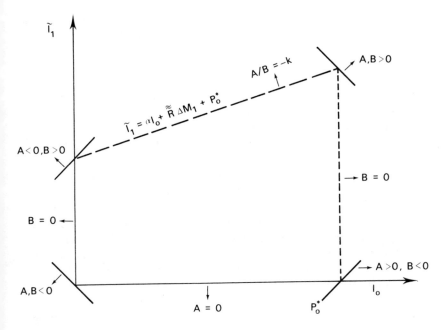

Figure 4.6.

4. PRICES REVISITED

In what follows the general ideas of section 2 on prices will be further developed, and an analyzed model pursued.

4.1. Prices of Raw Materials

The gradual development of the general world price level until 1972 was indeed a normal accompaniment to regular economic expansion. In the second half of 1972 this gradual development was interrupted unexpectedly by the increase of the oil prices to four times their former level. It is difficult to define exactly what had led up to that sudden steep increase. Many factors played a role but the most important factor was probably the growing conviction, particularly in Arab Countries, that the oil resources, as a source of energy and income, are finite, and that it was a matter of sensible policy in respect of their own countries to make the most of oil capital. Asking higher prices was one way to ensure a less steeply growing demand and thus keep the oil revenues coming in for a longer time.

Be that as it may, it is a fact that oil became four times as expensive, and that fact triggered off a series of events that changed the "creeping inflation" into a "marching inflation." To get an insight into the processes initiated, we have to examine carefully the phenomena of the typical cost-push inflation initiated by the terrific increase in the price of oil and stimulated further by similar, if more modest, rises in the price of the world's other essential raw materials.

Crude oil is one of the most vital raw materials; it is absolutely essential, at any rate in the medium term, for continued economic progress. For that reason, crude oil, and a few other raw materials in the same position, are sometimes called limitative raw materials. Because there are no adequate substitutes, less oil available implies in the short and medium run less production of very nearly all economic sectors all over the world. There is not a single sector, for the time being, that can make out without oil.

It is limitative as a raw material for production and, as a material either in primary or in secondary form (electricity), for heating and cooling purposes. But apparently its cost is only a fraction of the total cost; in most sectors energy accounts for no more than 3 or 4 percent of total costs. Only a few sectors, like the basic metal industry, chemical industry, and transportation industry, are different in that their energy percentages are higher.

As stated already in section 2, at first sight one tends to the conclusion that energy, though it is an essential production factor, represents such a modest proportion of total production costs that even large price increases can be met with relative ease.

At second sight, however, the above reasoning was found false.

It is true that the *direct* energy consumed by a certain sector represents only a minor proportion of that sector's total production costs, but this does not account for the "energy content" of the sector's inputs: products of other sectors worked up in the production process. Such energy content of inputs is called the sector's "indirect energy consumption."

The indirect energy consumption of a specific sector can be calculated with the help of so-called "input-output" tables, as explained in section 2.

As a result of the analysis presented there, further price increases as a result of the 1972 rise in the oil price must be expected, for a major part of the capital stock of 1972 has not yet been replaced. Its replacement will have to be effected at much higher costs than earlier ones. Indeed, the initial increase of the energy price will have prolonged after-effects.

With further rises in the price of energy imminent, and the example of the oil-producing countries likely to be followed by other countries that produce essential raw materials, it is obvious that the price of energy is going to be a dominant influence on the general price level.

4.2. Compensating for Price Increases

The extra rise in prices caused by the enormous increase in the price of crude oil affects, as we have shown in the previous section, the price level in two ways, viz., directly and indirectly — directly because electricity, petrol, gasoline, and so forth have become more expensive, and indirectly because increased energy prices have led to increased prices of all other products. Consequently, all over the world the price index of family consumption has started to rise, and for many countries "marching inflation," for some countries even "galloping inflation," has become a fact.

According to the compensation principle adopted under different circumstances, after the oil crisis wage compensation for employers was granted in very nearly all developed countries. One understands what was going to happen. The aim of compensation is to prevent the workers from being worse off than before, in other words, to make available to them an amount of money that, on top of the improvement resulting from productivity increase, enables them to buy exactly what they could buy before the increase. Now in this situation there are two equally interesting possibilities leading to the same ultimate result.

The first is that the oil countries apply only the price as an instrument and are prepared to supply any quantity at the price they fix. In that case, compensation leads to a rapid increase in import, jeopardizing the country's balance of payments. To keep afloat in the long run, devaluation of the money unit will have to be accepted. Because that means that imported products become dearer, the domestic price level goes up again and new compensation demands are made. Thus, the inflation spiral has become a vicious circle, capable of leading the country into economic breakdown.

The other possibility is for the oil-exporting countries not only to use the price as an instrument but also to carry through so-called quantitative restrictions. In that case, the compensation cannot be spent on oil-intensive products but will be used for other products, which thus will get an upward impulse. The result is further rise in prices, new demands for compensation, and so on, in fact a spiral similar to the one in the previous case.

Strictly speaking, the two situations do not differ very much in principle. Even when there are no quantitative restrictions, the shift in relative prices will still induce consumers to change their consumption patterns, substituting energy products that have become more expensive by other, relatively cheaper ones. In that case, too, at least part of the financial elbowroom will be directed towards other products than energy.

Looking at the problem from a very general point of view, we must admit that the oil crisis, though perhaps in part the result of a political action, is essentially a reflection of the fact that oil is an exhaustible material whose stocks are diminishing and whose increasing scarcity has caused its own and other prices to rise suddenly and sharply. If owing to the compensation mechanism the price increases have no real effect, further price increases cannot be avoided; after all, the raw material *has* become scarce and one cannot just pretend it hasn't. The inevitable consequence is an unwholesome inflation spiral whose economic consequence we shall have to discuss anew. Beforehand, we shall give some attention to a different form of compensation that is sure to start playing, or is already playing an important role.

However, that is not yet the whole story.

The "Advice about oil crisis and development cooperation"[14] contains an interesting passage. It reads:

"The World Bank estimates the *increase* in government revenues from oil destined exclusively to OPEC countries, from 1973 to 1974, at $62.5 milliard (from $22.7 to $85.2 milliard), if the oil prices of early 1974 are maintained.

"It is impossible for the governments involved to spend the whole of these additional revenues at short notice. That is predominantly a result of too little absorption capacity: the sudden enormous increase in available means cannot, even in poor, reasonably densely populated countries like Nigeria, immediately lead to a development program using up all that money. To that end, a comprehensive program of building infrastructure and enhancing the skills of the population is needed. The countries of the Arabian peninsula, which are the greatest oil producers, are relatively sparsely populated and will have even more trouble spending their extraordinarily large revenues.

"Estimates of the absorption capacity of all oil-producing countries have risen steadily since January 1974. It could be wishful thinking, though one thing is certain, viz., that the total increase in foreign currency revenues, which from 1973 to 1974 will come to at least $65 thousand million for all oil countries together (if the present prices are maintained, that is), cannot be spent entirely. The surplus current account of which these countries can dispose will, according to various estimations, lie somewhere between $25 and $50 thousand millions.

"The countries concerned — on the Arabian peninsula, and Libya, Nigeria, and Venezuela — will want to invest their surpluses in such a way as to make them as stable and profitable as possible. Investments will have to be largely in DAC countries; whether and how they will be accomplished will depend on the extent to which the two conditions mentioned can be met."

Apparently, OPEC countries put emphasis on their wish to make their investments in developed countries stable. The same holds for their imports: they do not wish the additional revenues they get from their oil to be partly swallowed up by price increases that set back their real investment volume, diminish the return on their investments, and make their imports from developed countries more expensive. Translated into practical terms that means that they wish to compensate price increases in developed countries by regular rises in the price of oil. Thus they add a new, reinforcing element to the inflationary spiral, completing the disastrous compensation mechanism and hence the automatism of future price increases.

It is easy to guess, after what has been written previously, what will be the effects of rises in the price of energy and resulting rises in the price of other inputs. The profitability of many industries is put in jeopardy owing to fast rising wages and input prices, and many of them find themselves forced to cut down their staff, either because they cannot maintain their production volume or because they switch to less labor-intensive methods. There is little doubt, therefore, that the cause of the current recession lies in the complicated compensation mechanism that marks the present inflationary spiral.

This recession, for that matter, has a few features that were almost or altogether lacking with former ones. The first is that the workers' associations, the trade unions, are not satisfied with price compensation; on top of that they demand a real improvement of the workers' income. That means that in a situation in which trade and industry are in the greatest difficulties, it is nevertheless demanded that the income of workers increases more than is required to maintain their real income. Such demands make for, first, an additional rise in prices to the extent they exceed the real productivity increase and, second, more unemployment, because even more industries, failing to attain the required increase in productivity, will get into trouble.

Such developments do not leave the authorities unaffected, for the government budget is unfavourably influenced in two ways. On the one hand, the increasing number of unemployed makes for considerably higher unemployment benefits, which can be a heavy burden on the budget. On the other hand, the decreasing profitability of trade and industry leads to diminishing government income from company or profit tax. At the same time, more and more demands are made upon the government in the way of social amenities, education, defense, and environmental control, so that ever higher outlays are confronted with ever lower revenues. Financing with loans appears to become harder and harder; thus, the temptation to fill the gaps by creating money becomes greater and greater. Needless to say, giving in to temptation of that kind would give a new impulse to both inflation and recession.

Such is, in fact, the precarious situation in which the Western world finds itself at the moment.

4.3. Measures Against Inflation

Measures to stop an inflationary process of the above description can be divided into two kinds: (1) measures abating the causes of inflation and (2) measures abating the consequences of inflation.

To the first group of measures belongs the elimination of the automatic price compensation for employed persons. As Zijlstra formulates it:

> In particular they (the oil-consuming countries) should avoid awarding wage increases to compensate for the specific rise in prices, which in each of the oil-consuming countries is felt as a deterioration in the terms of trade. If compensation *is* awarded, this may set in motion an overall process of price-inflation. [15]

Among economists the opinion is gradually gaining ground that this automatic compensation is one of the main causes of the current inflation and that its abolition is an *essential* condition to get the inflation under control. It would work in two ways: first, it stems directly the inflation in developed countries, and, second, compensation demands from oil-exporting countries would diminish as a result. Two important impulses that keep inflation going would thus be eliminated.

The measure seems simple, and easy to carry through, but in reality it is not for two reasons.

For one thing, compensation is a social acquirement, and its abolition, even if restricted to the part that relates to increased oil prices and such, would be looked upon as a politically hostile deed against people in employment. Trade unions, by agreeing, would risk getting into very serious difficulties; they might have their leaders simply voted away by their members. Indeed, politically the abolition of automatic compensation for all price increases hardly seems a feasible proposition. Still, slowly and reluctantly, trade unions and governments seem to come around to the idea that some mitigation to that effect could become inevitable; in the Netherlands, there is some talk of introducing a so-called refined (purified?) index figure, leaving, e.g., the recent VAT increase out of account.

For another thing, there is the practical problem how to ascertain to what extent the current rise in prices is due to normal and acceptable inflation and to what extent to inflation resulting from higher raw material prices. If it is assumed that the latter—being the result of progressive scarcity—(contrary to the former) does not qualify for wage compensation, then the rise of the price index of family consumption will have to be split up accordingly. To do so, the extremely complicated calculations referred to earlier would have to be carried out, and even so it is doubtful that an unequivocal outcome could be reached.

In spite of the obstacles, the present authors are convinced that the way of partial abolition of automatic compensation is the way along which to proceed, and that efforts must be made to convince workers how disastrous will be the long-term results, particularly for themselves, of proceeding in the present direction.

Among the measures that diminish the *results* of inflation belongs the cutting down of government expenditure. In political aspects that measure does not differ materially from the former one. Social expenditure is extremely difficult to diminish, if not impossible in a period when every self-respecting government is advocating redistribution of income and care of the poorest. Restriction of educational outlay meets with the same objection, so much so as far as higher education is concerned that, e.g., measures to curtail study time can be carried through only very gradually and with long delays. With respect to defense, the governments of the Western countries are committed by international agreements that leave small scope for maneuvering. In truth, such measures do not open any cheerful prospects either.

Price control also belongs to the category of measures to fight against the consequences of inflation. Attempts at controlling the prices in a period in which these are either determined by exogenous price increases, or follow from considerable wage demands, can do no more than prevent *excessive* price increases, i.e., increases over and above what is unavoidable. However, it is not these increases that constitute the essence of inflation, but the mechanism that causes the prices of essential cost categories to rise. Control of the last-mentioned prices would be even more fatal for trade and industry than the rises themselves.

Of the three types of government intervention described, there is only one that offers a real chance of improvement: stopping the mechanism in the inflation process, that is to say, doing away with automatic price compensation. It remains necessary, of course, to restrict government expenditure as much as possible and keep the price increases within reasonable bounds. But first and foremost, the compensation mechanism must be tackled.

Thus inflation, and the problem of how to control it, have become a political issue—and a very delicate one at that. Only very strong governments will be able to solve the inflation problem, for the solution will call for painful measures. No government particularly likes taking such measures; most of them prefer leaving them to their successors. They fear for the future; they are afraid to take unpopular measures that could cost them the support of the people. That is why in most countries the choice between further inflation and vigorous intervention might well be decided in favor of inflation.

4.4. A Model

In order to investigate the possibilities of extricating from a given observed price-level evolution the effects of at least some of the alternative sources of inflation, a small but operational model has been set up.*

The method was again taken up, and generalized to a four-equation dynamic model, which was as follows:

$$p_{1t} = \alpha \ p_{2,t-1} \tag{4.1}$$

$$w_t = \beta \ p_{3,t-1} \tag{4.2}$$

$$p_{3t} = \gamma \ l_{t-1} w_{t-1} + \delta m_{t-1} p_{1,t-1} \tag{4.3}$$

$$x_t p_{2t} + u_t p_{3t} \equiv w_t l_t + m_t p_{1t} \tag{4.4}$$

Equation (4.1) lays the link between export prices of oil-consuming developing countries (p_2) and oil prices (import price, p_{1t}).** Equation (4.2) is the price-compensation equation, w being wages and γ the national price level. Equation (4.3) is the government's price-policy equation, allowing for (partial) compensation of wages and import price (oil, raw materials) increase in proportion to the importance of labor and energy as production factors. Finally, (4.4) is the well-known production and expenditure identity. x, u, w, and m are the export, domestic-expenditure, wage, and import shares in the product; their time index will be omitted hereafter.

*See J.H.P. Paelinck (1975); the model has been partly implemented by G. Thiry (1976).
**The model was initially set up as

$$\frac{p_{it}}{p_{i,t-1}} = \epsilon \frac{p_{j,t-1}}{p_{j,t-2}} \tag{4.5}$$

or alternatively $\quad p_{it} = \dfrac{p_{i,t-1}}{p_{j,t-2}} \ \epsilon p_{j,t-1}$

$$\tag{4.6}$$

To simplify the analysis, we have put $p_{i,t-1} / p_{j,t-2} = 1$, $\forall$ i, j.

In matrix-vector terms the model reads as

$$\begin{bmatrix} 1 & 0 & 0 & 0 \\ 0 & 0 & 0 & 1 \\ 0 & 0 & 1 & 0 \\ m & x & u & -1 \end{bmatrix} \begin{bmatrix} p_1 \\ p_2 \\ p_3 \\ w \end{bmatrix}_t = \begin{bmatrix} 0 & \alpha & 0 & 0 \\ 0 & 0 & \beta & 0 \\ \delta_m & 0 & 0 & \gamma_1 \\ 0 & 0 & 0 & 0 \end{bmatrix} \begin{bmatrix} p_1 \\ p_2 \\ p_3 \\ w \end{bmatrix}_{t-1} \quad (4.7)$$

or, after multiplying by the inverse of the left-hand-side matrix

$$\begin{bmatrix} p_1 \\ p_2 \\ p_3 \\ w \end{bmatrix}_t = \begin{bmatrix} 0 & \alpha & 0 & 0 \\ -\dfrac{u}{x}\,\delta m & \dfrac{m}{x}\,\delta & \dfrac{1}{x}\,\beta & -\dfrac{u}{x}\,\gamma 1 \\ \delta m & 0 & 0 & \gamma 1 \\ 0 & 0 & \beta & 0 \end{bmatrix} \begin{bmatrix} p_1 \\ p_2 \\ p_3 \\ w \end{bmatrix}_{t-1} \quad (4.8)$$

The matrix of wages and prices if governed by the eigenvalues of the transition matrix in (4.8), which are solutions of the third-degree equation[16]

$$\left(\frac{m}{x}\,\alpha - \lambda\right)(\lambda^2 - \beta\gamma 1) + \alpha\delta m\left(\frac{u}{x}\lambda - \beta\,\frac{1}{x}\right) = 0 \quad (4.9)$$

Suppose first $\beta = 0$ (no interior price compensation); then

$$\lambda = \frac{m\alpha}{2x}\left(1 \pm \sqrt{1 - \frac{4\delta ux}{\alpha m}}\right) \quad (4.10)$$

leading to pure external inflation,[17] possibly activated by import-price compensations (δ).
Suppose now α to be zero; then

$$\lambda = \pm\sqrt{\beta\gamma 1} \quad (4.11)$$

a phenomenon of possible pure internal wage inflation activated through compensation, and showing alternatives (see the signs in (4.11); the rocketing depends on the product $\beta\gamma 1$ being $\overset{>}{<} 1$.
Suppose only the oil compensation (δ) is suppressed; then

$$\lambda = \pm\sqrt{\beta j 1} \text{ and } \lambda = \frac{m}{x}\,\alpha \quad (4.12)$$

an interplay of internal and external inflation.

Import-price compensation, δ, can dramatically change the picture, however. From (4.9) one can compute the total zero-preserving differential ratio

$$r = \frac{\triangle}{=} \frac{d\lambda}{d\delta} = - \frac{\alpha\lambda(\frac{u}{x}\lambda - \beta\frac{1}{x})}{\alpha\lambda m(2\frac{u}{x}\lambda - \beta\frac{1}{x}) + 2\lambda(\frac{m}{x}\alpha - \lambda) - (\lambda^2 - \beta\gamma 1)} \qquad (4.13)$$

for $\delta \to 0$, the denominator tends towards 0^{18} from (4.12). The numerator, on the other hand, can take two different signs, as (from [4.12]) there is always a negative eigenvalue. Suppose the eigenvalues to be in the neighborhood of $+1$ and -1; then the numerator takes the values $-(\underset{x}{u} - \beta\underset{x}{1})$ and $-(\underset{x}{u} + \beta\underset{x}{1})$. The former value can be positive for β and $\underset{x}{1}$ large relative to $\underset{x}{u}$.

This shows how adding an import-price-compensation element to the system, which in a number of cases is not justified on allocative grounds, can set in motion an otherwise stable (though perhaps oscillating) price subsystem.

5. CONCLUSIONS

In section 4 we have looked at inflation and its consequences essentially from the point of view of countries that import raw materials. Now let us consider the point of view of the countries that supply raw materials. Some countries, like the Netherlands, belong in fact to both categories. The Netherlands are importers of raw materials as well as exporters of natural gas. It is not quite clear how long they will keep their position; estimates of the stocks of natural gas vary widely. It is at any rate certain that sooner or later these stocks will become exhausted, and when that happens, the Netherlands could well be confronted with deficits on the balance of payments like those that have had such disastrous effects on the whole economic and political climate as well as on the value of the national currency in Italy, for example.

Some countries of the Third World are in more or less the same position as the Netherlands, exporting raw materials and products, importing other raw materials and other products. Evidently, a country in that situation may overcome some of the difficulties due to rises in the price of raw materials by linking the price of (scarce) raw materials to be exported to the price of products to be imported. The Netherlands has done just that, in a specific way, by linking the price of natural gas to that of oil: the product to be exported (gas) becomes automatically more expensive according as the product to be imported (oil) is raised in price. The case of some developing countries is perhaps somewhat different, but the difference is not essential.

A country like Surinam, which exports raw materials (bauxite and timber) while importing industrial products, could avoid increasing deficiencies on the balance of payments if one assumes that the price of export products, notably bauxite, could be linked to that of industrial products to be imported. In that way, at least one of the factors causing inflation in the country itself (deficient balance of payments) would be eliminated. But, while mitigating the effects of inflation at home, such a procedure—if adopted by many countries—would undoubtedly give a new impulse to world inflation.

Whether the linking of prices can be realized depends on the willingness of bauxite-producing countries to cooperate as well as on the degree to which aluminium can be replaced with something else. As a matter of fact, copper can replace aluminium for many uses. To realize the idea suggested above, a cartel would have to be set up in which all important producers of (raw materials for) both aluminium and copper are represented.

As we have seen, the deficit on the government's account is the second potential inflation factor. In a bauxite-producing country, that factor can be taken care of simply by letting the government share in the higher bauxite revenues. To that end, a higher tax could be imposed on the bauxite revenues, to be paid in foreign currency; or an extra levy per ton of bauxite could be claimed, progressing with the price of imported goods. In this way, the government would obtain additional means in foreign currency, which importers could use to buy goods abroad and whose countervalue would feed the exchequer. Thus another factor in the inflation process would, at least partially, be eliminated.

As far as the interior inflation problem—the compensation problem—is concerned, the situation in some developing countries may differ from that in the Netherlands in that the relative average income is so low that it cannot sustain any price increases. For that reason, compensation is even more of a hot potato in those countries than in the Netherlands. In the Netherlands the compensation problem is a matter of politics, while in developing countries it is one of politics *and* morality. Let us take a closer look at the problem and find out what it is all about.

Suppose a country is fully self-supporting, fully autarchic except for one product, one raw material. Imagine, moreover, that this country can export another raw material. There is no difficulty whatever: the interior price level can be kept entirely free of foreign influences. In theory, the government could even act as sole importer and, at the same time, as sole exporter. The balance of payment could be kept in reasonable equilibrium as long as the price evolutions of the two raw materials run parallel; but for one raw material, the above conditions should be met, of course.

Suppose further that this country has available for exportation another raw material, for which (oil, for example) demand is inelastic. That country will always be able, by dint of adapting the price level of its export material, to buy what it needs of the one material it lacks (theoretically, the government might be sole importer as well as sole exporter). As long as the price evolutions of the two raw materials run parallel, and the demand for the export material remains inelastic, the balance of payment can reasonably be kept in equilibrium, then the interior price level has become independent of the import. Price increases of the imported raw material need not be charged to the consumer, because the government can use the export surpluses to subsidize the imports.

In practice, such a case does not occur; importation and exportation of raw materials are always accompanied by exportation and importation of products. The price of imports will follow the world price level, and thus an inflationary element will be introduced into the domestic economy. So long as the exports of the domestic raw material balance the imports of the foreign one, no price impulse need be feared on that score, but the imported products will give such an impulse, and the country faces the same problem, albeit in a milder form, that it would have faced if it had no raw material to be exported. Consequently, the compensation problem presents itself too, if not as painfully as in countries that are poor in natural resources. But in this field, further research is in order.

6. NOTES

1. L.H. Klaassen (1976); L.H. Klaassen and J.H.P. Paelinck (1976); L.H. Klaassen, P.W. Klein, and J.H.P. Paelinck (1974); J.H.P. Paelinck (1975).

2. J. Paelinck and P. Markey. *Weerslag van de uitgaven voor energie en arbeid op de Belgische economie.* Brussel, Ministerie van Economische Zaken en Energie, Algemene Directie voor Studiën en Documentatie, Bijvoegsel bij het Maandschrift van de Algemene Directie voor Studien en Documentatie, 1963, 15e jaargang nr. 2, table X.

3. W. Isard. Some locational factors in the iron and steel industry since the early nineteenth century. *Journal of Political Economy*, 1948.

4. L.H. Klaassen and J.H.P. Paelinck (1976).

5. Rather: the autonomously developing part of this knowledge level.

6. For relevant literature, we refer to G.C. Chow (1975); M. Aoki (1976); L.-T. Fan and Ch.-S. Wang (1964); D. Cass and K. Shell (1976); G. Hadley and M.C. Kemp (1971); and J.-Y. Helmer (1972).

7. For the oil-producing countries, see, e.g., A. Schmalensee. Resource exploitation theory and the behavior of the Ail cartel. *European Economic Review*, vol. 7, no. 3, 1976, pp. 217–280.

8. L.H. Klaassen, P. Klein, and J.H.P. Paelinck (1974).

9. This feature was also used in a model TURCEDUC, developed at the Netherlands Economic Institute to study optimum professional training programs for Turkey.

10. Imports, essentially of energy, are considered below. This feature of the model is due to the fact that U refers to a *final* product balance, M (imports) referring to *strictly intermediate* (energy) imports. In this way it has been attempted to merge macroeconomic and (aggregate) sector approaches.

11. λ_i, μ_i, ν_i, $i = 1,2$, are the dual variables belonging to (3.13), the right-hand side of (3.14), and its left-hand size, respectively; deviations of the Lagrangean are presented in order of C_i, I_i, X_i, and M_i.

12. In case $(b - p_i^*) < 0$, one has to set up a program with an initial production level, p_i^*.

13. Cfr. OECD (1976).

14. Nationale Raad van Advies inzake hulpverlening aan minder ontwikkelde landen. National Advisory Board for Assistance to Less Developed Countries, Secretariat Ministry of Foreign Affairs, The Hague, June 1974, pp. 12–13.

15. Inflation and its impact on society, *De Economist*, vol. 123, no. 4, 1975, p. 498.

16. One eigenvalue is zero, the matrix of (4.8) not having full rank.

17. No monetary inflation is considered here.

18. The sign is uncertain, however.

7. REFERENCES

Aoki, M. *Optimal Control and System Theory in Dynamic Economic Analysis.* Amsterdam: North Holland Publishing, 1976.

Cass, D., and Shell, K. (eds.). *The Hamiltonian Approach in Dynamic Economics.* New York: Academic Press, 1976.

Chow, G.C. *Analysis and Control of Dynamic Economic Systems.* New York: Wiley, 1975.

Fan, L.-T. and Wang, Ch.-S. *The Discrete Maximum Principle.* London: Wiley, 1964.

Hadley, G., and Kemp, M.C. *Variational Methods in Economics.* Amsterdam: North Holland Publishing, 1971.

Helmer, J.Y. *La commande optimale en économie*, Paris: Dunod, 1972.

Klaassen, L.H., Enkele Beschouwingen over prijzen en inflatie, Nederlands Economisch Instituut, Rotterdam, December 1976. (Mimeographed)

Klaassen, L.H., Klein, P.W., and Paelinck, J.H.P. Very long term evolution of a system of regions. Introductory report in *6th International Congress of Economic History*, Copenhagen, 1974, pp. 93–108.

Klaassen, L.H., and Paelinck, J.H.P. Energie, grondstoffen, prijzen en groei (Energy, raw materials, prices and growth), *Preadviezen voor de Vereniging voor Staathuishoudkunde*, Utrecht, 1976, pp. 56–80.

OECD, *La production d'energie et l'environnement* [Production of energy and environment.] Paris, 1976.

Paelinck, J.H.P. Quartaire sector, groei, grondstoffen en milieu [Quaternary sector, growth, raw materials and environment.] *Extern*, no. 12, 1975, pp. 635–694.
Paelinck, J.H.P. A simple integrated model of price formation. Series: *Foundations of Empirical Economic Research*. Rotterdam: Netherlands Economic Institute, 1975/13.
Thiry, G. Le phénomène de l'inflation dans la CEE [The inflation phenomenon in the EEC.] Namur: Faculté des Sciences Economiques, 1976. (Mimeographed)

5 AN INTEGRATED INTERREGIONAL MODEL FOR POLLUTION CONTROL

Wim Hafkamp, *University of Amsterdam*; and
Peter Nijkamp, *Free University, Amsterdam*

1. INTRODUCTION

The study of externalities has had a long history in economics. Welfare theorists such as Marshall, Pigou, Scitovsky, Coase, and Mishan, especially, have claimed much attention for the external effects of economic decisions and actions in a market system.

During the last decade the analysis of externalities has been furthered by the failure of the market system to provide an adequate response to the complicated challenge of environmental deterioration, both on a global scale and on the local scale of the quality of daily life. These problems tend to become more intriguing as the extent and the intensity of external effects are increasing (for a further discussion see Nijkamp [1977a]).

The *spatial* transfer of external effects leads to basic frictions in our society, because precisely this phenomenon prevents polluters from suffering from their own negative externalities and leads to a difference between *private* marginal costs and *social* marginal costs. In this respect, the notion of a *spatial externality field* may be an important concept to describe the spatial patterns of externalities with a spatially varying intensity (see also Harvey

[1973]), so that the spatial distributive impacts of unpriced spill-overs can be represented in a more proper way.

The present paper is an extension of an earlier study (see Hafkamp and Nijkamp [1978]) and is devoted to spatial aspects of a multiregional production system. First, the notion of a *multidimensional welfare profile* will be introduced in order to describe the level of regional welfare in terms of multiple welfare indicators. Next, an interregional model will be described that links production, investment, employment, and pollution of all sectors of the multiregional system together. Third, this model will be used as a policy model on the basis of which various political options (such as a system of standards or charges) can be operationalized, so that the impacts of environmental policies upon the regional welfare profiles can be quantified. The final part of the paper is devoted to an *empirical illustration* of the above-mentioned ideas on the basis of an operational two-region model for the industrial heartland of the Netherlands (the Rhine Delta area) versus the remaining part of the Netherlands. This application will once more show the necessity of integrated economic-environmental-spatial models.

2. MULTIDIMENSIONAL WELFARE PROFILES

It has been emphasized by many authors that welfare is not a unidimensional variable but includes a wide variety of indicators that ultimately make up the economic health of a nation or region. The "social indicator movement" and the "environmental impact movement" reflect the fact that welfare is a multidimensional phenomenon that has to be characterized by a large set of underlying variables. Consequently, instead of a scalar welfare indicator a welfare *vector* has to be used. This vector, which will be called a *welfare profile* in the present paper, incorporates inter alia socioeconomic and environmental variables. Thus, a welfare profile may be divided into a series of subprofiles such as the (socio-)economic profile (average income, skewness of income, employment, investments, and the like) and the environmental profile (level of pollution, congestion, availability of natural areas, and so on). It is clear that a meaningful description of the level of welfare should be related to an adequate spatial scale (cf. the notion of externality field). Therefore, an appropriate representation of multidimensional welfare in a spatial system requires a matrix W:

$$1 \ldots \ldots \ldots \ldots \ldots R$$

$$W = \begin{matrix} 1 \\ \cdot \\ \cdot \\ \cdot \\ \cdot \\ \cdot \\ N \end{matrix} \begin{bmatrix} & & \\ & w_{nr} & \\ & & \end{bmatrix} \qquad (2.1)$$

where w_{nr} represents the level of variable n (n=1,..., N) in region r(r=1,..., R). Clearly, all N variables n are measured in different dimensions.

It should be noted that the elements of W are not completely independent: they are simultaneously determined by the evolution of the whole spatial system. Therefore, a proper analysis of the interdependencies in such a system requires the construction of an *interregional model* that links all variables together and that can be used to predict in a comprehensive manner the development of a set of spatial profiles:

$$W = F(W,E), \qquad (2.2)$$

where E stands for a matrix including exogenous variables and instrumental variables.

If such a model is to be used as a *policy model*, one may add to it a set of *side conditions* in order to control the spatial system within predetermined levels W^{min} and W^{max}:

$$W^{min} \leq W \leq W^{max}. \qquad (2.3)$$

Furthermore, one has to introduce a *criterion function* (an objective function or social preference function) on the basis of which a policymaker may judge the feasibility and desirability of a certain state of welfare:

$$\max \omega = \omega \ (W) \qquad (2.4)$$

Sometimes it may be more appropriate to use a *multidimensional* criterion function in order to take account of the variety of preferences in political decision making (for an extensive exposition see van Delft and Nijkamp [1977]).

Another question which has to be considered is how to measure discrepancies between spatial profiles.

First of all, one should be able to rank the outcomes w_{nr} by means of an (implicit) rank criterion. For example, up to a certain limit more employment is better than less employment; or more pollution is worse than less pollution, etc.

Next, one may carry out a *standardization* of the elements of the welfare profile in order to obtain comparable units of measurement (see also Paelinck and Nijkamp [1976]). The following standardization which proved to be rather appropriate will be used here (see also Nijkamp and Rietveld [1978a]).

$$z_{nr} = \frac{w_{nr} - w_n^{min}}{w_n^{max} - w_n^{min}} \quad , \text{if n is a benefit criterion} \tag{2.5}$$

and:

$$z_{nr} = \frac{w_n^{max} - w_n}{w_n^{max} - w_n^{min}} \quad , \text{if n is a cost criterion,} \tag{2.6}$$

where w_n^{min} and w_n^{max} are defined as:

$$w_n^{min} = \min_r w_{nr} \tag{2.7}$$

and:

$$w_n^{max} = \max_r w_{nr} \tag{2.8}$$

Now it is easily seen that $0 \leq z_{nr} \leq 1$. Moreover, it is clear that the most desirable state of a profile variable implies $z_{nr} = 1$, and the less desirable state $z_{nr} = 0$. Especially for the computational stage of a model such a standardization is rather efficient.

Then the *discrepancy* $d_{rr'}$ between the spatial profiles of any pair of regions r and r' can be measured as:

$$d_{rr'} = \sum_{n=1}^{N} | z_{nr} - z_{nr'} | \tag{2.9}$$

or as a more general Minkawski metric:

$$d_{rr'} = \{ \sum_{n=1}^{N} | z_{nr} - z_{nr'} |^{\lambda} \}^{1/\lambda} \quad , \lambda \geq 0 \tag{2.10}$$

Clearly, the elements of the discrepancy index can also be *weighed*, provided information is available on the trade-offs between these elements (see for a broader discussion on this subject Nijkamp and Rietveld [1978b]). It should be noted that the absolute level of a discrepancy index has no meaning; only its relative value with respect to other states of the economy is relevant.

Now the next section will be devoted to the way in which the elements of a spatial welfare profile can be linked together by means of an interregional model.

3. AN INTEGRATED INTERREGIONAL MODEL OF PRODUCTION AND POLLUTION

As set out before, the elements of a spatial welfare profile are not independent with respect to each other. Both at the *intraregional* and at the *interregional* level there is a high degree of mutual interaction due to sectoral linkages, technical relationships, behavioral conditions, and spatial spillovers. Therefore, in the present section a model will be developed that links production, consumption, investment, employment, income, and pollution together in a comprehensive framework. The model is an interregional and multisectoral model and parts of it have proved an empirical validity in a study of the Rhine Delta area near Rotterdam (see ESSOR [1977] and van der Werf [1977]). The structure of the model is kept rather simple in order to comply with the need of an operational approach for spatial welfare profiles.

The assumption will be made here that the welfare profile of each region contains three elements: production (q), employment (l) and pollution (p). This set of welfare elements can easily be extended, but for the sake of simplicity the analysis will be confined to these three elements. When (without loss of generality) the spatial system at hand is assumed to be composed of two regions, the interregional interaction scheme between q, l, and p may be created as shown in Figure 5.1. The vertical arrows represent *intra*regional linkages (viz., employment and pollution emission relationships), while the horizontal arrows represent *inter*regional linkages (viz., input-output and pollution diffusion relationships).

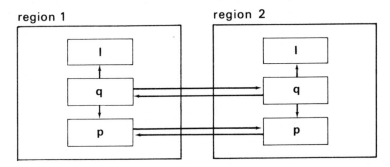

Figure 5.1.   Interaction Scheme of Welfare Elements of Two Regions

region 1   region 2

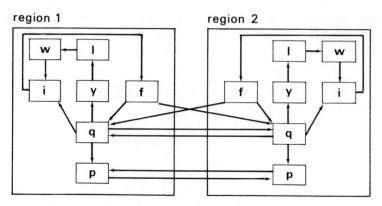

Figure 5.2.   Interaction Scheme for Two Regions

The structure of the latter scheme can easily be extended with relationships for the final demand, investments, value added, wages, and imports.
The formal structure of such a more extensive model including final demand
(f), wages (w), value added (y), and investments (i) will now be described
by means of an integrated scheme, followed by a formal mathematical representation (see Figure 5.2).

The interregional model employed here is a full information input-output
model, so that all flows of interregional deliveries of intermediate and final
commodities are known (see also Paelinck and Nijkamp [1976]). Therefore,
for each region r (r=1,..., R) the following input-output structure may be
constructed

$$q_r = \sum_{r'=1}^{R} A_{rr'} \ q_{r'} + \sum_{r'=1}^{R} f_{rr'} \quad , \tag{3.1}$$

where $A_{rr'}$ is the matrix of input-output coefficients for intermediate
deliveries between region r and r', q_r an Ixl vector of sectoral production
volumes, and $f_{rr'}$, a Ixl vector for final commodity flows from region r to r'.
It is clear that for all regions together this input-output model can be represented in a comprehensive manner as:

$$q = Aq + f \tag{3.2}$$

Final demand f is made up of the sum total of consumption c (both private and public), investments i (both private and public), exports abroad e,
and stock formation s; hence:

$$f = c + i + e + s \tag{3.3}$$

Regional and sectoral value added y_{ir} can be calculated by means of fixed value added coefficients v_{ir}:

$$y_{ir} = v_{ir} \, q_{ir} \, , \tag{3.4}$$

or

$$y = \hat{v} \, q \, , \tag{3.5}$$

where $\hat{v}$ is a diagonal matrix with the elements v_{ir} on the main diagonal. By means of (3.5) the value added of each region (y_r) and total value added (y) can be directly calculated.

The sectoral and regional demand for labor l_{ir} can be related to value added v_{ir} by means of a fixed employment coefficient λ_{ir}:

$$l_{ir} = \lambda_{ir} \, y_{ir} \tag{3.6}$$

or for the whole spatial system:

$$l = \hat{\lambda} \, y \, , \tag{3.7}$$

where $\hat{\lambda}$ is a diagonal matrix with employment coefficients. The impact of shifts in labor productivity upon the demand for labor can be taken into account as follows:

$$l_{ir} = d_{ir}^{-1} \, \lambda_{ir} y_{ir} \, , \tag{3.8}$$

where d_{ir} is an index for the annual rise in labor productivity per employee. Relationship (3.8) can be transformed into matrix notation as:

$$l = \hat{d}^{-1} \, \hat{\lambda} \, y \tag{3.9}$$

The total wage sum w can now easily be calculated on the basis of the regional sectoral wage rates u_{ir}:

$$w = \sum_{i=1}^{I} \sum_{r=1}^{R} u_{ir} \, l_{ir}$$

$$= u' \, l \tag{3.10}$$

The rise in annual wage rates may be assumed to be equal to the rise in labor productivity, when the foregoing model is to be used as a projection model.

The production factor labor is included as an endogenous variable in the previous model. In a similar way the production factor investments may be made endogenous. It should be noted, however, that i represents the investments produced by the sector of *origin*. It is clear, however, that the investment behavior of firms should be related to investments implemented by the sector of *destination*. The latter type of investments denoted by z can be related to the first ones by means of a distribution matrix T, which assigns the produced investments to sectors of destination:

$$i = T \ z \tag{3.11}$$

The investment relationship is based on both the accelerator principle and the complementarity principle. The accelerator principle links the investments to the rise in production volumes, while the complementarity principle involves a negative impact of the total wage sum upon the demand for investments. Therefore, the following investment model is assumed:

$$z = \hat{\kappa}\{(y - y_{-1}) - (w - w_{-1})\} \quad , \tag{3.12}$$

where $\hat{\kappa}$ is a diagonal matrix with marginal capital-output ratios on the main diagonal, w a vector with regional and sectoral wages, and where the lower index -1 refers to the value of a variable in the previous period.[1]

If necessary, imports m may also be included by means of the following import equation:

$$m = M \ q + N \ i \quad , \tag{3.13}$$

where M and N are matrices containing import coefficients for intermediate goods and investments, respectively.

Finally, the pollution sector may be related to the above-mentioned structural model for production. For each region r, the following pollution emission relationship may be assumed (see also Muller [1978]):

$$p_r = B_r \ q_r \quad , \tag{3.14}$$

where p_r is a Jx1 vector with volumes of pollutants p_{jr}, and B_r a matrix of order JxI containing the pollution emission coefficients. Matrix B_r is assumed to incorporate both the direct emission effects of production and the indirect effects (for example, the emission of carbon monoxide due to private transportation). For the moment, the assumption is made that the state of abatement technology is adequately reflected by the matrix B_r. In case of changes in abatement technologies due to pollution charges, one may assume that the relative decline in the emission rate of pollutant j in sector i of region r is equal to the relative increase in the pollution charge of pollutant j in sector i of region r. In case of a system of standards, the emission rates are also variables that can be adjusted on the basis of cost-minimizing principles. The latter model can be represented for the whole spatial system as:

$$p = \hat{B} \ q \quad , \tag{3.15}$$

where $\hat{B}$ is a block-diagonal matrix.

The diffusion of pollution can be represented by means of a diffusion matrix H, so that the emission of pollution g in all regions can be calculated as:

$$g = H\,p \quad , \tag{3.16}$$

where the elements of H reflect the average diffusion coefficients for each pollutant over all regions of the spatial system. Given a closed spatial system, it is easily seen that the additivity conditions should be satisfied by H, so that total pollution generated is equal to total emission of pollution.

In addition to the above-mentioned structural equations, it is possible to impose a set of side conditions on the development of the spatial system, for example, employment conditions, investment capacities, pollution standards, etc. This aspect will be dealt with in relation to political strategies and priorities regarding the state of the spatial system at hand. Price relationships might also be included in order to analyze the impacts of shifts in wage rates, costs of new technologies, and pollution charges.

4. INTERACTIVE COMPROMISE POLICY MODELS

In the preceding section the structure of an interregional production system has been presented. So far, however, no attention has been paid to political priorities, welfare choices, or optimizing behavior. It is clear that, after the *analytical* stage of interregional model building, now the attention has to be focussed on the *political* stage in which policy decisions and controls play a dominant role.

It is generally accepted that policymakers and planners have to base their decisions on a multiplicity of criteria (efficiency criteria, equity criteria, social criteria, ecological criteria, and so forth). Hence, in addition to a careful examination of the set of feasible solutions, decision makers have to evaluate the various alternative solutions. The existence of multiple decision criteria, the limited availability of information, the uncertainty about the set of feasible alternatives, and the gradually developing institutional procedures of decision and planning strategies usually preclude a straightforward application of traditional optimality principles.

In the present section this problem will be attacked by introducing the following elements in a political evaluation procedure:

a. *the existence of multiple objective functions*: for each element of the welfare profile described in section 3 a corresponding objective function will be assumed. Consequently, the following objective functions are distinguished: max q, max l, and min p. A further analysis of these problems requires the application of some principles from multiobjective decision theory (see van Delft and Nijkamp [1977] and Nijkamp [1978]).

b. *the existence of an interactive choice strategy*: due to uncertainty and limited information the choice-making process is a learning procedure. This implies that information about the set of feasible alternatives is provided in a stepwise way to the decision maker, so that he may formulate certain priorities regarding the outcome of the decision procedure. The latter information is used to truncate the set of feasible solutions and to specify some trial solutions that may again be judged by the decision maker. This procedure can be repeated until finally a (convergent) compromise solution can be identified.

When the set of all endogenous variables and instrumental variables incorporated in the model described in section 3 is represented by a vector x, and when the set of feasible solutions is represented by the symbol K, the multiobjective policy model corresponding to section 3 is:

$$\begin{cases} \max q \\ \max l \\ \min p \\ \text{s.t.} \\ x \in K \end{cases} \qquad (4.1)$$

where q, l, and p are assumed to be functionally related to the arguments x according to the structure specified in section 3.

The salient feature of (4.1.) is the existence of a multiplicity of conflicting criteria, viz., maximization of production *and* employment *and* minimization of pollution. Clearly, a simultaneous optimization of these objective functions leads to contradictory results due to the conflicting nature of these objectives. It has been exposed in Nijkamp [1977a] that several alternative approaches may be chosen to solve this problem, such as a utility maximization, a penalty approach, a goal-programming method, a constraint method, a hierarchical programming analysis, a min-max (game) approach, an efficiency point programming analysis, and a distance metric approach.

A central role in these types of models is played by *efficient* solutions (nondominated or Pareto-solutions). These solutions reflect the conflicting nature of multiobjective decision models: an efficient point is any point for

which the value of one decision criterion cannot be improved without affecting the value of the remaining criteria. In formal terms, an efficient solution
is a point x for which no other feasible solution x does exist such that:

$$
\begin{cases}
w_n (x) \geq w_n (x^*) & , \forall n \\
\text{and} \\
w_n (x) \neq w_n (x^*), \text{ for at least one n,} & (4.2)
\end{cases}
$$

where w_n $(n=1,\ldots, N)$ is assumed to be a certain decision criterion.

In this paper the multiobjective decision problem reflected by (4.1.) will
be attached by means of a *compromise* method based on a distance metric
which attempts to minimize the discrepancy between the set of efficient solutions and the "ideal" solution. The ideal solution of the nth objective function
is defined as:

$$
w_n^{max} = \max_{x \in K} w_n (x) \quad , \forall n \quad , \tag{4.3}
$$

so that the following vector of ideal solutions can be constructed:

$$
w^{max} =
\begin{bmatrix}
w_1^{max} \\
\cdot \\
\cdot \\
\cdot \\
\cdot \\
w_N^{max}
\end{bmatrix}
\tag{4.4}
$$

A straightforward application of a distance metric to the successive
objective functions, however, is precluded due to the *different dimensions*
of the objective functions. Therefore, a standardization has to be carried
out according to the lines exposed in section 2. When the standardized value
of w_n is denoted by z_n (see (2.5.) and (2.6.)), it is easily seen that the ideal
value of z_n is equal to 1, i.e.,

$$
z_n^{max} = 1 \tag{4.5}
$$

or

$$
z^{max} = \iota \quad , \tag{4.6}
$$

where ι is the vector with unit elements.

Therefore, a compromise solution between diverging priorities can be
calculated by minimizing the Euclidean distance between z_n and z_n^{max} ($\forall$n).[2]
This gives rise to the following quadratic programming problem:

$$\left\{ \begin{array}{c} \min \ \varphi_{\text{s.t.}} = \sum\limits_{n=1}^{N} \ \{1 - z_n \ (x)\}^2 \\[2mm] x \in K \\[2mm] (2.5.) \text{ and } (2.6.) \end{array} \right\} \quad (4.7)$$

The solution of this programming mode will be denoted by w^o, while the corresponding optimal elements of the decision variables will be denoted by x_i^0 ($i=1,\ldots,$ I).

Next, the following stage has to be taken into account, viz., the use of multiobjective decision models in interactive learning strategies. Such an interactive approach is necessary, because (4.7.) is only an unweighted minimization of quadratic discrepancies. A direct assessment of these weights, however, is generally impossible (except in case of an ex post revealed preference approach; see Nijkamp and Somermeijer [1971]). Therefore, a learning procedure has to be applied in order to gauge during a number of steps the decision maker's relative priorities attached to the elements of the welfare profile. This learning procedure is based on the following steps.

The elements of the optimal solution vector x^o for model (4.7.) are presented to the decision maker as a first trial solution. Then the decision maker has to indicate whether or not he is satisfied with this trial solution. The easiest way to deal with this method is to use a check list:

	satisfactory	
	yes	no
w_1^o $\cdot$ $\cdot$ $\cdot$ $\cdot$ $\cdot$ $\cdot$ w_N^o		

The elements for which the decision maker is not satisfied are included in a set S. This gives rise to the specification of the following additional constraint:

$$w_n' \ (x) \ge w_n^{o'} \ (x) \ , \quad n' \in S \qquad (4.8)$$

The latter side condition is added to the model represented in (4.3.), so that the following adjusted programming model is obtained for each objective function n:

$$\left.\begin{array}{ll} \max \; w_n\,(x) & , \quad \forall\, n \\[2mm] x \in K & \\[2mm] w_n{}'\,(x) \geq w_n^{o\prime}\,(x) & , \quad n' \in S \end{array}\right\} \qquad (4.9)$$

The optimal solutions of the latter model are denoted as $w^{\max}_{(1)}$. Then the compromise procedure described in (4.5.) – (4.7.) is again applied. This leads to a new set of trial solutions $w^{o}_{(1)}$. Next, the steps implied by (4.8.) and (4.9.) are again carried out and so forth, until finally a satisfactory compromise solution is obtained. These steps are briefly represented in Figure 5.3.

This procedure implies in fact that instead of an optimizer concept a "satisficer" concept is used, so that the ultimate compromise result complies with certain achievement levels specified by the decision maker (cf. also Simon [1957]). A further elaboration of this approach, sometimes called the method of displaced ideals, can be found in van Delft and Nijkamp [1977] and Nijkamp [1978].

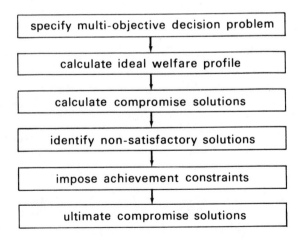

Figure 5.3.   Representation of the Steps of an Interactive Multiobjective Decision Model

5. AN EMPIRICAL ILLUSTRATION OF AN INTERACTIVE COMPROMISE MODEL

As said before, the model used in this section is the extended input-output model developed for the Rhine Delta area by ESSOR [1977]. In the framework of our approach this model is extended with pollution and diffusion relationships. The model can be used as an intertemporal model, so that future options can also be taken into account. The data and parameters of this model will not be presented here, because they can be found elsewhere (see ESSOR [1977]). Only the emission coefficients will be presented here.

The model itself contains twenty-seven different sectors, which are linked together by means of a full-information input-output table, both within the area itself (R) and between the remaining part of the Netherlands (N). Therefore, the model is essentially a two-region model. The number of pollutants taken into account is equal to 4, viz., sulfur dioxide (SO_2), carbon monoxide (CO), nitrogen oxide (NO_x) and particulates. Information about emission coefficients was derived inter alia from Muller [1978] and from a report "Milieuverontreiniging en Productiestructuur in Nederland" [1978]. Table 5.1 shows the 4 x 27 matrix of emission coefficients B that was obtained (this matrix is assumed to be equal for both regions R and N). As set out in section (4.1.), the model is a multiobjective programming model with production value, employment, and environmental quality as successive objective functions. In order to arrive at a suitable set of constraints for each programming variant of this interregional model, some minor adjustments had to be carried out:

- the input-output model was specified as an inequality condition such that the production has to meet at least a prespecified minimum level of final demand. This minimum achievement level was supposed to be equal to 90 percent of the known (observed) final demand level in the year 1970.
- For all regions together a minimum and maximum employment level was fixed. These minima and maxima were equal to 90 percent and 110 percent of the observed total employment levels in 1970, respectively.
- For each region and each sector a minimum employment condition was introduced. This minimum value was assumed to be equal to the observed sectoral employment level in 1970.

It is clear that many other adjustments might have been performed, but for the moment these adjustments are sufficient to guarantee a meaningful and feasible decision area. According to the procedure sketched in section 4,

Table 5.1. Emission Matrix for the Sectoral Production Structure

Sectors

Pollutants	1	2	3	4	5	6	7	8	9
SO_2	2.74	0.54	3.21	2.24	3.44	2.07	1.71	2.30	2.30
CO	1.43	0.54	0.38	0.41	1.11	0.46	0.53	0.45	0.45
NO_x	1.86	0.02	0.90	0.38	0.19	0.47	0.65	0.40	0.40
part.	0.19	3.29	22.19	0.04	0.37	0.04	0.05	0.04	0.04

	10	11	12	13	14	15	16	17	18
SO_2	4.02	4.02	4.02	1.33	2.37	1.49	18.41	0.91	4.65
CO	1.52	1.52	1.52	0.88	3.04	0.27	1.41	10.00	1.86
NO_x	1.31	1.31	1.31	0.54	11.16	0.19	3.55	9.02	0.41
part.	1.19	1.19	1.19	0.04	1.09	0.09	1.85	2.83	3.16

	19	20	21	22	23	24	25	26	27
SO_2	4.63	3.95	2.35	2.35	2.35	2.35	0	0	0
CO	0.53	0.31	0.34	0.34	0.34	0.34	0	0	0
NO_x	0.16	0.09	0.24	0.24	0.24	0.24	0	0	0
part.	0.76	0.13	0.05	0.05	0.05	0.05	0	0	0

Table 5.2a. Results of Separate Optimization Models for Region R

Sectors	Maximization of q			Maximization of l			Minimization of p^3		
	q_1	l_1	p_1	q_1	l_1	p_1	q_1	l_1	p_1
1	0.386	5.167	2.404	0.386	5.167	2.404	0.316	4.225	1.966
2	0.000	0.000	0.000	0.000	0.000	0.000	0.000	0.000	0.000
3	0.015	0.110	0.392	0.015	0.110	0.392	0.012	0.090	0.320
4	0.379	2.640	1.162	0.379	2.640	1.162	0.310	2.105	0.952
5	1.760	12.427	8.995	1.760	12.427	8.995	1.440	10.166	7.358
6	0.668	4.840	2.029	0.668	4.840	2.029	0.546	3.959	1.660
7	0.060	0.880	0.175	0.060	0.880	0.175	0.049	0.725	0.144
8	0.059	2.417	0.189	0.059	2.417	0.189	0.049	0.204	0.156
9	0.006	0.329	0.018	0.006	0.329	0.018	0.005	6.057	0.016
10	0.128	4.289	1.030	0.128	4.289	1.030	0.105	3.415	0.844
11	0.124	2.750	0.999	0.124	2.750	0.999	0.102	6.481	0.820
12	0.358	7.809	2.876	0.358	7.809	2.876	0.293	156.587	2.356
13	8.767	25.627	24.461	8.767	25.627	24.461	7.173	4.151	20.013
14	0.174	2.750	3.069	0.174	2.750	3.069	0.142	17.972	2.508
15	1.389	20.345	2.972	1.389	20.345	2.972	1.136	19.792	2.431
16	1.651	29.700	41.636	1.651	29.700	41.636	1.351	6.962	34.072
17	0.473	4.617	24.934	0.473	4.617	24.934	0.387	16.130	12.678
18	2.018	56.985	20.340	2.018	56.985	20.340	1.651	80.823	16.642
19	3.498	24.300	21.265	3.498	24.300	21.265	2.862	144.577	17.401
20	4.972	85.261	22.272	4.972	85.261	22.272	4.068	11.593	18.225
21	0.826	16.937	2.461	0.826	16.937	2.461	0.676	13.783	2.014
22	0.822	20.898	2.449	0.822	20.898	2.449	0.672	9.002	2.003
23	0.433	18.810	1.290	0.433	18.810	1.290	0.354	2.650	1.005
24	0.074	2.638	0.221	0.074	2.638	0.221	0.061	9.230	0.182
25	0.318	30.239	0.000	0.318	30.239	0.000	0.260	10.925	0.000
26	0.014	0.000	0.000	0.014	0.000	0.000	0.115	0.000	0.000
27	0.000	0.000	0.000	0.000	0.000	0.000	0.000	0.000	0.000

Table 5.2b. Results of Separate Optimization Models for Region N

Sectors	Maximization of q			Maximization of l			Minimization of p³		
	q_2	l_2	p_2	q_2	l_2	p_2	q_2	l_2	p_2
1	14.213	356.761	88.409	14.213	356.761	88.409	11.629	291.888	72.332
2	0.448	0.000	1.970	0.448	0.000	1.970	0.367	0.000	1.611
3	0.345	4.289	9.207	0.345	4.289	0.207	0.282	3.505	7.524
4	10.057	54.512	30.877	10.057	54.512	30.877	8.229	44.601	25.263
5	12.979	120.706	66.324	12.979	120.706	66.324	10.619	98.757	54.263
6	3.014	27.063	9.162	3.014	27.063	9.162	2.466	22.145	7.497
7	4.778	87.103	14.047	4.778	87.103	14.047	3.909	71.261	11.492
8	2.211	71.283	7.054	2.211	71.283	7.054	1.809	58.322	5.771
9	0.744	16.169	2.374	0.744	16.169	2.374	0.609	13.234	1.943
10	2.528	67.209	20.322	2.528	67.209	20.322	2.068	54.988	16.771
11	2.379	34.656	19.124	2.379	34.656	19.124	1.946	28.353	15.646
12	4.248	83.508	34.152	4.248	83.508	34.152	3.476	68.338	27.947
13	11.538	124.028	32.190	11.538	124.028	32.190	9.439	101.469	26.335
14	3.019	54.456	53.308	3.019	54.456	53.308	2.470	44.559	43.620
15	18.289	269.950	39.139	18.289	269.950	39.139	14.964	220.869	32.023
16	13.386	199.051	337.760	13.386	199.051	337.760	10.952	162.856	276.209
17	4.684	42.668	247.107	4.684	42.668	247.107	3.832	34.910	125.536
18	18.191	498.429	183.363	18.191	498.429	183.363	14.883	407.794	150.021
19	25.856	909.355	157.204	25.856	909.355	157.204	21.154	743.986	128.616
20	10.461	250.217	46.863	10.461	250.217	46.863	8.559	204.731	38.344
21	3.046	118.364	9.077	3.046	118.364	9.077	2.492	96.839	7.426
22	7.402	127.611	22.058	7.402	127.611	22.058	6.056	104.405	18.047
23	5.123	184.681	15.266	5.123	184.681	15.266	4.191	151.086	12.489
24	0.989	31.461	2.948	0.989	31.461	2.948	0.809	25.726	2.411
25	3.739	311.861	0.000	3.739	311.861	0.000	3.059	255.121	0.000
26	1.090	0.000	0.000	1.090	0.000	0.000	0.892	0.000	0.000
27	0.000	0.000	0.000	0.000	0.000	0.000	0.000	0.000	0.000

the first step is to carry out for each objective function a separate optimization. The results of this separate optimization are included in Tables 5.2a and 5.2b, where the solution for the key variables of the decision model are represented. The following conclusions can be inferred from Table 5.2a. and 5.2b.

- the separate optimization of production value and employment appears to lead to the same results for all sectors due to (1) the linear dependency between production and employment and (2) the fact that in the first run of the model the employment constraints act as the only upper bounds. This situation, however, will change during subsequent stages of the interactive procedure, when additional constraints are introduced.
- the minimization of total pollution leads to a significant lower level of production and employment due to the linear character of the model, so that a minimum pollution corresponds to a minimum production and employment. In fact, the production constraints and the employment constraints act simultaneously as lower bounds and determine the pollution levels in the same proportion.
- the calculated results correspond to a high extent to the relative share of actual production, employment, and pollution among the two regions at hand.

The following stage of the analysis is the calculation of a first best compromise solution as exposed in section 4. The results of this procedure are contained in Table 5.3.

The results in table 5.3 show a linear correspondence to those presented in tables 5.2a and 5.2b. The reason for this linear correspondence is that the model used has a linear structure with constant production coefficients. Hence the minimization of pollution will also imply a minimization of employment, so that in the present model the optimal outcomes of a minimum pollution correspond to a production level related to a 90 percent employment level (both at the aggregate level and at the sectoral level).

Similarly, the maximization of production leads to maximum pollution outcomes. The same holds true for the employment option. Because the scores in the quadratic distance metric with respect to the ideal point are equal, the first compromise solution will be located at a point where the production falls in between its minimum and its maximum value such that the distance to the minimum is twice the distance to the maximum.

Assume next that the decision-making committee wants to increase the employment levels such that the sectoral unemployment rates do not exceed

Table 5.3.   Results of the First Compromise Procedure for Regions R and N

Sectors	Region R			Region N		
	q_1	l_1	p_1	q_2	l_2	p_2
1	0.362	4.835	2.250	13.309	334.050	82.780
2	0.000	0.000	0.000	0.420	0.000	1.844
3	0.014	0.103	0.366	0.323	4.011	8.611
4	0.355	2.409	1.090	9.418	51.043	28.912
5	1.648	11.634	8.421	12.153	113.022	62.101
6	0.625	4.531	1.900	2.822	25.344	8.580
7	0.056	0.830	0.165	4.474	81.554	13.152
8	0.056	0.233	0.179	2.070	66.746	6.605
9	0.006	6.932	0.018	0.697	15.146	2.224
10	0.120	3.908	0.966	2.367	62.931	19.193
11	0.117	7.417	0.938	2.227	32.448	17.906
12	0.335	179.205	2.696	3.978	78.209	31.984
13	8.209	4.751	22.904	10.802	116.126	30.139
14	0.163	20.568	2.870	2.827	50.995	49.921
15	1.300	22.651	2.782	17.125	252.772	36.649
16	1.546	7.968	38.994	12.534	186.380	316.106
17	0.443	18.460	14.509	4.386	39.953	143.669
18	1.890	92.497	19.046	17.033	466.698	171.691
19	3.275	165.460	19.914	24.210	851.451	147.194
20	4.656	13.268	20.857	9.795	234.303	43.883
21	0.774	15.774	2.305	2.852	110.827	8.499
22	0.769	10.302	2.292	6.931	119.486	20.654
23	0.405	3.033	1.150	4.796	172.910	14.293
24	0.070	10.563	0.208	0.926	29.442	2.759
25	0.298	12.503	0.000	3.501	291.972	0.000
26	0.132	0.000	0.000	1.021	0.000	0.000
27	0.000	0.000	0.000	0.000	0.000	0.000

5 percent. The latter side condition can be incorporated as a constraint in model [4.9.], so that a new run of the model can be made. Under the new set of constraints maximization of value added and of employment leads to the same results as those contained in tables 5.2a and 5.2b under the heading "maximization of q" and "maximization of l" respectively. The upper bounds on sectoral labor demand remain unchanged and hence the production maxima and the employment maxima also remain unchanged. The results of this compromise procedure are included in tables 5.4a and 5.4b.

Table 5.4a.   Results of Second Compromise
Procedure for Region R

	Minimization of p		
Sectors	q_1	I_1	p_1
1	0.369	4.929	2.294
2	0.000	0.000	0.000
3	0.014	0.105	0.373
4	0.362	2.456	1.111
5	1.680	11.860	8.584
6	0.637	4.619	1.937
7	0.057	0.846	0.168
8	0.057	0.238	0.182
9	0.006	7.066	0.019
10	0.122	3.984	0.985
11	0.119	7.561	0.957
12	0.342	182.685	2.749
13	8.368	4.843	23.348
14	0.166	20.967	2.926
15	1.325	23.091	2.836
16	1.576	8.122	39.751
17	0.451	18.818	14.791
18	1.926	94.293	19.416
19	3.339	168.673	20.301
20	4.746	13.525	21.262
21	0.789	16.080	2.350
22	0.784	10.502	2.337
23	0.413	3.092	1.172
24	0.071	10.768	0.212
25	0.303	12.746	0.000
26	0.134	0.000	0.000
27	0.000	0.000	0.000

These compromise procedures appear to lead to the same conclusions as discussed above, viz., linear compromise solutions between pollution, production and employment. Clearly, several alternative experiments and scenarios can be constructed to generate satisficing compromise solutions.

Table 5.4b.   Results of Second Compromise
Procedure for Region N

	Minimization of p		
Sectors	q_2	l_2	p_2
1	13.567	340.536	84.387
2	0.428	0.000	1.879
3	0.329	4.089	8.778
4	9.600	52.034	29.473
5	12.389	115.216	63.307
6	2.877	25.836	8.746
7	4.560	83.138	13.407
8	2.110	68.042	6.733
9	0.710	15.440	2.267
10	2.413	64.153	19.566
11	2.270	33.078	18.254
12	4.055	79.728	32.605
13	11.012	118.380	30.724
14	2.882	51.985	50.890
15	17.458	257.680	37.360
16	12.777	189.999	22.244
17	4.471	40.728	46.459
18	17.363	475.760	75.024
19	24.680	367.984	50.052
20	9.985	238.853	44.735
21	2.907	112.979	8.664
22	7.065	121.806	21.055
23	4.889	176.267	14.571
24	0.944	30.014	2.813
25	3.569	297.641	0.000
26	1.041	0.000	0.000
27	0.000	0.000	0.000

6. CONCLUDING REMARKS

The foregoing sections have demonstrated the usefulness of multiobjective
decision models for integrated spatial-environmental-economic models. The

analysis has shown that the traditional maximizing paradigm is not a pre-requisite for operational decision making. On the contrary, the introduction of a satisficer principle seems to be realistic and offers better opportunities to integrate policy making and model building. Thus, this extension of traditional economic theory provides much more flexibility for alternative ways of thinking (for example, the steady-state idea, the entropy philosophy, and so on).

The impacts of public policy may be further studied either by means of a system of charges or of standards. Charges may be related to the cost structure of an input-output framework; standards may be incorporated via constraints. Clearly, in both cases in the long run a shift in technology will take place so that then the input-output model is no longer valid. This would require an extension forward, a completely dynamic model that has essentially a nonlinear character.

For the moment, it is sufficient to conclude that models of the foregoing type provide the opportunity to integrate in a meaningful way spatial-economic and environmental profiles such that they yield the necessary information for rational economic-environmental policies.

7. NOTES

1. This relationship presupposes a complementarity between capital and labor; this assumption may be valid when there is a close link between the marginal labor productivity and the rise in wage rates. Otherwise, the assumption of fixed labor coefficients may be invalidated [see 3.8]. In the latter case, equation (3.8) has to be extended also with a complementary term.

2. It is clear that an alternative approach may be the specification of a most pessimistic provisional solution, such that the distances with respect to this solution are maximized.

3. Total pollution is defined here as the unweighted aggregate pollution over all four pollutants. If necessary, a weighted pollution indicator may be calculated (see "Milieuverontreiniging en Productiestructuur in Nederland" [1978]). The units of measurement of production, employment and pollution are 10^9 Dfl., 10^3 man-years and 10^3 tons per year, respectively.

8. REFERENCES

van Delft, A., and P. Nijkamp. *Multi-Criteria Analysis and Regional Decision-Making.* The Hague: Martinus Nijhoff, 1977.

ESSOR, *Een Prognose van Economische Ontwikkelingen in het Rijnmondgebied tot 1980.* Rotterdam: Openbaar Lichaam Rijnmond, 1977.

Hafkamp, W., and P. Nijkamp. Environmental Protection and Spatial Welfare Patterns. *Spatial Inequalities and Regional Development,* H. Folmer and J. Oosterhaven, eds. The Hague: Martinus Nijhoff, 1978.

Harvey, D. *Social Justice and the City.* London: Arnold, 1973.

Milieuverontreiniging en Productiestructuur in Nederland. Amsterdam: Institute for Environmental Studies, Free University, 1978. (Mimeographed)

Muller, F. *Energy and Environment in Interregional Input-Output Models.* The Hague: Martinus Nijhoff, 1978.

Nijkamp, P. *Theory and Application of Environmental Economics.* Amsterdam: North-Holland Publishing, 1977a.

Nijkamp, P. New Decision Models for Multiple Goals, Research Memorandum no. 69. Amsterdam: Department of Economics, Free University, 1977b.

Nijkamp, P. A Theory of Displaced Ideals, Research Memorandum. Amsterdam: Department of Economics, Free University, 1978.

Nijkamp, P. and P. Rietveld. Conflicting Social Priorities and Compromise Social Decisions. *London Studies in Regional Science,* I. Cullen, ed. London: Pion, 1978a.

Nijkamp, P., and P. Rietveld. A Multivariate Analysis of Spatial Inequalities, Research Memorandum. Amsterdam: Department of Economics, Free University, 1978b.

Nijkamp, P., and W.H. Somermeijer. Explicating Implicit Social Preference Functions. *Economics of Planning,* vol. 11, no. 3, 1971, pp. 100–119.

Paelinck, J.H.P., and P. Nijkamp. *Operational Theory and Method of Regional Economics.* Farnborough: Saxon House (jointly with D.C. Heath, Lexington, MA), 1976.

Simon, H.A. *Models of Man.* New York: Wiley, 1957.

van der Werf, D. Developing the Rijnmond Model. *Relevance and Precision,* J.S. Cramer, A. Heertje, and P.E. Venekamp, eds. Amsterdam: North-Holland Publishing, 1977, pp. 159–204.

6 THE ENVIRONMENTAL IMPACT ISSUES IN ENERGY DEVELOPMENT IN THE UNITED STATES

Peter House, *Director, Office of Technology Impacts*
Office of the Assistant Secretary for Environment
U.S. Department of Energy

1. INTRODUCTION

Possibly the most interesting policy confrontations of recent years could be found in those areas where environmental and energy choices clash (or appear to) head on. Both areas are of the nature of political sacred cows to some constituency or other, and both have been preferred to the general public as being in "crisis." It is in situations such as these, where problematical and emotionally charged issues meet, that the more interesting and difficult policy analyses lie. In this paper we shall, in a general fashion, catalog the environmental aspects of the energy problem from the point of view of one observer in the U.S. Department of Energy. Of necessity, both because of limited perspective and information, the viewpoint is flawed. However, the opinion of the evolution of environmental/energy analyses gets more accurate toward the present, as my own experience is greater. Nonetheless, I hope the reader will permit me a minimum of philosophy.

Although numerous specific examples exist to disprove the generalization, it is possible to see how one might characterize the two major previous bureaucracies that combined to make up the current Department of Energy (DOE). Such musing is important, because from these roots grows an understanding of the current situation in the Department. One of these groups, the Federal Energy Administration (FEA) was put together specifically to respond to the 1974 oil embargo and had as its mission the realization of "energy independence" for our nation. Throughout its existence, the focus of the FEA was on short- to medium-term issues. A decade was its longest perspective. In such a milieu, it is possible to speculate how environmental matters could be perceived as "barriers" to the immediate implementation of energy supply policies.

The second Agency, the Energy Research and Development Agency (ERDA), was born somewhat later and had a less than two-year life span. As opposed to policies of regulation or taxes (a la FEA), ERDA's efforts were largely concentrated on research to develop energy technologies. Its perspective was research, development, and demonstration over a longer time frame, as long as the year 2000 (or 2050 in a few cases). In this latter case, it is possible to perceive the environmental problem, as it relates to emerging energy technologies, as being largely irrelevant. Given lead times of decades, the energy technologists could justify propositions that no environmental "problem" was insurmountable.

All issues were reduced to a question of cost. Therefore, because the cost of energy was expected to be ever increasing, all solutions were judged reasonable. As extremes, these positions could be characterized as one agency doing its best to ignore or subjugate environmental questions and the other to assume the questions away.

The birth of DOE has tended to do away with these extremes. Figure 6.1 lists the duties and responsibilities of the Assistant Secretary for Environment in DOE. As is clear, these duties are in the areas of basic research, assessments, and in overview of the environmental concerns of the Department at large. In a nutshell, the environment is no longer apt to be ignored and, in fact, takes an increasingly active role in the day-to-day policy life of the DOE. Let us turn to some specifics.

2. THE 1977 ERDA NATIONAL PLAN

In 1977, the Assistant Administrator for Environment and Safety (AES) of ERDA, to enhance the accomplishment of its mission, decided to perform an analysis of the ERDA National Energy Plan (ERDA-77). To help manage this effort, it released in March 1977 a Plan for the Development of an Annual Environmental Assessment Report (AEAR).[1] In general, the authors of the methodology (of whom I was one) decided that the AEAR would take the form of a true impact analysis. Specifically, this meant that no effort would be made to generate original energy or economic scenarios;

The Assistant Secretary for Environment Will Be Responsible to the Secretary to Provide Policy Guidance to Assure Department-wide Compliance with Environmental Laws and Procedures

- Review and Assess Environmental Analytical and Technical Products Prepared by Other DOE Program Offices
- Review and Assess DOE Policies and Strategies for Environmental Impacts
- Act as Link to Environmental Agencies and Environmental Community

The Assistant Secretary for Environment Will Exercise Independent Review and Approval of Environmental Impact Statements Prepared within the Department

- Provide NEPA Technical Assistance and Policy Guidance to DOE Program and Regulatory Offices
- Review, Exercise Quality Control Over, and Approve NEPA Documents
- Prepare Policy and Legislative EISs
- Develop DOE NEPA Policies and Internal Directives
- Review and Comment Upon EISs From Other Agencies

The Assistant Secretary Will Also Be Responsible for Policy Guidance with Respect to Health and Safety Issues Involved in DOE Programs

- Assure Adequate Health and Safety Measures in DOE Programs
- Provide Policy Guidance on DOE/Contractor Employee Health and Safety Measures
- Assure Implementation of Health and Safety Measures by DOE Contractors

The Assistant Secretary Will Also Have Program Responsibility for Research and Development Programs regarding the Impact of Energy on the Environment and Will Be Responsible to the Under Secretary for the Management of These Programs

- Conduct Environmental R&D
- Assure Implementation of Practical Substantive Environmental Mitigating Measures Into DOE Programs Subject to NEPA Review

Figure 6.1. Responsibilities and Functions of the Office of the Assistant Secretary for Environment

rather, this information would be obtained from the designers of the Energy Plan and taken as given. From this perspective, a national assessment of the environmental impact of the Plan would be prepared. Figure 6.2 is the earlier perspective of how this project would be carried out (see pages 176–177).

During the early summer of 1977, the White House announced its National Energy Plan (NEP). This plan was to be the basis for the forthcoming National Energy Act. The NEP was comprehensive in scope and replaced all existing plans of the FEA and ERDA. As a consequence, the AES made a policy decision to shift from using ERDA-77 to the President's NEP. As a refinement of the more straightforward environmental analysis of the Plan itself, the White House also developed a Base Case to compare the energy impacts of its policies. This Base Case was also analyzed for its environmental impacts and provided a comparative analysis of the President's policies. The following are some summary statements from a fact sheet published in 1978.[2]

Before going into a discussion of these results, however, let us turn to a very brief statement of our country's energy objectives as stated in the National Energy Plan to better understand both what drives the models, and what has, in part, developed from them.

Quoting from our National Energy Plan (NEP), the United States has three overriding energy objectives:

- as an immediate objective that will become even more important in the future, to reduce dependence on foreign oil and vulnerability to supply interruptions;
- in the medium term, to keep United States imports sufficiently low to weather the period when world oil production approaches its capacity limitation; and
- in the long term, to have renewable and essentially inexhaustible sources of energy for sustained economic growth.

The salient features of this Plan are:

- conservation and fuel efficiency;
- rational pricing and production policies;
- reasonable certainty and stability in Government policies;
- substitution of abundant energy resources for those in short supply; and
- development of nonconventional technologies for the future.

To carry out these objectives and components of the Plan, we have set a series of goals. These goals are:

SOURCE | INFORMATION | EVENT (& RESPONSIBILITY) | INFORMATION

Inputs (SOURCE / INFORMATION):

- ASEV — • Provide ERD's
- DOE — • Determine Relative Priority of Energy Program Technologies

- DOE, EPAS — • EDP Topical Areas
- US — • Modified Tech. Timing
- EPAS/TO — • Technology Process Parameters • Segment Timing
- EPAS/TO — • Projects for Current Examination
- EV — • EV Functional Statement
- EPAS/TO/EV — • Judgemental Concerns
- EPAS/TO — • Measurable Concerns
- EPAS/TO — • "TRAK" System Requirements • Bibliography of Environmental Reference Data

EVENT (& RESPONSIBILITY):

- TECHNOLOGY DESCRIPTIONS (Joint EPAS/TO)
- TECHNOLOGY "SCREENING"
- IDENTIFICATION OF ENVIRONMENTAL CONCERNS (Joint EPAS/TO)
- SORTING OF CONCERNS
- DETERMINATION OF CONCERN SIGNIFICANCE (BER, ECT, OES)

Outputs (INFORMATION):

- • Technology Process Parameters
- • Segmented Technology Schedules and Decision Points
- • Projects for Examination this cycle
- • Projects for Examination next cycle
- • H&S, Socioeconomic, Ecological, Legal Issues
- • Bibliography of Environmental Reference Data
- • Concerns Requiring Judgment
- • Concerns Requiring Measurement
- • Nonsignificant Concerns
- • Significant Known Concerns
- • Significant Unknown Concerns

176

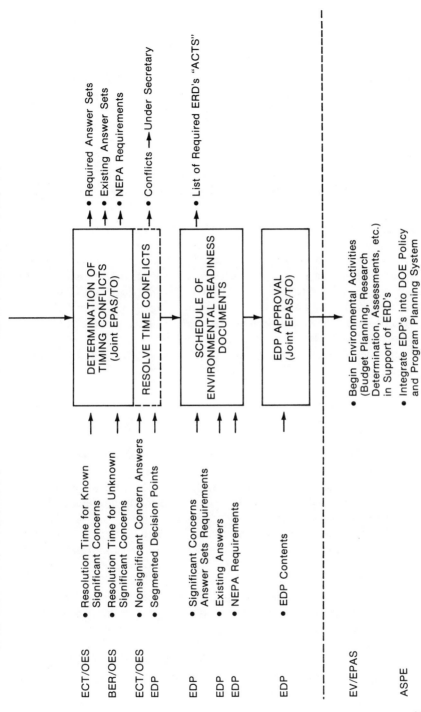

Figure 6.2. EDP Process

177

- reduce the annual growth of total energy demand to below 2 percent;
- reduce gasoline consumption 10 percent below its current level;
- reduce oil imports from a potential level of 16 million barrels per day to 6 million, roughly one-eighth of total energy consumption;
- establish a Strategic Petroleum Reserve of 1 billion barrels;
- increase coal production by two-thirds, to more than 1 billion tons per year;
- bring 90 percent of existing American homes and all new buildings up to minimum energy efficiency standards; and
- use solar energy in more than 2½ million homes.

These goals and the detailed Plan developed to accomplish them were analyzed and at least partly created by the use of two models — Brookhaven National Laboratory and Project Independence Evaluation System.

Further, after the Plan was published, another group of analysts in the Office of the Assistant Secretary for Environment (then in ERDA) did an environmental impact analysis of the Plan using a third model, Strategic Environmental Assessment System (SEAS) (see Chap. 1), called the Annual Environmental Analysis Report (AEAR).

From the NEP assessments and AEAR, the following R&D priorities emerged:

- To decrease expected short-term and long-term increases in SO_x and NO_x, pollution control technology for coal combustion facilities should be accelerated.
- The large quantities of sludge that will be produced from more efficient pollution control systems contain trace heavy metals and other toxic chemicals. Environmentally sound methods of disposal of this sludge waste need to be developed to protect ground water and public health.
- The expected increase in underground mining in the East will increase subsidence and acid drainage problems. Improved mine sealing techniques need to be developed to protect the environment and the public from these mining hazards.
- To ensure environmentally sound land use, water use, and water quality in the West, rapid reclamation techniques must be developed for surface mines to prevent the runoff of alkaline solids from exposed areas.
- Detailed and comprehensive research and assessment will be required on all energy-related environmental factors which will affect the environmental quality of the North Central Region (Region 8). The

environmental quality of that region should be given special consideration.

• Reliable radioactive waste storage systems need to be developed to ensure that the environment will be protected from radioactive leaks to local air and water as storage requirements expand in the near future.

Future efforts to update the AEAR will involve developing procedures for directly incorporating AEAR findings in environmental R&D and policy recommendations for the Assistant Secretary for Environment in the Department of Energy.

The success of these activities indicates rather clearly that large policy models will be used in the energy-environmental decision-making process, along with other methodologies, to link energy, economics, and environmental policies and plans closely together.

3. TO THE PRESENT

Since the publication of the AEAR report, several new efforts have been undertaken. The Department undertook the development of several new supply initiatives (an effort called NESS) and this required the production of an environmental assessment. Currently, an agency-wide effort is underway in the area of commercialization of energy technologies and each of these also requires environmental assessment. Finally, the forthcoming National Energy Plan is underway and this effort requires further AEAR analysis. Although all these are merely a sampling of the major assessment activities, they are enough to indicate that such efforts are becoming a major part of Environment's activities.

Possibly the greatest impact on environmental assessment of energy technologies has come through the formal institutionalization of procedures for putting environmental perspectives into the decision-making stream. A brief discussion of two of these would be illustrative.

The first is the newly formed Environmental Issues Committee (EIC). The second is the technique designed to track the environmental side of energy technology development, the Environmental Development Plan (EDP).

4. EDP SYSTEM

The major objective of the DOE EDP system is to provide environmental information at the time of energy program decision points. This information will allow DOE management to include environmental considerations, as well as technical and economic factors, in decision making.

The EDP system will coordinate DOE's environmental research with energy program decision points, by assessing the environmental status of energy technologies and by scheduling activities required for the determination of environmental acceptability. The EDP system will continue to provide mechanisms for coordinating and integrating technology and Office of Environment (EV) program planning efforts, with an increased emphasis on the assignment of tasks and responsibilities to support environmental decision making.

The EDP system will result in the preparation of Environmental Readiness Documents (ERDs), NEPA documents, and other environmental analyses. The ERD analysis will provide assessments of the environmental readiness of the energy program technologies to move to the next development stage. The ERDs will be scheduled and monitored by an Environmental Coordinating Committee (ECC).

The evolving EDP system is designed to meet the planning needs of internal DOE offices and interested external groups. There are four major users.

- *Assistant Secretary for Environment.* The EDPs and supporting ERDs provide a decision mechanism for the environmental readiness of a technology. EDPs also provide a basis for planning EV environmental activities.
- *Energy Program Offices.* EDPs provide a basis for planning the environmental activities that are the responsibility of the energy program offices.
- *Assistant Secretary for Policy and Evaluation.* EDPs are incorporated into the DOE Policy and Program Planning System.
- *General.* EDPs provide information to groups interested in the environmental status of DOE energy programs.

The contents, procedures, and timing of the EDP system are described in more detail below.

5. EDP CONTENTS AND PROCEDURES

The EDP system assumes the establishment of relative priorities for DOE energy programs, based principally on information from the energy programs and the Assistant Secretary for Policy and Evaluation. The major difference between the Fiscal Year (FY) 1977 EDP system and the FY 1978 system is that environmental analyses associated with energy program decision points will be scheduled and summarized in the EDPs.

EDPs will contain the following information:

- *Introduction and Summary.* The EDP objectives will be introduced and the process for identifying the environmental concerns and implementing mitigating measures will be summarized.
- *Technology Description and Program Schedules.* Technology descriptions and schedules will be used to develop timing schedules by major development stages and their preceding budget authorization decision points. The description will contain sufficient engineering information and process parameters to identify environmental concerns for current and future stages of development.
- *Significant Environmental Concerns and Resolution Times.* Significant environmental concerns associated with the forthcoming and future technology development stages and the times required to resolve these concerns will be described.
- *Environmental Strategy.* A coordinated schedule, including responsibilities for conducting environmental analyses to address the concerns and for preparing NEPA documents will be presented in the EDPs. A summary of results from previous analyses will also be included. (Environmental Readiness Documents will contain more details on the assessments of environmental impacts or acceptability, and on the research recommendations.)

Figure 6.2 summarizes the major events, information flows, and responsibilities associated with the EDP process. External activities related to the EDP process are also indicated. The following paragraphs further describe the major steps in the process.

6.   TECHNOLOGY DESCRIPTIONS

Preparation of an EDP begins with an examination of the technology description and program schedules for the priority program areas. The examination, a joint activity conducted by the energy program offices and the EV Division of Technology Overview (TO), allows the identification of:

- major stages of technology development,
- budget authorization decision points at which EV should provide a statement as to the environmental readiness of a particular technology program to proceed to the next stage,[3] and

- sufficient engineering information and process parameters to allow identification of environmental concerns for the current development stage and the one immediately following.

For technology programs containing numerous projects or process options, it may be necessary to examine the projects or process options in detail for the periods preceding the next decision point. This examination will determine which EH&S concerns should be examined in detail within the current EDP and which concerns can be examined in the next EDP update.

7. IDENTIFICATION OF ENVIRONMENTAL CONCERNS

For each technology program area or project, a comprehensive list of potential environmental concerns will be developed.[4] A supporting bibliography of pertinent technology-related environmental reference data (including existing standards and regulations, potentially relevant Federal inventory projects, emissions and effects data, and technology assessments) is compiled where appropriate. Concerns are identified jointly by the energy program offices and TO.

Based on applicable standards, regulations, and guidelines, concerns are grouped into two categories:

- judgmental concerns which, due to a lack of existing standards or guidelines (e.g., ALARA and BACT),[5] require a judgment of health and safety effects to determine their significance or severity; and
- measurable concerns, the significance of which may be determined by measurement against a standard or guidelines.

A single technology may generate both types of concerns.

8. DETERMINATION OF SIGNIFICANCE OF ENVIRONMENTAL CONCERNS

The significance of both judgmental and measurable concerns is determined by EV divisions. The energy program offices and the Office of Technology Impacts (OTI) will provide appropriate reference data to the EV divisions and will specify the reply time and format requirements for the significance determination. This determination produces three types of concerns:

1. *Nonsignificant Concerns*—those concerns that do not exceed standards or are judged to have "nonsevere" effects.
2. *Significant Known Concerns*—those concerns that exceed standards or are judged to have potentially severe effects.
3. *Significant Unknown Concerns*—those concerns that have not been adequately characterized or measured or are judged to have effects with unknown severity.

For each concern determined to be significant, an estimate of the time needed to answer or to resolve the concern will be provided by the EV divisions and others (e.g., Office of General Counsel), as appropriate. These estimates will be subject to revision as the EH&S research proceeds.

9. TECHNOLOGY ASSESSMENT

The Technology Assessment (TA) discipline, developed over the last decade, is considered of such importance in our national policymaking that the U.S. Congress has, among its four major analysis support elements, an Office of Technology Assessment. As a classical definition, Technology Assessment is a class of policy-oriented research, aimed at the anticipation, identification, and evaluation of the potential impacts of a technology (or project) on society or on a region or community. TA considers secondary (unplanned or derivative) impacts and consequences—that is, it goes beyond questions of technical feasibility, direct or internalized costs, and safety considerations. It has the following primary characteristics:

- TA focuses on long-range impacts or consequences of a technology—i.e., an application of scientific knowledge to affect changes in the environment or to solve problems; the impacts may be physical, biological, or social.
- It addresses a wide range of possible consequences (social, economic, environmental, legal, institutional, cultural, behavioral). Prior selection of a narrow range of impacts or of a few specific impacts to be investigated does not constitute a TA.
- It is oriented toward providing a broad information base for determining policy options and alternatives, that is, toward decision making and policy formulation. Therefore, it integrates and points out trade-offs or issues that will arise in implementation or dissemination of a technology.

- It identifies potentially affected parties and segments of society beyond those who would be investors, manufacturers, and customers — TA is not market research.
- It includes qualitative as well as quantitative data wherever this is appropriate and significant to potential decision makers.

Within the Department of Energy and its Office of Environment, the discipline of Technology Assessment continues to maintain its general classical characteristics but with emphasis on environmental impacts as related to emerging energy technologies. To do this properly requires consideration of much more than pollutants and ambient air and water quality. The full scope of environmental issues involves the socioeconomic impacts, indirect community and regional needs and institutions, and induced economic and labor stimuli. Additionally, resource usage as well as environmental quality degradation enter the assessments. Land use and urban form may also be involved.

The conduct of a set of integrated analyses and data collection activities that cut across this full set of impacts and pertain to a family of technologies has been demonstrated as a major policy support tool, expanding the definition of issues from the purely technological scope to a wider set of issues that impact and motivate the citizenry to accept or reject technological options in meeting our energy supply needs.

Recent technology assessments of EV include consideration of both long-term fuel sources (e.g., coal) and the emerging geothermal fuel resource and associated conversion systems.

Both these techniques, and the major applications cited above, are but a few of the constantly evolving methods and instances where environmental concerns are melded into the energy policy planning process. Numerous others exist. Still more are being developed.

10. SUMMARY AND CONCLUSIONS

The evaluation of environmental/energy analyses has come a long way from the FEA and ERDA days. Some of this has to do with the changed perception at the Federal level of the role of the environment relative to national priorities. Other reasons include the changed internal perception of the energy planners who now are concerned with policies that are an amalgam of the short- and long-term strategies of FEA and ERDA. The perceptions of "barrier" and "technological fix for a price" still exist, but melded together they assume the same guise as numerous other trade-off options — (solution for price in time and resources) — and so are more familiar and comfortable to deal with. The day is within sight when DOE's treatment of environmental issues will be about the most sophisticated around and when environmental issues will be intimately tied to the rest of the energy policy network — a far cry from the reported adversary past reported in the composite agencies — and an interesting model for others in the future who must deal with similar trade-offs.

11. NOTES

1. The MITRE Corp.,/METREK Division, CONSAD Research Corp., Control Data Corp., and International Research and Technology, Inc., *Annual Environmental Analysis Report*, MTR-7626, Vol. I Technical Summary, September 1977.

2. U.S. Department of Energy, Assistant Secretary for Environment, Office of Technology Impacts, *Environmental Assessment Report*, (DOE/EV-0012/1) April 1978.

3. Examination of mature technologies, in a few cases, may not yield analogous major development stages and their associated decision points. For these technologies, readiness will be interpreted as status.

4. Environmental is defined to include public and occupational health and safety, socio-economic, ecological, and legal factors.

5. As Low as Reasonably Achievable, and Best Available Control Technology.

7 DUTCH ENERGY POLICIES FOR THE FUTURE
A.A.T. van Rhijn

1. INTRODUCTION

The interaction of energy, the environment, and the economy is a subject of great interest to the Netherlands, whose own position in each of these three areas has been especially privileged during the last ten to fifteen years. However, the continued existence of the current comparatively favorable situation is not taken for granted. Dutch energy policy is being carefully planned on the basis of intensive national and international research and the evaluation of numerous significant trends and factors.

More than half of total energy consumption in the Netherlands has been in the form of natural gas, compared to 15 percent in the European Economic Committee (EEC) as a whole. At the same time the Netherlands has a per capita energy consumption in 1975 of 5,784 Kgms of coal equivalent as compared with 5,345 Kgms in Germany and 3,944 Kgms in France. Thus, the Netherlands has been the highest energy consumer in the EEC, most of which has been in the form of natural gas. This has been possible because the Netherlands possesses huge natural gas reserves that can generally be exploited at a low cost. The existence of such reserves has significantly boosted the post-World War II economy. Because of the availability and use

186

of natural gas the Netherlands has been able to avoid the negative consequences usually associated with a high per capita consumption of energy,
because the environmental effects of natural gas are minimal. However,
about 40 percent of the existing proven reserves has already been committed
for exports, and there is little probability that considerable additional
volumes will be found.

At this moment oil and gas together comprise 93 percent of primary
energy consumed in the Netherlands. Approximately half of the total energy
supply consumed in this country — mainly in the form of oil and a small
quantity of coal — is imported, despite the fact that the Netherlands itself
is a net exporter of energy. Moreover, imports will increase considerably in
the future even if the demand for energy increases only moderately, because
of the established policy of decreasing the use of natural gas in order to save
indigenous natural supplies for unforeseeable strategic or humane reasons.

Dutch energy policy is being carefully planned on the basis of intensive
national and international research and the evaluation of numerous significant trends and factors. On the one hand there are uncertainties about
future energy supplies; on the other there is the desire to be able to use
natural gas over the long term wherever this seems to be necessary for
environmental or social benefit. Consequently, in order to conserve natural
gas the consumption of oil will increase from 40 to about 55 percent by 1985;
during the same period the consumption of natural gas will decrease from
the 52 percent now consumed to 38 percent — an undesirable development
since the Netherlands should try to diminish, rather than to increase, its
consumption of oil. Nonetheless, if there ever should be a shortage in the
supply of oil, the Netherlands will be able to switch back to natural gas since
practically all of the big users of natural gas, including electricity plants and
the big industrial factories, have dual firing installations.

Energy conservation plays a fundamental role in Dutch energy policies
for the future, serving to decrease both energy consumption and dependency
on imports. While conservation is an instrument that is applicable in the
short run, its true effects show on a massive scale only in the long run. Moreover, conservation policy can be implemented without purposely limiting
the growth of GNP. In fact, limiting growth to limit energy consumption is
not a viable policy: many urgent needs will still have to be satisfied, and a
no-growth policy would have many disruptive effects on society and international trade, in the developed as well as the developing countries. Of
course, a situation might evolve at some time in the future in which there are
compelling reasons for zero economic growth, but one ought in the first
place to make maximum efforts to see that this does not happen. Moreover,
it is mandatory that we study how the very serious disruptive effects that
would accompany new growth could be overcome. There is no basis what-

soever for optimism about solving this problem, and perhaps there are grounds for pessimism about the consequences of continued economic growth.

Regardless of policy, risks are always present, but there is no good reason to overestimate the environmental problem of finality of resources while at the same time underestimating the social problems — especially since the latter have very often proven extremely difficult to solve.

Thus, even when the positive effects of a vigorous conservation policy are taken into account, the demand for energy will still increase, although the rate of increase will depend largely on the rate of growth in the economy as a whole.

2. ENERGY SUPPLY AND ENERGY POLICY IN THE NETHERLANDS

To supply sufficient energy to meet demand, the following sources may be considered: gas, oil, coal, and nuclear power are primary sources, and solar, wind, and geothermal energy are alternative sources. However, until 1985 there is hardly a choice to be made: the development of economically feasible alternative sources of energy that are available for large-scale use will take time, and a large-scale introduction of either coal or nuclear energy is now impossible — if only because the lead times for building new capacity are considerable, especially in the case of electricity plants. Additionally, any intentions of the Dutch government to expand its existing nuclear capacity are entirely conditional upon the solution of the waste disposal problem. Oil and gas, both indigenous and imported, are therefore the only realistic alternatives at the present, in addition to a small increase in the use of coal.

After 1985 there will fortunately be more of a choice. Dutch energy policy for the longer run is based upon four criteria which are applied to possible sources of energy. The results are used to determine the extent to which any one source should be used. The criteria for determining the energy mix over the long run are as follows:

1. the availability and security of supply;
2. the feasibility of application of the source, including the problems of lead time and practicality of wide usage;
3. the economics of the various sources of energy; and
4. the environmental impact and the possible risks that accompany the use of any particular source.

It should be stressed that it is not possible to single out any one of these four elements as the decisive one. Each covers only one aspect of our complicated, and thereby fragile, modern society. A decision based on a choice of only one element could and would lead to unacceptable consequences. Considering the various criteria separately, the following comments can be made.

3. AVAILABILITY AND SECURITY OF SUPPLY

According to all experts, the estimates of ultimate reserves of oil and gas will be more than sufficient to supply the Netherlands and the world with the necessary volumes well into the twenty-first century, even with a continuation in the growth of energy consumption such as we have been experiencing over the last decades. (By then, admittedly, they will be consumed entirely.) Coal could supply all energy needs far beyond this date. Proven reserves for uranium are still rather modest; but with further exploration, and taking into account recent and expected price rises, we may anticipate that ultimate uranium reserves will undoubtedly be much higher. If breeders are ever introduced, then energy produced from uranium could be multiplied by sixty. Geothermal sources will be of only limited relevance, while flow energies, which of course have tremendous potential, will not be available in significant quantities until after the year 2000.

The foregoing assessment applies only to physical availability. A clear distinction must in any case be made between sheer physical availability—indicating potential—and the actual supply made available to meet demand at a particular time and in the particular location where demand exists. If one can first be sure of such a practical availability, then one can speak of security of supplies. When we look at the security of supply, the picture is quite different from that for physical availability.

All studies by such organizations as the International Energy Agency, the Workshop on Alternative Energy Strategies (WAES), the Central Intelligence Agency (CIA), and the Organization of Petroleum Exporting Countries (OPEC) point out (with different nuances) that there is a real danger of a shortage in oil supplies within the next five to fifteen years. This is because oil reserves are very unevenly spread over the countries of the world and because a number of major exporters will limit production in order to advance national goals and priorities, avoid disrupting the national economy, prevent excessive surpluses on balance of payments, and so forth. It is not just the countries in the OPEC that might do this—Saudi Arabia, Norway, and Britain, and probably Mexico, will do exactly the same.

Since there has so far been such a strong preference for oil, switches to other fuels are necessary. Since everybody has been lazy in respect to implementing such shifts, the security of future oil supplies remains very doubtful, even with a lower rate of increase in energy consumption and at a slightly increased time scale than is assumed in many of the just-mentioned scenarios. Political action by the OPEC is less probable since industrialized countries in the IEA have developed an effective scheme for sharing in case of emergencies, as well as a plan to supply stocks for ninety days to individual countries in trouble.

Although the reserves of oil are spread very unevenly, with the Middle East having by far the most important reserves, the infrastructure for transporting natural gas (especially in the form of LNG) is extremely capital intensive. There is a rather general feeling that once contracts have been concluded and the necessary infrastructure has been installed, the contracts will be fulfilled, in general, for twenty to twenty-five years. This would give a much greater security of supply than oil.

The security of the coal supply must be viewed in a different light. Although coal reserves are also not well spread over the globe, security of supply is not as much endangered by national economic considerations as in the case of oil. Rather, the problems are the following:

a. strikes such as we experience regularly in the United Kingdom and the United States, which lead to shortages in supply and therefore to government curtailment of exports;

b. uncertainties about whether the population of any country involved will be prepared to accept the heavy environmental effects caused by coal—and especially by strip mining—simply for the sake of exporting coal;

c. the unwillingness to make the heavy investments involved in mining, transporting to seaports, and building and maintaining the seaports themselves. With pay-out times so very long, investors will be most reluctant to make decisions as long as they are not sure about their markets; and

d. international political developments such as, for example, the tensions between South Africa—potentially one of the major coal-supplying countries—and the rest of the world with respect to apartheid policy.

Uranium resources are more limited but have a much wider spread. Moreover, uranium is far easier and far cheaper to store. The further possibility of using breeders to multiply energy production makes uranium highly attractive as a secure source of energy to big countries that largely depend on energy imports, such as France, Germany, Italy, Japan, the United Kingdom, and even the United States. Although the government of the United States does not currently plan to introduce the breeder, it has committed itself to a heavy program for building light water reactors (LWRs) in order to avoid a continued dependency on oil imports from the OPEC—which is seen as highly undesirable for the United States in international politics.

To summarize, we may say that insofar as supplying most sources of energy implies taking risks in regard to the volumes to be made available, it is highly desirable that energy supplies be diversified both as far as sources and as far as regions of origin are concerned, thereby minimizing the risks for securing the supplies essential to the sustenance of the national economy.

4. FEASIBILITY OF APPLICATION

Lead times are much longer in the energy sector and flexibility is therefore less than in most other sectors. This is not only because of construction times and the time needed for getting the necessary permits and licenses, but also because the volumes of energy needed for consumption are so enormous that every switch requires tremendous efforts and easily requires about ten to fifteen years to accomplish.

In the Netherlands the switch from gas and oil to coal or nuclear power is additionally hampered by the impressive overcapacity of about 35 percent that exists presently in the electricity sector of the Netherlands, as well as in many other countries. Electricity plants ordered well before the oil crisis are still coming into operation, with the result that virtually no new electric capacity is required before the end of the eighties. Any large-scale introduction of coal—say around twenty million tons or more—will be conditional upon measures to prevent serious pollution. Whether such measures can be taken soon enough, and within reasonable budgetary limits, remains uncertain.

The expansion of nuclear capacity in the Netherlands depends very much on whether the Dutch government can find a solution to the problem of the final disposal of highly radioactive waste and on the outcome of a prior broad general public discussion on the role of nuclear energy. Studies must still be made of flow and geothermal energy sources so they may be developed to whatever extent is possible. Inevitably energy supplied by the sun and wind will have only limited application in the Netherlands because of the climate and the large spatial effects of wind power. Nor is the exploitation of the rather large coal reserves in the Netherlands a possibility given existing technology and available manpower. If underground gasification becomes feasible, this would create good prospects for the exploitation of gas reserves, but in any case this will take a very long time.

Thus, while flow and geothermal energy sources should play a major role in the research and development program of the Netherlands, they will certainly not contribute more than a very small percentage of total energy supply before the year 2000. There will therefore be more reliance on imported pipeline or LNG gas, on coal, and on uranium. There is thus far less immediate applicability and flexibility than one would have liked, and from that point of view one should keep as many options open as possible. Neither coal nor nuclear energy can be easily discarded, but at the same time it should be realized that problems connected with the exploitation of these sources must be very carefully studied.

5. ECONOMICS OF ENERGY SOURCES

Assuming that oil is still the price leader for at least the coming ten to fifteen years, how do prices of other energy sources compare? Are they at all competitive with oil prices? This is the first of two economic problems still to be solved. The second problem is concerned with a distortion of competition caused by nationalistic policies of the oil-producing nations. In a number of cases serious distortion of competition is caused when industries in specific countries are able to profit from lower energy prices than those that prevail elsewhere.

To take the first problem first. Comparing the prices and competitiveness of different sources of energy, one can first conclude that flow energies are not yet available on a commercial scale and from an economic point of view cannot be taken into account, although this will change in the longer term. Unhappily, natural gas is apparently available only in limited quantities. Additional imports from Norway and the Soviet Union are possible but impractical due to the relatively high prices likely to result from the fierce competition for additional supplies within Western Europe. Imports from African and Middle Eastern countries are generally possible only in the form of LNG. But since the costs of liquefaction and transportation are extremely high in such cases, the difference between cost and selling price will leave only a rather low to very low margin for the producing countries when contrasted to crude oil parity—this being one of the major reasons that, apart from Algeria, gas-producing countries are reluctant to sell, and, if they do, it is only at relatively high prices with a very high indexation on price rises of crude oil.

Coal is comparatively cheap, for the moment. One tends to forget that coal prices have to be lower than oil parity because of the extra costs involved in using coal compared with using oil, on the one hand, and that, on the other, coal prices are low because sea transport tariffs are low and because the big industrial consumers and electricity plants cannot switch to coal with existing equipment. However, once these two aspects change, coal prices will certainly rise considerably. Since coal accounts for almost 60 percent of the production costs of electricity at present, it is clear that future price developments will be decisive in defining the competitiveness of coal. Moreover, there is an additional uncertainty regarding the future cost of coal: we simply do not know how much it will cost to develop techniques and measures to prevent pollution and protect the environment from the hazards of coal mining.

In the recent past many studies have been undertaken to compare the production costs of electricity based on coal with those based on uranium. Presently, this depends very much on such specific conditions as location of the plant to the coal-mining site and the degree of antipollution measures necessary. Beyond this, however, one conclusion is very safe to draw. Although nuclear plants are vulnerable to inflation because of high investment costs, they are intensive expenditures since the price increase of uranium is only 10 percent of the total, compared to the 60 percent of the total price for coal that must be calculated for inflation. From the point of view of competitiveness, one should conclude that it is not wise to put all one's efforts and resources into the production of any one energy source, but rather to use a mix of sources.

This leads us to the second problem—the distortion of competition that is especially relevant to West European countries because their economies are so closely linked and transportation costs from one country to another are of minor importance. In this respect the United States and Japan are better off than other countries, although from time to time Canada and the northern United States are also in fierce competition. In the Netherlands we are presently having difficulties because of the lower gas and electricity prices available to large industrial consumers in other countries, and particularly in Germany. The competitiveness of our energy-intensive industries has been reduced in the struggle to attract new industries and sell to large industrial consumers of gas and electricity. Lower energy prices for large consumers make Germany distinctly more appealing than the Netherlands for the location of new production units.

The lower gas prices are partly due to the fact that gas contracts made according to the old, more favorable price formula are rapidly expiring in the Netherlands, and in the new contracts the payment of a premium is now required. In Germany, however, the introduction of gas was three to five years later than in the Netherlands; thus, the increases in price expected to accompany renewal of contracts with large consumers will come a few years later in Germany. Unfavorable competition is therefore to some extent a temporary problem.

The situation that affects the price of electricity is more structural. For example, in Germany about 30 percent of the electricity is generated by cheap lignite, although an increasingly larger part — 7.5 percent in 1976 — is being generated in German nuclear plants. In Belgium about 20 percent of the total electricity consumed is already generated in nuclear plants — thus giving Belgium a very comfortable position in the event that energy prices rise again. Under such circumstances, large consumers of electricity in the Netherlands will be forced into an uncompetitive position unless they take into account developments in other countries when making decisions about primary energy sources to be used for producing electricity in the future.

From an economic point of view, it is clear that the Netherlands must be extremely careful if it is to avoid a situation in which its energy prices are structurally higher than those in surrounding countries, even if the difference amounts to no more than one or two Dutch cents per m^3 or kwh. Failure to do this can cause serious distortions of competition and may even result in critical levels of unemployment in important segments of Dutch industry. That is why the electricity industry, for example, favors a 1:1:1 policy for the use of coal, oil, and gas combined, and nuclear power; such a ratio allows one to spread the economic risks attendant upon any unforeseeable developments affecting either the prices of various energy sources or the environment as evenly as possible among the major sources.

6. ENVIRONMENTAL IMPACT AND RISKS OF THE SOURCE

One of the major problems with energy is that the use of any of its sources implies some very undesirable consequences. Oil, and especially coal, have serious implications from the environmental point of view — pollution of the air and water among them. Natural gas and nuclear fuels are, in contrast, reputedly clean while being used; but their possible consequences cause some concern. LNG is a gaseous substance with the capability of seriously harming the environment, and the waste products created by nuclear energy are deadly.

Therefore, if one regards risks as simple chance effects, then oil and especially coal have a worse record than nuclear energy or LNG. With the latter two the chances of an accident are minimal, but if the accident takes place the effects might under certain circumstances be very considerable indeed. It is clear that in a small, densely populated country this danger must be evaluated especially carefully. Moreover, it should be added that there is a far from uniform valuation of this type of risk.

Even though the chance that an accident will occur is minimal, the resulting massive effects of an accident are so great that many believe this creates an extra dimension that must be decisive in any evaluation of the acceptability of risk. Others are willing to concede some extra weight to the size of the effects, but they do not regard it as decisive.

Recently, a serious debate has taken place about the location of the future terminal for LNG that Algeria will export to this country in the early 1980s. The final choice has been the northern part of the Netherlands. In the past two years risk analyses have gained increasing attention in the Netherlands as well as in many other countries. While most of these studies have been concerned with nuclear energy, LNG, coal, and other sources are being examined carefully to determine the risks involved in their use. I would like to observe that the social sciences have not yet created a more scientific background for the interpretation of the results of such risk analyses or provided a basis for making decisions about risks in general and especially about large-scale effects. It seems to be absolutely necessary that more attention be given to the problem of risks in our highly technological society, particularly as our awareness of such risks is growing very rapidly. It has often been assumed, for instance, that alternative energy sources would involve fewer risks than the traditional sources. However, a recent Canadian study based on historical data gathered for the United States has reached quite different conclusions, especially if the materials used must be imported. I do not say that such results should be accepted automatically, but it is important that we not be too optimistic about the levels of risk from such alternative sources as the sun and wind without further study.

In Holland, close cooperation between the Ministry for the Environment and Social Health and the Ministry of Economic Affairs has developed over the past few years in regard to these issues. The environmental impact of oil, coal, and nuclear energy is being carefully studied, and much time has been devoted to the integration of the environmental aspects with other aspects that also must be taken into account. One of the major problems with which they are concerned is the deterioration in current levels of air pollution that we may expect if coal is exploited on a large scale. There is also the very considerable problem of the disposal of the ashes, which equal 10 to 20 percent of the weight of the coal used. Every 700 MW coal-fired station needs a space of at least one hectare (10,000 meters), ten meters high, for its ashes. Moreover, the ashes may contaminate water, and therefore location of disposal facilities must be carefully considered. Special preventive measures will have to be taken.

One might question whether there would in fact be a real pollution problem if oil and coal were reintroduced on a massive scale. As early as 1956 there was a coal consumption of eighteen million tons. It should be pointed out that this was only a temporary peak, that the general level of pollution was then much lower than it is now, and that ash deposits were not a problem because we did not know their potential danger and they were largely dispersed over a wider area. A large part of the coal was used for domestic heating and by small industrial consumers.

More generally, there is a close relationship between the environmental and economic aspects of the production and use of energy. One of the major difficulties about antipollution measures is that they considerably increase the cost of producing energy. We have insufficient knowledge about the real effects of pollution as well, and we in general lack well-developed technologies that can prevent pollution effectively.

7. THE ENERGY MIX POLICY: SPREADING NEGATIVE EFFECTS

To create optimum conditions in the energy sector it is necessary to spread the negative effects that might come from unforeseeable developments affecting any one source. We therefore use as broad a mix of energy as possible and do not exclude any source unless the reasons are extraordinarily compelling.

One of the important considerations before implementation of measures to prevent pollution or reduce risks is economics, both of the particular source and of the Dutch energy industry as a whole—and most especially its competitiveness. Such a focus, it will be seen, shifts the emphasis from an analysis of the previously cited four criteria (security of supply, feasibility of application, economics of the source, and environmental impact) to a broad synthesis of the pros and cons of various elements. However, it was concluded for three of the four elements there was a need to minimize negative effects and risks (both technological and economic) by using as broad a mix of energy sources as possible, and this judgement is only reinforced if we consider the situation as a whole. If we weigh the various outcomes carefully, the only reasonable conclusion is that no single source of energy should be excluded, since they are all a mixture of both pros and cons. Admittedly, some of the negative features are very serious and may even be conditional, as, for example, in the case of further nuclear expansion in the Netherlands, which is dependent upon the solution to the problem of waste disposal. Urgent action must be taken to find solutions to such problems. Nevertheless, such difficulties do not weaken the conclusion that the supply policy for the Netherlands in the future should foster a broad energy mix, not excluding a priori nuclear energy or any other source.

Such a broad policy statement has not been fully elaborated, nor has it matured in all respects. However, a number of policy guidelines have developed on the basis of the four elements in Dutch energy policy. Three important guidelines for future energy policy follow.

8. GUIDELINES FOR FUTURE ENERGY POLICY

8.1. Natural Gas

Even if we try to import a great quantity of gas, we should limit its use to those situations in which higher principles demand or confirm its use, e.g., where air pollution is so high as to justify the use of another energy source. In the context of so-called noble uses, priority is given to the use of gas for domestic heating or for environmental reasons. We have also been negotiating with the electricity industry, the provincial licensing authorities who determine permissible emissions, and the gas supply firm, Gasunie, to develop a plan to spread the use of available natural gas within the limits of the existing contracts: $\pm$ 100 10^9 m^3, with an extra volume of 25 10^9 m^3 as a bonus over the next twenty years, and with the agreement that the gas shall be used only for $\pm$25 percent of their yearly energy consumption (instead of 80 percent). This will in many cases enable the electricity industry to use gas if required for reasons of air pollution.

A portion of the total available volume will be reserved for those who do not have sufficient gas but are faced with air pollution as a particular problem. The result will be as follows: on the one hand, natural gas is being conserved for the period in which shortfalls in energy supplies might arise; on the other hand, from the environmental point of view high levels of air pollution after 1985 can be eased considerably. (This implies a more rapid increase in air pollution during the next few years.) It is hoped that by the summer of 1979 arrangements will be agreed upon for the use of gas.

8.2. Coal

Particular attention will in future be given to the gasification of coal in order to minimize the pollutive effects of coal and at the same time to use the already existing very elaborate pipeline system for distribution of natural gas. The existence of this infrastructure gives the Netherlands a privileged position for coal gasification compared to other countries. A study group has recently recommended coal gasification for electricity generation provided the total amount of coal used does not exceed 30 million tons a year. This limitation is stipulated for reasons of pollution and security of supply.

8.3. Nuclear

We hope to initiate a broad discussion in this country about the further expansion of nuclear capacity for generating electricity. But the final decision is conditional upon finding a solution to the problem of nuclear waste disposal.

It is along these and similar lines that the energy policies of the Netherlands are being shaped. The interactions between energy, economics, and the environment are of the utmost importance in the formulation of this policy, as they affect the outlook for any particular source and for all possible combinations of sources. The seriousness and challenge of this responsibility are not being taken lightly in the Netherlands.